Advances in Japanese Business and Economics

Volume 26

Advances in Japanese Business and Economics (AJBE) showcases the work of Japanese and non-Japanese scholars researching the Japanese economy and Japanese businesses. Published in English, the series highlights for a global readership the unique perspectives of Japan's most distinguished and emerging scholars of business and economics. It covers research of either theoretical or empirical nature, in both authored and edited volumes, regardless of the sub-discipline or geographical coverage, including, but not limited to, such topics as macroeconomics, microeconomics, industrial relations, innovation, regional development, entrepreneurship, international trade, globalization, financial markets, technology management, and business strategy. At the same time, as a series of volumes written by Japanese and non-Japanese scholars studying Japan, it includes research on the issues of the Japanese economy, industry, management practice, and policy, such as the economic policies and business innovations before and after the Japanese "bubble" burst in the 1990s.

AJBE endeavors to overcome a historical deficit in the dissemination of Japanese economic theory, research methodology, and analysis. The volumes in the series contribute not only to a deeper understanding of Japanese business and economics but to revealing underlying universal principles.

Overseen by a panel of renowned scholars led by Editor-in-Chief Professor Ryuzo Sato, AJBE employs a single-blind review process in which the Editor-in-Chief, together with the Managing Editors and specialized scholars designated by the Editor-in-Chief or Managing Editors, rigorously reviews each proposal and manuscript to ensure that every submission is a valuable contribution to the global scholarly readership.

All books and chapters in AJBE are indexed in Scopus.

More information about this series at http://www.springer.com/series/11682

Naoto Jinji · Xingyuan Zhang · Shoji Haruna

Deep Integration, Global Firms, and Technology Spillovers

Springer

Naoto Jinji
Faculty of Economics
Kyoto University
Kyoto, Japan

Xingyuan Zhang
Faculty of Economics
Okayama University
Okayama, Japan

Shoji Haruna
Faculty of Economics
Okayama University
Okayama, Japan

ISSN 2197-8859 ISSN 2197-8867 (electronic)
Advances in Japanese Business and Economics
ISBN 978-981-16-5209-7 ISBN 978-981-16-5210-3 (eBook)
https://doi.org/10.1007/978-981-16-5210-3

This Springer imprint is published by the registered company Springer Nature Singapore Pte Ltd.
The registered company address is: 152 Beach Road, #21-01/04 Gateway East, Singapore 189721, Singapore

Preface

This monograph investigates interactions among deep regional economic integration, activities of global firms, and international spillovers of technological knowledge. Each of these three and their interactions are significant factors that have a strong influence on the current world economy. In particular, the relationship between global firms and international technology spillovers and the impact of deep integration on the spillovers are very interesting issues from both academic and practical points of view. In each chapter of this monograph, we address some specific issues in the broad theme of the book. Therefore, depending on readers' interest, each chapter can be read separately without worrying about the order of reading the chapters. However, the entire book has a structure, and the reading order is arranged to properly explore the broad theme of the book.

This is an output of our collaborative research for more than 10 years. When our joint research project started, we were colleagues at Okayama University. The first research topic was technology spillovers. Specifically, we tried to investigate the relationship between the trade specialization of countries/economies and technology spillovers across countries/economies in Asia. At that time Zhang was working on empirical studies of innovation using patent data. He had just started employing patent citation data as a proxy of spillovers of knowledge and technology. Haruna mainly engaged in theoretical analysis of research and development spillovers in the industrial organization literature. As Jinji's specialty was international economics, we considered that the three of us could tackle the above topic through working together. Our first paper was published in 2010. By that time Jinji had already moved to Kyoto University, but our collaborative project still continues. The focus of our research has been extended to the globalized activities of firms, regional trade agreements, and their relationships with international technology spillovers. The outputs of our collaborative research on these issues have been published in a number of journal articles.

Some of the chapters in this monograph are closely related to the papers that were published before, but none of them is a reprint of the published paper. Chapters 3 and 4 extend our research published in the *North American Journal of Economics and Finance* in 2019 by investigating the relationship between a firm's choice of globalization mode and various measures of firm performance including labor productivity, total factor productivity, and intangible asset intensity, as well as Tobin's *q*. We also employ a number of different estimation techniques to cope with particular characteristics of our data. Chapter 5 examines the relationship between bilateral trade patterns and technology spillovers, which is the main topic of our paper published in *Review of World Economics* in 2015. In Chap. 5 we conduct theoretical analysis to derive testable hypotheses, which is not included in the published paper. In addition, we extend our previous empirical analysis by employing additional data at Japanese and European patent offices. Finally, Chap. 7 provides an extended analysis of the paper published in the *World Economy* in 2019. The issue in Chap. 7 is the impact of deep regional integration on international technology spillovers. We extend the coverage of countries/economies and the period targeted in the analysis. Moreover, we enrich the measurement of deep regional trade agreements.

Research funding was provided by the Japan Society for the Promotion of Science under Grants-in-Aid for Scientific Research (B) 23330081, 16H03619, 19H01481, and 20H01507, the Japan Center for Economic Research, and the Murata Science Foundation. The analysis in Chaps. 3 and 4 uses firm-level data extracted from surveys conducted by the Ministry of Economy, Trade and Industry (METI). We thank the Research and Statistics Department of the METI for granting permission to access the surveys' firm-level data. Part of Chap. 6 is based on the research conducted through a research project at the Research Institute of Economy, Trade and Industry (RIETI). We are grateful to Xin Cen, Rinki Ito, and Shunya Ozawa for their excellent research assistance. They also read the entire manuscript of this book and gave comments. In addition, we have benefited a great deal from discussion and/or comments from a large number of colleagues and participants at numerous conferences, workshops, and seminars.

We would like to thank Prof. Kazuo Mino for recommending that our work be published by Springer and Ms. Juno Kawakami for her editorial assistance. We would like to express our sincere gratitude to Prof. Ryuzo Sato, the Editor in Chief of the Advances in Japanese Business and Economics book series, and the editorial board members for accepting our book into the series. Finally, we would like to express our deepest gratitude to the late Prof. Keizo Nagatani, who had provided intellectual stimulation to us and encouraged our research activities for many years.

Kyoto, Japan — Naoto Jinji
Okayama, Japan — Xingyuan Zhang
Okayama, Japan — Shoji Haruna
May 2021

Contents

About the Authors

Naoto Jinji is Professor of Economics at Kyoto University and a Faculty Fellow of Japan's Research Institute of Economy, Trade and Industry (RIETI). He received his Ph.D. in economics from the University of British Columbia in Canada. His major is international economics, industrial organization, and environmental economics. He has published numerous papers on international trade and trade policy, regional trade agreements, international technology spillovers, topics in industrial organization and environmental economics, and other related topics in international refereed journals, including *Canadian Journal of Economics*, *Journal of Environmental Economics and Management*, *Review of International Economics*, *Review of World Economics*, and the *World Economy*. He was awarded the 14th Kojima Kiyoshi Prize from the Japan Society of International Economics.

Xingyuan Zhang is Professor in the Faculty of Economics at Okayama University. He received his Ph.D. in economics from Kobe University. His major is applied econometrics and industrial organization. He has published numerous papers in international refereed journals, including *Journal of Productivity Analysis*, *Journal of Technology Transfer*, *Contemporary Economic Policy*, and *Economics of Innovation and New Technology*.

Shoji Haruna is Professor Emeritus and Specially Appointed Professor at Okayama University. He received his Ph.D. in economics from Hitotsubashi University. His major is Industrial Organization and Applied Microeconomics. He has published numerous papers in journals such as *Canadian Journal of Economics*, *International Journal of Industrial Organization*, *Journal of Comparative Economics*, and *Southern Economic Journal*.

Acronyms

AC	Area-covered
ASEAN	Association of South-East Asian Nations
BBP	Behind-the-border policy
BEA	Bureau of Economic Analysis
BIT	Bilateral investment treaty
BSJBSA	Basic Survey of Japanese Business Structure and Activities
BSOBA	Basic Survey of Overseas Business Activities
CACM	Central American Common Market
CARICOM	Caribbean Community and Common Market
CIF	Cost, insurance, and freight
CQR	Censored quantile regression
CT	Communication technology
CU	Customs union
EC	European Community
EEC	European Economic Community
EMS	Electronics manufacturing services
EU	European Union
FDI	Foreign direct investment
FO	Foreign outsourcing
FOB	Free on board
FTA	Free trade agreement
GATS	General Agreement on Trade in Services
GATT	General Agreement on Tariffs and Trade
GDP	Gross domestic product
GVC	Global value chain
HFDI	Horizontal foreign direct investment
HIIT	Horizontal intra-industry trade
ICT	Information and communication technology
IIP	Institute of Intellectual Property
IIT	Intra-industry trade (or two-way trade)
IPC	International Patent Classification
IPR	Intellectual property right

IT	Information technology
IV	Instrumental variable
JPO	Japanese Patent Office
LAD	Least absolute deviations
LAV	Least-absolute value
LE	Legally-enforceable
LP	Labor productivity
METI	Ministry of Economy, Trade and Industry
MNE	Multinational enterprise
NAFTA	North American Free Trade Agreement
NBER	National Bureau of Economic Research
NEEDS	Nikkei Economic Electronic Database Systems
NEP	Non-economic policy
NTB	Non-tariff barrier
OECD	Organization for Economic Co-operation and Development
OLS	Ordinary least squares
OP	Other policy
OWT	One-way trade (or inter-industry trade)
PATCRA	Agreement on Trade and Commercial Relations between the Governments of Australia and Papua New Guinea
PATSTAT	Patent Statistical Database
PC-TAS	Personal Computer Trade Analysis System
PPML	Poisson pseudo-maximum likelihood
PVI	Pandemic vulnerability index
QR	Quantile regression
R&D	Research and development
RCA	Revealed Comparative Advantage
RCEP	Regional Comprehensive Economic Partnership
ROLS	Robust ordinary least squares
RoO	Rules of origin
RTA	Regional trade agreement
SPS	Sanitary and phytosanitary
TBT	Technical barriers to trade
TFP	Total factor productivity
TRIPS	Trade-related aspects of intellectual property rights
USPTO	United States Patent and Trademark Office
VFDI	Vertical foreign direct investment
VIIT	Vertical intra-industry trade
WTO	World Trade Organization

List of Figures

List of Tables

Chapter 1
Introduction and Overview

The world economy was severely hit by the COVID-19 pandemic in 2020. It was estimated that the annual growth in the world's real gross domestic product (GDP) in 2020 would be −3.3% (International Monetary Fund (IMF) 2021). World trade simultaneously contracted sharply. It was estimated that the growth in the world's trade volume of goods and services would be −8.5% in 2020 (IMF 2021). According to the statistics released by the Johns Hopkins Coronavirus Resource Center, by the end of 2020 the cumulative number of infected people worldwide is over 83 million and the cumulative number of worldwide deaths is over 1.81 million. However, the decline in global manufacturing was short-lived and both advanced and emerging economies showed V-shaped recoveries in manufacturing output in the second half of 2020 (IMF 2021, Fig. 1.1.1). Moreover, thanks to vaccines and various policy supports, the world economy is projected to grow at 6% in 2021 (IMF 2021), but still faces great uncertainty. Its recovery depends on the path of the health crisis.

Although the COVID-19 pandemic proved that the world economy is vulnerable to health risks, at the same time it shows its good adaptability. The size of the COVID-19 recession is expected to be smaller than the 2008 Global Financial Crisis (IMF 2021). Its influences are different from one country to another. Low income countries with limited capacity for policy support were hit relatively harder than advanced economies. Furthermore, countries that rely on tourism and commodity exports were particularly severely damaged. Those countries are expected to suffer more significant medium-term losses. Using the pandemic vulnerability index (PVI), which is calculated by national data on COVID-19 morbidity and mortality rates and other related information, Shrestha et al. (2020) show that certain countries are more vulnerable to the COVID-19 pandemic than others. According to their analysis, the top 10 highly vulnerable countries include Brazil, India, the United States, Russia, South Africa, Chile, Mexico, Iran, Peru, and Pakistan.

It is argued that globalization was a major driving force behind the fast spread of COVID-19 from China to the rest of the world. For example, Farzanegan et al. (2021) show that countries with higher levels of socio-economic globalization are exposed to a higher case fatality rate due to COVID-19, according to the KOF

N. Jinji et al., *Deep Integration, Global Firms, and Technology Spillovers*,
Advances in Japanese Business and Economics 26,
https://doi.org/10.1007/978-981-16-5210-3_1

Globalization Index (the ratio of confirmed deaths to confirmed cases), covering more than 150 countries in July 2020. Shrestha et al. (2020) argue that "trade and travel, essential components of globalization, are significant contributors to the spread of infectious diseases" (p. 1). Historically, pandemics have repeatedly emerged together with human activities and movements.[1] By reviewing the history of pandemic influenza, Saunders-Hastings and Krewski (2016) argue that pandemic influenza is a consequence of human development and that globalization in relation to human behavior, demographics, and mobility has enhanced the threat of pandemic emergence and accelerated the spread of novel viruses. Conversely, they point out that globalization has also facilitated international cooperation in disease prevention, control, and treatment by promoting advances in disease research and surveillance.

In this book we pay attention to the proliferation of regionalism from the mid-1990s and the globalized activities of multinational enterprises (MNEs) as important elements of recent globalization and explore interactions between these two elements of globalization and diffusion of knowledge in the world. Diffusion of knowledge across countries is important because it affects the speed at which the world's technology frontier expands. For example, Eaton and Kortum (1996) show that more than 50% of the economic growth in 19 advanced countries in the 1980s derived from innovation in the United States, Japan, and Germany. Moreover, diffusion of knowledge contributes to income convergence across countries (Keller 2004).

This chapter starts by presenting the background of the study in this book and then provides an overview of the book.

1.1 Background of the Study

1.1.1 Globalization and the Proliferation of Regionalism

The term "globalization" is commonly used, but it means different things to different people. Globalization in the economic sense means the "integration of national economies into international economy" (Bhagwati 2004, p. 3) through international trade, foreign direct investment (FDI), and international flows of workers and technology. Alternatively, economic globalization can be defined as "the increased interdependence of national economies, and the trend towards greater integration of goods and factor markets" (Neary 2003, p. 246). There has been a heated debate about the pros and cons of globalization among economists (e.g., Bhagwati 2004; Rodrik 1997, 2011, 2018; Samuelson 2004; Stiglitz 2002, 2006, 2018). For example, Samuelson (2004) uses a Ricardian model and numerical examples to illustrate the possibility of a country suffering a welfare loss from a trading partner's productivity growth in the country's export good sector. But he supports globalization by arguing that "free trade may turn out pragmatically to be still best for each region in comparison with

[1] See Diamond (1997) for the relationship between human activities and viruses in history.

lobbyist-induced tariffs and quotas which involve both perversion of democracy and nonsubtle dead-weight distortion losses" (p. 143). Whereas Bhagwati (2004) defends globalization by answering many criticisms from the anti-globalism side over the issues of its impacts on poverty, child labor, culture, labor standards, and the environment, Stiglitz (2002, 2018) emphasizes that globalization has been mismanaged and argues what should be done to make globalization more equitable.

The current wave of globalization is not the first. The world economy reached a peak of globalization just before World War I, when trade and FDI attained for then unprecedented levels (Deardorff and Stern 2002). Baldwin (2006, 2011, 2016a) explains the waves of globalization by the theory of "unbundling." According to him, the first unbundling, which is the unbundling of production and consumption across national borders, occurred when the transportation revolution—railroads and steamships—dramatically lowered transport costs in the first half of the nineteenth century. Since then, until around 1990, countries engaged mainly in trade in final consumption goods, according to their comparative advantage as traditional international trade theory such as the Ricardian model and Heckscher-Ohlin model predicted, and experienced gains from international trade.[2] Baldwin calls the first unbundling "old globalization." Then, the second unbundling, which is the "spatial unbundling of production stages previously clustered in factories and offices" (Baldwin 2011, p. 5), was derived from the information and communication technology (ICT) revolution around 1990. Not only transport costs but also communication costs were substantially reduced, so that stages of production that previously had to be performed in close proximity could be performed in geographically distant locations. Due to the second unbundling, production processes were fragmented, FDI in production facilities increased, and trade in parts and intermediate goods was greatly expanded. A theory of fragmentation developed by Jones and Kierzkowski (1990) explains these changes in production and trade.[3] Baldwin calls the second unbundling "new globalization." Moreover, the third unbundling, which is the unbundling of tasks to individuals located in different countries due to a reduction in face-to-face communication (Baldwin 2016a, 2019), may have already started. Further advances in both information technology (IT) and communication technology (CT) will lead to this third unbundling. "Telemigration" (i.e., virtual presence of foreign workers through the advancement of CT) and "globotics" (i.e., a combination of globalization and a new form of robotics by the advancement of IT such as artificial intelligence) characterize the third unbundling (Baldwin 2019). Baldwin (2016a) calls the third unbundling "future globalization."

The trend of globalization after 2000 can be seen by comparing bilateral trade in the world between 2000 and a recent year (2017). Figures 1.1 and 1.2 show the amount of bilateral trade in 2000 and 2017, respectively (Ministry of Economy, Trade, and Industry (METI) 2019). Comparing these two figures, the changes in the

---

[2] For details of traditional international trade theory, see the standard textbooks on international economics such as Dixit and Norman (1980) and Feenstra (2016).

[3] Venables (1999) and Deardorff (2001) also analyze fragmentation theoretically. Kimura and Ando (2003, 2005) provide empirical evidence on fragmentation.

Fig. 1.1 Bilateral trade accounting for over 0.1% of the value of global trade (2000). *Notes*: This figure is created from the IMF's Direction of Trade Statistics. Trade between Hong Kong and other countries is excluded. *Source*: METI (2019), Fig. II–1–1–1–9

Fig. 1.2 Bilateral trade accounting for over 0.1% of the value of global trade (2017). *Notes*: This figure is created from the IMF's Direction of Trade Statistics. Trade between Hong Kong and other countries is excluded. *Source*: METI (2019), Fig. II–1–1–1–10

hub countries of bilateral trade within eighteen years are significant. In the figures, countries in a blue and red circle are a developed and an emerging/developing country, respectively. A red-filled circle represents bilateral trade that accounts for over 0.1% of global trade, and it exceeds $1 trillion in total. A blue-filled circle represents bilateral trade, and it exceeds $500 billion in total, and a green-filled circle represents bilateral trade, and it exceeds $100 billion. Blue lines indicate ties between developed countries, red lines represent ties between emerging/developing countries, and green lines ties between developed and emerging developing countries. The thickness of lines between two countries represents the size of the total trade amount on a scale, from the thickest to the thinnest, of (1) over $200 billion, (2) over $100 billion, (3) over $50 billion, and (4) below $50 billion.

From the figures we can observe the following five transitions (METI 2019):

(1) The number of large-scale bilateral trades between emerging and developing countries around China expanded, and the trade in itself greatly increased in amount.
(2) The network of bilateral trade in the East Asian region became dense, and the trade simultaneously increased in amount. Particularly, Vietnam was a rising country in trade.
(3) The number of large-scale trade and the amount of trade within the European Union (EU) expanded.
(4) The center of trade in the East Asian region moved from Japan to China.
(5) Economic linkage between the East Asian region and the North American region strengthened.

We next turn to the issue of trade policy in the progress of globalization. Deardorff and Stern (2002) argue that both steady increases in international trade and international capital flows in the second half of the twentieth century, which are much of what has come to be called globalization, were caused by technology and policy. Baldwin's theory of unbundling mainly focuses on changes in technology. On the other hand, policies that have enhanced both trade and investment are multilateral trade liberalization through the General Agreement on Tariffs and Trade (GATT)/the World Trade Organization (WTO) after World War II and the recent proliferation of regional trade agreements (RTAs) from the mid-1990s.[4]

Baldwin (2016b) illustrates how countries have succeeded in liberalizing trade through the GATT rounds of negotiations after World War II.[5] Mainly, advanced countries, such as the United States, Western European countries, and Japan, reduced their import tariffs and non-tariff barriers until the start of the WTO in 1995. By contrast, the trade negotiation at the Doha Round that started in 2001 has been deadlocked. For the last two decades, little progress has been made on multilateral trade liberalization at the WTO. Baldwin (2016b) argues that the most commonly cited cause of the WTO's difficulties is "the lost dominance of the advanced economies" (p. 106). The share of major advanced countries in world imports declined due to the rapid growth of emerging economies. At the same time, the sheer number of developing country members has shifted power in the WTO and made negotiations more difficult. In addition, Baldwin argues that regionalism and unilateral tariff-cutting by developing countries also created challenges to multilateral trade liberalization

[4] The world trading rules under the GATT/WTO are mainly characterized by the principles of reciprocity and non-discrimination (Bagwell and Staiger 2002). A series of research by Kyle Bagwell and Robert W. Staiger (e.g., Bagwell and Staiger 1999, 2002, 2005, 2010) illustrate how world trade is governed by the rules of GATT/WTO. Whereas the formation of RTAs is permitted under the GATT Article XXIV, it essentially violates the non-discrimination principle of the GATT/WTO.

[5] Eight rounds of multilateral trade negotiations were held between 1947 and 1994: Geneva (1947), Annecy (1949), Torquay (1950–1951), Geneva (1956), the Dillon Round (1960–1961), the Kennedy Round (1964–1967), the Tokyo Round (1973–1979), and the Uruguay Round (1986–1994).

through the WTO. RTAs involve tariff cutting that would otherwise have had to be achieved through the WTO. Moreover, many of the new RTAs are "deep" in the sense that "they went beyond tariff-cutting and included legally binding assurances aimed at making signatories more business-friendly to trade and investment flows from other signatories" (Baldwin 2016b, p. 107). On the other hand, an expansion in offshoring from advanced economies opened a new pathway to industrialization through joining an international production network and expanding the amount and range of tasks performed (Baldwin 2016b). Since tariffs hinder rather than help industrialization in this new development model, developing countries started to cut their import tariffs unilaterally, independently of the WTO negotiations.

Because of the malfunctioning of the WTO in the 2000s for trade liberalization and rule setting, RTAs have been playing a more important role in the world economy than before.[6] With regard to the impact of RTAs on bilateral trade, existing studies have obtained very different estimates. Cipollina and Salvatici (2010) investigate by a meta-analysis why the ex post measurements of the trade impact of RTAs are volatile. For this research, they use 1,827 point estimates of the impact of RTAs on bilateral trade from 85 studies (38 published journal articles and 47 working papers) and run meta-analysis regressions. After filtering out the publication impact and other biases, they find a robust, positive trade impact of RTAs equivalent to an increase in trade of around 40%. Since the estimates tend to become larger for more recent years, they argue that the tendency could be a consequence of the recent evolution from "shallow" to "deep" integration.

1.1.2 Global Firms and Production Networks in the East Asian Region

For the last two decades, empirical studies on international trade have provided evidence of firm heterogeneity in trade, as Melitz (2003) demonstrates theoretically (e.g., Bernard and Jensen 1995, 1999; Bernard et al. 2007, 2009, 2012, 2018). A

[6] There has been much debate over the issue of regionalism versus multilateralism. Originally, the classic work by Viner (1950) demonstrates that, using the concepts of trade creation and trade diversion, the formation of a customs union (CU) is not necessarily welfare-improving not only for world welfare but also for member countries of the CU. Ohyama (1972) and Kemp and Wan (1976) show the possibility of forming a Pareto-improving CU by adjusting external tariffs and making internal transfers—the Kemp-Wan-Ohyama theorem. Then, since the early 1990s the question of the dynamic time-path has attracted great attention (Bhagwati 1992; Panagariya 1999). That is, scholars have investigated whether RTAs under regionalism are, in the terminology of Bhagwati (1991), "building blocks" or "stumbling blocks" to global free trade. Studies on this issue include Aghion et al. (2007), Baldwin (1995), Freund (2000), Furusawa and Konishi (2007), Krishna (1998), Mukunoki and Tachi (2006), Ornelas (2005), and Saggi and Yildiz (2010). However, because of the stagnant negotiation at the WTO and the "deepened" nature of the recent RTAs, it seems that the direction of the debate over the issue of regionalism versus multilateralism has changed, so that the focus of research is on the more active role of RTAs. See Panagariya (2000), Freund and Ornelas (2010), Maggi (2014), and Limão (2016) for surveys of the literature.

large number of studies that employ micro data in many different countries have suggested that "global firms" play a dominant role in each market. Bernard et al. (2018) define "global firms" as "firms that participate in the international economy along multiple margins and account for substantial share of aggregate trade" (p. 566).

Bernard et al. (2018) use US firm and trade transactions data and show that only a subset of firms participate in international markets. These trading firms indicate superior performance characteristics: they are larger and more productive than other non-trading firms. Moreover, a large fraction of firms that export or import actually engage in both exporting and importing. "More successful firms export more of each product to each market, export more products to each market, export to more markets, import more of each product from each source country, import more products from each source country, and import from more source countries" (Bernard et al. 2018, p. 607). Global firms are likely to be MNEs. Bernard et al. (2009) report that US-based MNEs mediate more than 90% of US trade. Consistent with the model of heterogeneous firms (Helpman et al. 2004), Yeaple (2009) shows that more productive US firms tend to own affiliates in a larger number of countries and that these affiliates generate greater revenue from sales in their host economies.

Studies of Japanese firms have also provided evidence consistent with theories of heterogeneous firms (e.g., Head and Ries 2003; Kimura and Kiyota 2006; Todo 2011; Wakasugi 2014; Wakasugi and Tanaka 2010, 2012). Thus, global firms are likely to hold a dominant position in the globalized activities of Japanese firms. In some of the chapters in this book, we employ micro data on Japanese firms and focus on their globalized activities. Since Japanese MNEs play an important role in production networks in East Asia, it is worth looking at the situation of the supply networks in this region, as the background of the study.

According to METI (2019), about two thirds of annual intra-regional exports (of raw materials, intermediate goods, and final goods) in East Asia from 2011 to 2017 were shared by intermediate goods, whereas their export ratios in the 1990s were a little over one half. Annual intra-regional exports amounted to $1,400–1,600 billion in 2011–2017, while they ranged between $170 and $400 billion in the 1990s.[7] Both amount and ratio of intra-regional exports have increased greatly for the 1990–2017 period. If we focus on the machinery industry in East Asia, in which the international division of labor is most developed,[8] the ratio of intermediate goods in its intra-regional export during 1998–2017 was at 60–65% except for 2012, while its ratio in 1990 was less than 50% (METI 2019).[9] In contrast, the amount of its trade increased rapidly from $40 billion in 1990 to about $830 billion in 2017. These results unambiguously substantiate that the production network is formed in the machinery industry in East Asia.

The system of typical international division of labor between the United States (developed country) and Mexico (developing country) focusing on intra-firm trans-

7 See Fig. II–1–1–1–15 in METI (2019).

8 Machinery industry includes general machinery, electric machinery, electric household machinery and equipment, transportation machinery, and precision machinery.

9 See Fig. II–1–1–1–15 in METI (2019).

actions was established by around the year 1990 (Ando and Kimura 2014). Later, this system developed into the one including East Asia in the machinery industry (mainly electrical and electronic sectors): parts and intermediated goods are exported from East Asia to Mexico, and then final goods and parts that are manufactured in Mexico are exported to the United States and Canada. After the Central and Eastern European countries—such as Poland, Czech Republic, Slovakia, Hungary, and Romania—became EU members in the fifth enlargement of the EU, industrial clusters were accelerated in these countries. As a result, the supply of machinery parts and intermediates from East Asia rapidly expanded (Ando and Kimura 2013). Among others, the import of electrical and electronic parts and intermediates increased remarkably. The production network between the EU and East Asia was consolidated via the Central and Eastern European countries (Ando and Kimura 2013). These countries have an active role as a catalyst, like Mexico in North America. The fact that East Asia is deeply related to the other two global production networks attracts our interest.

The enlargement of production networks in a region makes it possible to supply goods efficiently, while it may make the supply of goods vulnerable to shocks. In fact, it has been shown that production networks in East Asia are relatively resilient to severe shocks (Ando and Kimura 2012; Obashi 2011; Todo et al. 2015).[10] Specifically, Ando and Kimura (2012) analyze the impact of the 2008–2009 Global Financial Crisis and of the 2011 Great East Japan Earthquake on Japanese exports, focusing on the characteristics of domestic/international production networks in machinery industries. They show that these two massive shocks generated common and different adjustments in production networks and trade. In the face of such severe shocks, trade within the production networks of machinery final products and other products demonstrates distinctive stability and resiliency. However, the magnitude and duration of the shocks were fairly different: the impact of the Financial Crisis was huge and prolonged, whereas that of the Japan Earthquake was much smaller and more temporary. They argue that the cause of such a difference is that the Financial Crisis was primarily a demand shock in the US and EU markets, while the Japan Earthquake was a supply shock due to the destruction of production plants in the impacted area.

The effects of the 2011 Great East Japan Earthquake on supply chain networks within Japan are examined by Todo et al. (2015).[11] Using firm-level data, they show that extensive supply chain networks are not always harmful to disaster recovery.

[10] The production networks in East Asia may also be resilient to shocks caused by pandemics. Early assessments of the impact of the COVID-19 pandemic on international production networks and global value chains include Ando (2021), Espitia et al. (2021), and Hayakawa and Mukunoki (2021).

[11] With regard to the macroeconomic impact of the 2011 Great East Japan Earthquake, see, for example, Carvalho et al. (2021). They quantify the role of input-output linkages as a mechanism for the propagation and amplification of shocks. According to their estimates, the earthquake resulted in a 3.8% point decline in the growth rate of firms with disaster-hit suppliers and a 3.1% point decline in that of firms with disaster-hit customers. Then, using a general equilibrium model of production networks, they estimate that the disaster resulted in a 0.47% point decline in Japan's real GDP growth in the year after the earthquake.

More specifically, they find that having more suppliers and customers outside of the disaster area tends to shorten the recovery time, though it affects sales growth in the medium term only weakly. By contrast, having more suppliers and customers in the disaster area has no effect on the recovery time but tends to improve medium-term sales growth. In addition, they identify a negative effect from supply chains on recovery through the disruption of supply and demand and two positive effects through support and substitution. Overall, they conclude that the positive effects from extensive supply networks typically outweigh the negative effects, resulting in a net positive effect. Moreover, Obashi (2011) investigates the resilience of international production network in the Asian region to the 1997–1998 Asian Currency Crisis. She conducts a series of survival analyses and finds that transactions of machinery parts and components within the production network are more likely to be stable and resilient to a temporary disruption, compared to transactions of finished products. More specifically, during the Asian Currency Crisis, machinery parts and components were more likely to be traded through long-lived trade relationships than finished products. Besides, many of the trade relationships for machinery parts and components were restored shortly after the break caused by the Asian Currency Crisis, as compared to those for finished products.

1.1.3 Innovation and Diffusion of Knowledge

It is Joseph A. Schumpeter (1883–1950) who first asserted the importance of innovation for economic development in industrial society. These days, it is well recognized that innovation has a significant influence on the rise and fall of an enterprise. After his assertion, it has been extensively investigated and discussed in the literature whether firm size and market power have an effect on firm innovation. Schumpeter (1942) argued that a large-scale establishment is the most powerful engine of progress and that firms in concentrated markets have a stronger incentive to invest in innovation. Many theoretical and empirical studies have explored the relationship between market structure and innovation. Specifically, the Schumpeterian endogenous growth models, the pioneering work of which is Aghion and Howitt (1992), formalize Schumpeter's argument. In contrast to the Schumpeterian theory, Arrow (1962) argues that a firm's gains from innovation at the margin are larger in an industry that is more competitive ex ante. Assuming that property rights over invention are fully protected, he shows that a monopolist that is not exposed to competition under both old and new technologies has less incentive to invest in research and development (R&D) for a process innovation than does a firm in a competitive sector. Blundell et al. (1999) examine the relationship between a firm's ex ante market power and innovation and find that the market share has a positive effect on innovation, whereas that of overall market concentration is negative, suggesting that, while a higher market share stimulates innovation, concentrated industries may innovate less. Many other empirical studies find a positive relationship between competition and innovation.[12] To reconcile the Schumpeterian theory with empirical evidence, Aghion et al. (2005) develop a simple model in which competition discourages laggard firms from innovating but encourages neck-and-neck firms in innovating and derive an inverted-U shaped relationship between competition and innovation. They provide strong empirical support for their theory using data on publicly listed manufacturing firms in the United Kingdom. In contrast, Hashmi (2013) finds evidence of a mildly negative relationship between competition and innovation from the US data. He modifies the model of Aghion et al. (2005) in such a way that the average technology gap is higher in the country where the relationship is negative and then show that the modified model can explain both negative and inverted-U shaped relationships. Some empirical studies provide evidence to support the Schumpeter's hypothesis more strongly. For example, focusing on publicly traded US industrial firms in the 1910s and 1920s, Nicholas (2003) finds that both firm size and market power have significantly positive effects on patenting and, moreover, that financial markets reward firms for their innovative behavior with increasing their market values. He shows that all of these effects worked strongly during the 1920s.

Innovation is one of the important sources of competitive advantage for global firms (e.g., Aw et al. 2011; Atkeson and Burstein 2010; Costantini and Melitz 2008). Those firms make enormous investments in R&D. Then, both global firms and other firms benefit from diffusion of knowledge (Keller and Yeaple 2013; Sampson 2016). A large number of existing studies have shown that even for highly advanced economies like the United States, the outcomes of R&D in foreign countries play an important role in its own technical progress. Most of the other countries in the world are far more dependent on foreign R&D (Sveikauskas 2007). Therefore, innovation and diffusion of knowledge are both strongly related to globalization.

A common measure of the state of innovation is the number of patent applications. Patent applications worldwide were 3.224 million in 2019 (World Intellectual Property Organization (WIPO) 2020). A breakdown of the total applications by country is as follows: China was top-ranked, with 1.4 million applications and a 43.4% share of the world total, followed by the United States (0.621 million, 19.3%), and Japan (0.308 million, 9.6%). China's share has increased considerably over the last decade from 17% in 2009 to 43.4% in 2019. Although Japan's share has decreased from 18.8% in 2009 to 9.6% in 2019, Japan is still ranked in the top three.

In terms of the share of patent applications by region, Asia accounts for 65.0% (50.9%) in 2019 (2009), followed by North America 20.4% (26.6%), and Europe 11.3% (17.4%) (WIPO, 2020). Over the past 10 years, Asia's share increased greatly by 14% points, whereas those of North America and Europe decreased by 6.2% points and 6% points, respectively. The main factor in the increase in Asia is an increase in the number of the applications in China in this period.

Furthermore, among 35 technology fields the largest share in the total of published patent applications worldwide in 2017 (3.199 million) was computer technology (7.3%), followed by electrical machinery/apparatus/energy (6.7%), measurement

[12] See Gilbert (2006) and Cohen (2010) for detailed surveys of the literature.

technology (5.1%), and medical technology (4.6%): the first two of these are in the field of electrical engineering and the other two are in the field of instruments.

The effects of R&D on firms themselves and on the economy in general can be measured by the returns on R&D. There have been many empirical studies to estimate the private and social returns on R&D. Sveikauskas (2007) reviews the estimates of the private and social returns on R&D shown in the previous studies. The private return on R&D has generally been estimated by comparing productivity growth or profitability in different firms with R&D expenditures or the growth of the research stock within these firms (Sveikauskas 2007). On the other hand, in order to estimate the returns to an industry or a national economy or even the returns to the world economy, the spillover effects of R&D and complementary investments have to be taken into account (Sveikauskas 2007). An example of complementary investment is that when a new computer is introduced, purchasing firms must deploy considerable resources to use the new equipment effectively. According to Sveikauskas (2007), the estimates of the private return on R&D in the previous studies range from 10% to 43%, whereas those of the social return range from 11% to 147%. He concludes that the private returns of 25% and the social returns of 65% seem reasonable. Since the social rates of returns include returns due to spillovers of knowledge in addition to private returns, the estimates become two or three times as large as the private rates of returns.[13]

Spillover channels of R&D performance are various. They are, for example, disclosure of patents, reverse engineering of newly developed products, movements of researchers and technical experts among organizations, research exchanges among them, industrial espionage, outsourcing, FDI, and so on.[14]

Two major channels of international diffusion of knowledge are international trade and FDI (Keller 2004, 2010). A number of studies confirm significant spillovers of knowledge through trade, but the empirical findings on spillover effects through FDI vary substantially. Spillovers of knowledge from foreign investors to local firms in the same sector are called horizontal spillovers, while knowledge spillovers from foreign investors to local firms in upstream and downstream sectors are called vertical spillovers. A large number of existing studies show that vertical spillovers from FDI tend to be positive and large, whereas horizontal ones from FDI are almost negligible (Keller 2004). However, the results vary substantially across countries, sectors, and estimation methods.[15] Therefore, spillovers from FDI have attracted great attention from economists, and a number of studies using meta-analysis approaches have been

[13] Two recent studies (Neves and Sequeira 2018; Ugur et al. 2020), both of which conduct meta-analysis regressions, provide somewhat conflicting results. The former finds that the average spillover effect is high (less than but close to one) and highly significant, whereas the latter shows that the average spillover effect is positive but heterogeneous and usually smaller than the own-R&D effect. Thus, it seems that the magnitude and significance of the spillover effect should be investigated.

[14] Patents excluding secret patents disclose their technology information after their application: although secret patents have already been introduced in many developed countries, their contents are not disclosed within a certain period of time to keep their technology information secret.

[15] See Murakami and Otsuka (2020) for a recent survey of the literature on spillovers from FDI.

conducted to figure out what factors cause differences in estimates (Görg and Strobl 2001; Havránek and Iršová 2011; Iršová and Havránek 2013; Meyer and Sinani 2009). With regard to horizontal spillovers, Iršová and Havránek (2013) find that investments through joint ventures between foreign investors and domestic firms tend to bring more positive spillovers than full foreign-ownership ones. The degree of technology gap is also important. They find that spillovers get smaller when the technology gap between foreign investors and domestic firms is too large. Moreover, Meyer and Sinani (2009) show that horizontal spillovers are related to a U-shaped form to the host economy's level of development in terms of income, institutional framework, and human capital. As for vertical spillovers, Havránek and Iršová (2011) find that spillovers tend to be larger for host economies open to international trade and underdeveloped financial systems. In addition, greater spillovers seem to be generated by FDI from more distant countries with slight technological advantages over domestic firms.

The majority of the existing empirical studies on international diffusion of knowledge have analyzed the spillover effects of foreign knowledge on the productivity of domestic firms, but there is another type of equally important spillover effect. That is, the R&D activities of some firms or researchers may benefit from spillovers of knowledge that originated from innovation or the outcomes of R&D by other firms or researchers. To distinguish these two types of spillover effects, we call the former type "international productivity spillovers" and the latter type "international technology spillovers."[16] Although both types of spillovers capture flows of knowledge across countries, the exact effects differ. In this book we focus on the latter type. In the industrial organization literature, there are a large number of theoretical studies on the latter type of spillover among firms located in the same country (e.g., d'Aspremont and Jacquemin 1988; Haruna and Goel 2017; Kamien et al. 1992; Leahy and Neary 1997; Suzumura 1992). Moreover, theoretical studies on international technology spillovers and policies to address these spillovers include Goel and Haruna (2011), Haruna and Goel (2015), Leahy and Neary (1999), Neary and Leahy (2000), Neary and O'Sullivan (1999), and Qiu and Tao (1998). As we will explain in Chaps. 5–7, there are a number of existing empirical studies that investigate international technology spillovers, such as Branstetter (2006), Cappelli and Montobbio (2020), Haruna et al. (2010), Hu and Jaffe (2003), Jinji et al. (2013, 2015, 2019a), Li (2014), MacGarvie (2006), Mancusi (2008), Peri (2005), and Singh (2007).

1.2 Overview of the Book

In this book we explore interactions among deep integration, global firms, and technology spillovers. The structure of the book is as follows. In Chap. 2 we illustrate

[16] In the literature the latter type is often called international R&D spillovers, but sometimes the same term is used for the former type as well. Therefore, we use the term "international technology spillovers" rather than international R&D spillovers for the latter type.

the trend of regional trade integration by distinguishing deep integration from shallow one. We clarify what deep regional integration means and discuss how we can measure shallow and deep integration.

In Chaps. 3 and 4 we focus on the behavior of global firms using micro data on Japanese MNEs. Specifically, we empirically investigate how firm performance, such as productivity and Tobin's q, affects the choice of globalization mode. As for the modes of globalization, we consider export, FDI, and foreign outsourcing (FO). In Chaps. 5 and 6, we examine the relationship between global firms and technology spillovers. Specifically, we consider how trade patterns influence technology spillovers among countries/regions in Chap. 5. First of all, trade patterns can be classified into one-way trade (OWT or inter-industry trade) and two-way trade (or intra-industry trade: IIT). IIT is, furthermore, decomposed into horizontal intra-industry trade (HIIT) and vertical intra-industry trade (VIIT). These trade patterns arise from the behavior of heterogeneous firms. On the other hand, technology spillovers among countries/regions are measured by citations of patents. As we will explain later, patent citation data are used as a direct measure of technology spillovers (Hall et al. 2001).

Chapter 6 is devoted to the analysis of how FDI promotes technology spillovers. Employing detailed data on Japanese MNEs and their foreign affiliates, we measure the types of FDI (i.e., vertical and horizontal FDI). Then, we examine how differences in the types of FDI affect the degree of technology spillovers between Japanese MNEs and their host economies. Again, we utilize patent citation data.

Finally, we analyze the relationship between deep integration and technology spillovers in Chap. 7. Deep RTAs include a number of provisions that may directly affect flows of knowledge among countries/regions. We examine which aspects of deep integration contribute to enhance technology spillovers among members of RTAs.

To consider how deep integration facilitates technology spillovers, we need to take various channels of technology spillovers into consideration. Deep integration stimulates globalized activities of firms in a number of ways, which facilitates technology spillovers through various channels. For example, as for international trade, firms can obtain the necessary technology information from imported goods by dismantling them and making imitations. Moreover, when enterprises establish their operations overseas, this causes the transfer of production and business management technology to local enterprises in the host country. Experts, employees, and managers that are locally hired by the enterprises make their technologies, know-how, and knowledge with respect to their production and process management diffuse through their movements. In contrast, offshoring creates more direct diffusion of technological information. A representative example of offshoring is electronics manufacturing services (EMS) in Taiwan. In recent years, the number of firms without fabrication facilities ("fabless companies") has increased. They specialize their activities in the design, development, and sales of products, and outsource their manufacturing. Apple Inc., which commissions the manufacturing of iPhone to enterprises in Taiwan and China, is one of the well-known fabless enterprises. Local enterprises overseas can acquire and accumulate information on the content and ways of manufacturing products through such commissioning.

Chapter 8 concludes and provides policy implications. Furthermore, it discusses some issues for future research in connection with this book.

Let us now look at each of these chapters in more detail.

Chapter 2 "The Trend of Deep Regional Integration"

The main purpose of this chapter is to illustrate the current trend of regional trade integration by distinguishing deep integration from shallow one and to shed light on the causes and impacts of recent deep regional integration. We explain what shallow and deep RTAs mean and why countries have recently pursued deep integration. Next, we argue how we can measure the degree of deep RTAs and what data are available to analyze the content and effects of deep RTAs. Moreover, we examine the state of deep RTAs in the world generally and in the Asia-Pacific region specifically.

The concept of shallow and deep integration is originally proposed by Lawrence (1996). Shallow integration is simply trade liberalization involving the removal of trade barriers. By contrast, deep integration "moves beyond the removal of border barriers" (Lawrence 1996, p. 8). Deep RTAs contain a variety of provisions including those on investment, labor, the environment, and intellectual property rights (IPR).

Horn et al. (2010) identify 52 policy areas covered by RTAs and classify them into two groups, i.e., WTO-plus (WTO+) and WTO-extra (WTO–X). The WTO+ group includes 14 provisions and the WTO-X group includes 38 ones. Limão (2016) recategorizes the WTO+ and WTO–X policy areas from the viewpoints of the depth and breadth of RTAs. The depth of RTAs measures the degree of bilateral economic cooperation. As for the definition of the depth of an RTA, he proposes that the depth of RTAs is measured by four categories of policy areas in the WTO+ and WTO–X groups: (a) import tariffs, (b) non-tariff barriers (NTBs), (c) behind-the-border policies (BBPs), and (d) other policies (OPs). On the other hand, the breadth of RTAs measures how wide the coverage of policy areas is. Policy areas are classified by (i) the type of trade (goods/services), (ii) technology (innovation/spillovers/IPR), and (iii) factors of production (capital/labor). As the definition of the breadth of an RTA, he proposes that the breadth of RTAs is measured by five categories: (a) services, (b) technology, (c) investment/capital, (d) labor, and (e) non-economic policies (NEPs).

We examine the characteristics of deep RTAs in the Asia-Pacific region. The contents of RTAs signed by the Association of South-East Asian Nations (ASEAN) countries, China and Japan are fairly different in their depth and breadth. Specifically, there are significant differences in the NTB and BBP areas in the depth measure and in the investment/capital and labor provisions in the breadth one. The degree of deep RTAs in the Asia-Pacific region is still not so high in both the OPs in the depth measure and the NEPs in the breadth one, compared with those in OP areas.

Chapter 3 "Which Aspect of Firm Performance is Important for the Choice of Globalization Mode?"

In this chapter we attempt to compare the effects of various measures of firm performance on firms' globalization activities. Japanese firm-level data (covering the period 1994–1999) are used. Information on corporate balance sheets and patent applications are included in the data. Then, following Jinji et al. (2019b), we estimate the degree of engagement in each globalization mode by calculating the ratio of a mode of globalization activities such as export, FDI, and FO to the domestic sales of headquarters companies. Besides, we estimate the relative choice of the globalization mode by taking the ratio of the volume of direct export by the headquarters company to FDI (i.e., sales of foreign affiliates) and the ratio of costs of FO to FDI. As the measures of firm performance, we use three variables. First, labor productivity (LP) is used as a measure of productivity. Further, we employ two measures to capture the importance of the knowledge-capital intensity: one measure, as the second variable, is Tobin's q (Tobin 1969) estimated by a simple approximation version; and the other, as the third variable, is the intangible asset intensity, which is the ratio of intangible to tangible assets. Intangible assets include patents, copyrights, trademarks, trade names, goodwill, and other items that lack physical substance and provide long-term benefits to the company. By using the stock of patent applications as a direct measure of intangible assets we regress the indexes of a firm's choice of globalization mode on these variables.

By using Japanese firm-level data, we investigate empirically which measure of performance is important when a firm chooses one from various modes of globalization activity. As a result, it is found that an increase in LP or Tobin's q motivates a firm to engage in export and FDI more, but does not enhance the engagement in FO. Secondly, it is found by using quantile regression that a difference in LP is important to a choice between exporting and FDI, but not to a choice between FDI and FO. In contrast, a difference in Tobin's q is important to a choice between FDI and FO, but not to the one between exporting and FDI. Interestingly, a difference in the intangible asset intensity is important to a choice between exporting and FDI as well as to the one between FDI and FO.

Chapter 4 "Does Tobin's q Matter for a Firm Choice of Globalization Mode?"

Previous theoretical research on the relationship between the productivities of firms and their globalization modes includes, for example, the following: Melitz (2003) presents a model in which the most productive firms export goods to foreign markets, whereas less productive firms supply goods only to their domestic market; and Helpman et al. (2004) extend the framework of Melitz and predict that only the most productive firms find it profitable to serve foreign markets via FDI and that medium productivity firms serve foreign markets through exports (the HMY prediction).

We attempt to sort firms into three modes of globalization by Tobin's q (Tobin 1969). Our study is motivated by a theoretical analysis by Chen et al. (2012), who examine how the relative importance of knowledge capital over physical capital affects a firm's choice between FDI and FO for offshore production. They then show that firms with a higher physical-capital intensity tend to choose FO, whereas firms with a higher knowledge-capital intensity tend to conduct FDI. An interesting testable hypothesis is obtained from this result: firms with a high Tobin's q tend to conduct FDI, whereas firms with a low Tobin's q tend to choose FO (the CHM hypothesis). Given that the book value of capital reflects only physical assets, a firm with a higher knowledge-capital intensity will have a higher Tobin's q, because the firm's market value reflects both knowledge-based and physical assets.

We employ detailed Japanese firm-level data (covering the period 1994–1999) to sort firms into three modes of globalization by Tobin's q. The data include information on sales, employment, capital, R&D expenditure, direct exports, the costs of domestic production and FO of the companies headquartered in Japan, and the sales of their foreign affiliates. Corporate balance sheet data are also included. The advantage of the data over previous studies allows us to recognize not only whether a firm engages in a particular globalization activity among exports, FDI, and FO, but also the extent to which it is involved in that activity. By utilizing the feature of the data, we construct indexes to measure the relative choice of globalization mode through calculating both ratios of the costs of FO to the total FDI and of the volume of direct exports by the headquarters company to horizontal FDI. We then regress these indexes of globalization activity on Tobin's q, of which measurement is based on the simple approximation proposed. To demonstrate how sorted patterns by Tobin's q are different from those by a firm's productivity, we regress the indexes of globalization activity on the total factor productivity (TFP) of each individual firm. Our analysis focuses mainly on firms engaging in multiple globalization modes and attempts to reveal whether Tobin's q (and TFP) motivates the firms to select more FDI relative to FO or exports.

The main findings are as follows. Both quantile and endogenous quantile regressions indicate that an increase in Tobin's q significantly reduces the ratio of FO to the total FDI across different quantiles, which strongly supports the CHM hypothesis that an MNE reduces its ratio of FO to FDI, as Tobin's q increases. Besides, Tobin's q has a positive effect on the ratio of exports to horizontal FDI at some quantiles, but is not strong. This implies that the imperfect contractibility of knowledge capital and a higher cost of technology transfer actually matter for knowledge-capital intensive firms. These effects of Tobin's q on a firm's choice of globalization mode are apparently different from those of TFP. An increase in TFP motivates a firm to enhance its engagement in horizontal FDI relative to exports, which supports the HMY prediction and concurs with existing empirical findings, but a difference in TFP does not significantly affect the choice of a firm between FDI and outsourcing.

Chapter 5 "Trade Patterns and International Technology Spillovers: Theory and Evidence from Japanese and European Patent Citations"

The international trade of goods and services is considered to be a major channel of technology spillovers. A simple explanation for this is that firms in an importing country can obtain information on advanced technology by, for example, reverse engineering of imported goods, patent information, and the movement of business persons. However, the relationship between bilateral trade patterns (such as inter-industry and intra-industry trade) and international technology spillovers has received little attention in the literature. It is intuitively conceivable that the flow of international knowledge could be different, depending on whether a good is only imported, exported, or both imported and exported. We have a look at the relationship between trade patterns and technology spillovers. It is worth considering the relationship from a theoretical point of view. To address this issue, we develop a two-country model of monopolistic competition with quality differentiation, in which inter- and intra-industry trade patterns endogenously arise. Our model is an extension of Melitz and Ottaviano (2008). It is assumed that firms randomly draw their product quality and hence are heterogeneous in product quality even if their productivity is identical. We investigate how technology spillovers are associated with trade patterns.

One theoretical feature of our model is that it can explain OWT, HIIT, and VIIT in a unified framework. Then our framework can provide the three testable hypotheses: the first hypothesis is that technology spillovers are larger when the trade pattern between the two countries is HIIT than when it is VIIT; the second one is whether or not technology spillovers from the country exporting higher quality products to that exporting lower quality ones are larger than those in the opposite direction is ambiguous when the trade pattern is VIIT; and the third one is that technology spillovers are lower when the trade pattern is inter-industry trade (i.e., OWT) than when it is VIIT.

Secondly, we empirically examine whether the three hypotheses theoretically derived hold. Our empirical analysis in this chapter complements Jinji et al. (2015): we use patent citation data at Japanese and European patent offices, whereas Jinji et al. (2015) employ US patent data. Our estimation results basically confirm the predictions of our theoretical model. An increase in the shares of HIIT and VIIT has a significantly positive effect on international technology spillovers. In addition, HIIT has a larger effect on them than VIIT does. In contrast, the relative magnitudes of technology spillovers between the country exporting high quality products and the country exporting low quality ones under VIIT are generally ambiguous. It is derived that the effect of OWT on technology spillovers tends to be much weaker than that of other trade patterns. Finally, we concluded that intra-industry trade plays a significant role in technology spillovers.

Chapter 6 "Vertical versus Horizontal Foreign Direct Investment and Technology Spillovers"

In this chapter we attempt to identify how MNEs' activities in terms of horizontal and vertical FDI affect technology spillovers between themselves and host countries. Then, we combine the Japanese firm-level data on the business activities of Japanese MNEs' foreign affiliates and the data on the patent citations at the US patent office between MNEs and their host countries. We now define a measure of "pure horizontal FDI" as the extent to which affiliates' purchases of intermediate inputs and sales of final goods are concentrated in the local market and a measure of "pure vertical FDI" as the extent to which their purchases of intermediate inputs and sales of final goods are linked to the home country. We then estimate how the two types of FDI affect both technology spillovers from Japanese MNEs to the host country and from the host country to them by utilizing a negative binomial model. Moreover, to deal with a potential endogeneity problem we employ an endogenous switching model.

We obtain interesting results concerning technology spillovers under vertical and horizontal FDI through empirical analysis. First, an increase in the degree of pure vertical FDI has significantly positive effects on technology spillovers captured by patent citations when technologically advanced economies host Japanese MNEs (call this "result V"). Technology spillovers occur in both directions between the MNEs and their host countries. These positive effects of pure vertical FDI on them are robust for different specifications, and partially vertical FDI has significantly positive effects on technology spillovers from the (high-income) host countries to the MNEs. By contrast, an increase in the degree of pure horizontal FDI has no significant effects or significantly negative effects on technology spillovers between the MNEs and their host countries (call this "result H"). Partially horizontal FDI has significantly positive effects on them from the MNEs to the (high-income) host countries, but this result is not robust for different estimations. It is concluded from these results that pure vertical FDI plays a dominant role in the technology spillovers in both directions between the MNEs and the high-income host countries.

To explain the observed results between the structure of FDI and technology spillovers, we develop a simple partial-equilibrium model of FDI and technology spillovers among developed countries, in which differentiated goods are produced in three stages. The market is characterized by monopolistic competition. Depending on parameter values, firms may have an incentive to engage in horizontal or vertical FDI. Given the same factor costs in the two countries, there is no possibility of vertical FDI in the usual sense. However, vertical FDI does occur if there are technology gaps in some production stages between the countries and if firms can take advantage of the superior technology of the foreign country by fragmenting its production process and conducting some intermediate production in the foreign country. This explains result V observed in the empirical analysis. The technology gaps are the source of technology spillovers through FDI. Technology spillovers may occur in one way or two ways if firms engage in vertical FDI, depending on how the three production stages are located in the two countries. It is also shown that horizontal FDI does not necessarily induce technology spillovers, because it is mainly motivated by saving transportation costs and appears even in the absence of technological difference. This result corresponds with result H.

Chapter 7 "Do Deep Regional Trade Agreements Enhance International Technology Spillovers?: Depth, Breadth, and Heterogeneity"

A rapid proliferation of RTAs has been observed during the last two decades. RTAs are primarily aimed at expanding trade in goods by reducing tariffs on imports and removing non-tariff barriers, but many recent RTAs pursue deeper integration, and include liberalization of investment and harmonization of IPR protection policy. It seems that RTAs affect the diffusion of knowledge (i.e., technology spillovers) across countries. We empirically investigate this issue.

We use patent citation data as a proxy for technology spillovers. Previous research shows that technology spillovers measured by patent citations decrease as geographical distance extends, but has paid little attention to the effects of "economic distance" on the localization of technology spillovers. Economic distance is a measure of proximity between two locations in an economic sense, which is affected by not only geographical distance but also other factors such as membership of RTAs, infrastructure, a transportation mode, and public policy. A given geographical distance between two countries (or regions) is constant, although the economic distance can vary, depending on such factors. Therefore, economic distance seems to be more meaningful to a measurement of technology spillovers than geographical distance. In particular, the membership of the same RTA or any other organization to facilitate international trade of goods will affect the economic distance between two countries and be of importance for the localization of technology spillovers.

Peri (2005) and Jinji et al. (2019a) have investigated the effects of RTAs on technology spillovers. Using a sample of 18 countries with 147 subnational regions in Western Europe and North America for the period of 1975–1996, Peri (2005) estimates a gravity-like model to examine the effects of several resistance factors on patent citations. He shows that regional, national, and linguistic borders have a significantly negative effect on technology spillovers, whereas the effect of "trade blocs" on them is insignificant. By contrast, Jinji et al. (2019a) find a significantly positive effect of RTAs on technology spillovers for the sample of 114 countries/regions during 1991–2007.

In comparison to these studies, we conduct a more comprehensive analysis of the effects of RTAs on technology spillovers by extending the sample to 243 countries/regions and the coverage of RTAs to 110. Specifically, we extend the research of Jinji et al. (2019a). For example, we construct a panel for 11,667 pairs of the citing and cited countries/regions from the sample of 243 countries/regions for 25 years from 1991 to 2015 by patent application and citation data from the US patent office.

We focus both on the impacts of the depth and breadth of RTAs and the heterogeneous effects of individual RTAs on international technology spillovers. With regard to the depth of RTAs, we use indexes in the areas of tariffs, NTBs, BBPs, and OPs. As for the breadth of RTAs, we construct indexes for services, technology, investment/capital, labor, and NEP areas. On the other hand, the heterogeneous effects of individual RTAs are captured by various RTA dummies. In addition to the usual RTA dummy, we use separate dummy variables for RTAs signed by the United States and European countries, such as the North American Free Trade Agreement (NAFTA), the European Community (EC)/European Union (EU), RTAs with the United States, and FTAs with the EC/EU.

The main findings are as follows. First, we confirm the result of Jinji et al. (2019a) that RTAs increase international technology spillovers measured by bilateral patent citations. Second, we demonstrate that deep RTAs with higher coverage of policy areas in the depth categories and those with higher coverage of policy areas in the breadth categories both have positive effects on international technology spillovers. Third, we show that the NAFTA has a strongly positive effect on such spillovers in comparison with the effects of the EU and EU enlargement.

Chapter 2
The Trend of Deep Regional Integration

2.1 Introduction

The last quarter century until around 2016 has witnessed "unprecedented trade integration" (Baier et al. 2019) in the world. There has been a rapid proliferation of regional trade agreements (RTAs). Figure 2.1 shows the evolution of RTAs in the world since the World War II. The red bar indicates the number of RTAs in force notified to the General Agreement on Tariffs and Trade (GATT)/the World Trade Organization (WTO) in each year and the gray bar indicates the number of inactive RTAs notified to the GATT/WTO in each year. Moreover, the gray line indicates the cumulative notifications of RTAs in force and inactive RTAs, the red line the cumulative notifications of RTAs in force, and the black line the cumulative number of RTAs in force. For any of these indexes to show the evolution of RTAs, it is evident that a proliferation of RTAs started around 1992. More than 15 new RTAs were notified to the WTO each year. More than 35 new RTAs were notified to the WTO in 2009 when their number peaked. The high level of the proliferation had been maintained until 2015, but the momentum seemed to be paused from 2016 to 2020. The main causes of the momentary pause are the anti-globalization sentiment in many countries and the implementation of protectionism policies by the Trump Administration in the United States and other countries (Jinji 2021). Moreover, since 2020 the COVID-19 pandemic may have affected the momentum of globalization.

The unprecedented trade integration over the last quarter century involved not only a rapid increase in the number of RTAs but also the "deepened" and "widened" nature of trade integration (World Trade Organization (WTO) 2011). As one of the stylized facts about RTAs, WTO (2011) points out that the coverage of RTAs in terms of policy areas has been deepened and widened over time. That is, many of the recent RTAs go beyond traditional tariff-cutting and include a wide array of non-tariff policy areas, both at the border and behind-the-border, such as services trade, investment, labor market regulation, intellectual property rights (IPR) protection, and technical

N. Jinji et al., *Deep Integration, Global Firms, and Technology Spillovers*,
Advances in Japanese Business and Economics 26,
https://doi.org/10.1007/978-981-16-5210-3_2

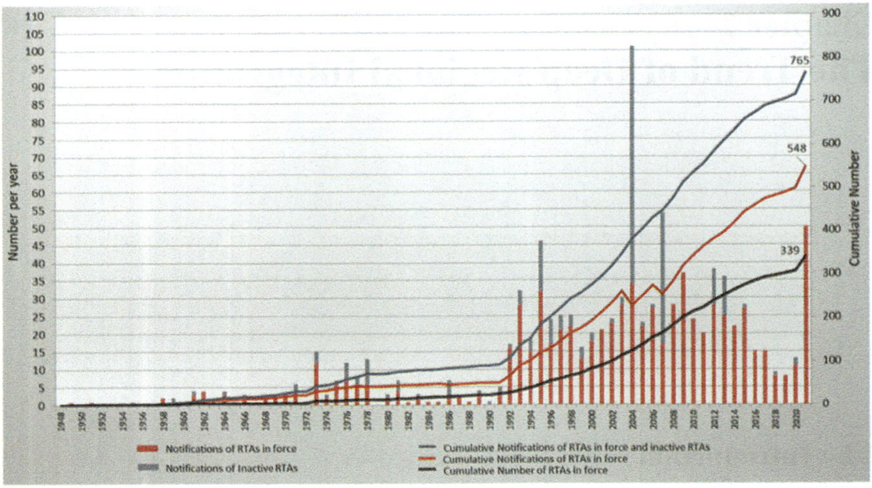

Fig. 2.1 Evolution of RTAs in the World, 1948–2021. *Notes*: Notifications of RTAs: goods, services and accessions to an RTA are counted separately. The cumulative lines show the number of RTAs/notifications that were in force for a given year. The notifications of RTAs in force are shown by year of entry into force and the notifications of inactive RTAs are shown by inactive year. *Source*: RTA Section, World Trade Organization Secretariat

barriers to trade. For example, according to WTO (2011), about one third of RTAs in force in the 2000s contain services commitments, compared to less than a tenth in 1990.

The main purpose of this chapter is to illustrate the current trend of regional integration in terms of the contents of RTAs by distinguishing between shallow and deep integration and to shed light on the causes and impacts of recent deep regional integration.

In Sect. 2.2 we explain what shallow and deep RTAs mean and why countries have recently pursued deep integration. In Sects. 2.3 and 2.4 we argue how we can measure the degree of deep RTAs and what data are available to analyze the content and effects of deep RTAs. In Sect. 2.5 we examine the state of deep RTAs in the world and in the Asia-Pacific region using the measurement and data introduced in Sect. 2.3. In Sect. 2.6 we review existing studies on the effects of deep regional integration on global firms and technology spillovers. Finally, in Sect. 2.7 we provide the concluding remarks of this chapter.

2.2 Shallow and Deep Regional Integration

2.2.1 The Concept of Shallow and Deep Regional Trade Agreements

The concept of shallow and deep integration is originally proposed by Lawrence (1996). Shallow integration is simply trade liberalization, which involves the removal of trade barriers. By contrast, deep integration "moves beyond the removal of border barriers" (Lawrence 1996, p. 8). Deep RTAs contain a variety of provisions including on investment, labor, the environment, and IPR.

It is said that recent RTAs tend to be deeper than old ones. A good comparison of an old RTA with a recent RTA in terms of the degree of the depth is provided by Rodrik (2018). He compares two RTAs signed by the United States: the United States–Israel Free Trade Agreement (FTA) and the United States–Singapore FTA. Both Israel and Singapore are small nations. The United States–Israel FTA, which entered into force in 1985, was the first bilateral trade agreement that the United States signed in the postwar period. The legal text of the United States–Israel FTA contains only 22 articles and three annexes, and consists of fewer than 8,000 words. Thus, it is "quite a short agreement" (Rodrik 2018, p. 75). By contrast, the United States–Singapore FTA entered into force in 2004. Its legal text is much longer than that of the United States–Israel FTA. It contains 20 chapters with many articles in each and more than a dozen annexes. The total length is about 70,000 words. These two agreements are distinct in the coverage of policy areas. Most of the articles in the United States–Israel FTA are devoted to trade liberalization issues, such as the elimination of duties and other restrictive regulations, free of import licensing requirements, and rules of origin (RoO). On the contrary, only the first seven chapters in the United States–Singapore FTA cover trade issues, and the remaining 13 chapters address a variety of policy areas including financial services, anti-competitive business conduct, e-commerce, investment, IPR, labor, and the environment. Based on the coverage of the policy areas, the United States–Singapore FTA can be considered to be "deeper" than the United States–Israel FTA.

2.2.2 Countries' Motivation for Deepening Regional Trade Agreements

Given the fact that recent RTAs tend to be deeper than older ones, one may ask why countries have recently pursued deep integration. Lawrence (1996) argues that the development of regional production systems and the promotion of service investment became important in the 1990s. Deeper forms of economic integration such as the elimination of differences in national production and product standards that make regionally integrated production costly are required in order to facilitate international investment and the operation of multinational enterprises (MNEs).

Baldwin (2011, 2016a) explains in detail why countries have been pursuing deep regional economic integration. He calls the second phase of globalization initiated by the information and communication technology (ICT) revolution in the 1990s the "second unbundling," which is the geographic separation of factories. The fragmentation of production processes and offshoring occur in the second unbundling. The ICT revolution enabled know-how in rich (North) countries to be combined with low-wage labor in poor (South) countries. Baldwin (2016a) calls this combination the *high-tech/low wage mix*. In this era of the second unbundling, the so-called *trade–investment–services–intellectual property nexus* (Baldwin 2016a) emerged because of this mix. That is, MNEs from rich countries bring their intangible property to the factories built in poor countries and conduct part of the production process there. Parts and components are traded between parent firms and their foreign affiliates. Thus, the trade of goods, the movement of capital, services that connect unbundled factories, and intellectual property are all involved in the production of branded goods under the above nexus. Baldwin (2016a) argues that this nexus thus requires a new package of disciplines, which can be provided by deep RTAs.

Another motivation for countries to pursue deep regional integration is to address a number of important issues that have been debated in the international community, but that have been difficult for countries to agree to include in the GATT/WTO rules. Those issues include IPR protection, the environment, and labor market regulation.[1] Those countries that are active in addressing those issues try to construct international regulatory rules on these issues by including them in RTAs.

2.3 Measurement of Deep Regional Integration

2.3.1 WTO-Plus and WTO-Extra Policy Areas

We need some measurement of the depth of RTAs in order to know how deep each RTA is.

Horn et al. (2010) propose a systematic method to measure the depth and nature of the economic integration of RTAs, which examines the policy areas covered by their provisions and legal enforceability of these obligations. They identify 52 policy areas covered by RTAs of which either the United States or the European Community is a member, classifying them into two groups: WTO-plus (WTO+) and WTO-extra (WTO-X). The WTO+ group includes provisions that fall under the current mandate of the WTO, but go beyond commitments at the multilateral level. By contrast, WTO-X policy areas include issues that fall outside the current WTO mandate. The WTO+

[1] With regard to studies on trade and the environment, see, for example, Cherniwchan et al. (2017) and Copeland and Taylor (2003, 2004).

Table 2.1 List of WTO+ and WTO–X areas in RTAs

WTO+ Areas (14)	WTO–X Areas (38)	
FTA Industrial Goods	Anti-Corruption	Health
FTA Agricultural Goods	Competition Policy	Human Rights
Customs Administration	Environmental Laws	Illegal Immigration
Export Taxes	IPR	Illicit Drugs
SPS	Investment	Industrial Cooperation
TBT	Labor Market Regulation	Information Society
State Trading Enterprises	Movement of Capital	Mining
Anti-dumping	Consumer Protection	Money Laundering
Countervailing Measures	Data Protection	Nuclear Safety
State Aid	Agriculture	Political Dialogue
Public Procurement	Approximation of Legislation	Public Administration
TRIMs	Audio Visual	Regional Cooperation
GATS	Civil Protection	Research and Technology
TRIPS	Innovation Policies	SME
	Cultural Cooperation	Social Matters
	Economic Policy Dialogue	Statistics
	Education and Training	Taxation
	Energy	Terrorism
	Financial Assistance	Visa and Asylum

Source: Horn et al. (2010)

group includes 14 policy areas and WTO-X group includes 38 policy areas, as shown in Table 2.1.

The method developed by Horn et al. (2010) evaluates the coverage and legal enforceability of each policy area in RTAs using two indexes: the area-covered (AC) and legally-enforceable (LE) indexes. The AC index simply indicates whether a policy area is covered by an RTA. It takes the value 1 if a policy area is mentioned and 0 otherwise. On the contrary, the LE index evaluates the legal enforceability of each policy area on a three-point scale: 0 for not mentioned in the agreement or not legally enforceable, 1 for legally enforceable but explicitly excluded by a dispute settlement provision, and 2 for legally enforceable.

2.3.2 *Depth and Breadth*

Limão (2016) proposes recategorizing the WTO+ and WTO-X policy areas from the viewpoints of the *depth* and *breadth* of RTAs (see Table 2.2). The depth measures the level of bilateral economic cooperation. In general, the lower the applied tariffs are the deeper is the level of bilateral economic cooperation. Moreover, various non-tariff

Table 2.2 Depth and breadth of RTAs

Depth		Breadth	
Field	Policy area	Field	Policy area
(a) Import tariffs	FTA industrial goods FTA agricultural goods	(a) Services	General Agreement on Trade in Services
(b) Non-tariff barriers	Customs administration Export taxes Sanitary and phytosanitary measures Technical barriers to trade Anti-dumping Countervailing measures	(b) Technology	TRIPS IPR Innovation policies Economic policy dialogue Information society Research and technology
(c) Behind the border policies	State trading enterprises State aid Public procurement Anti-corruption Competition policy	(c) Invest-ment/capital	Trade-related investment measures Investment Movement of capital
(d) Other policies	Consumer protection Data protection Agriculture Approximation of legislation	(d) Labor	Labor market regulation Illegal immigration Social matters Visa and asylum
	Civil protection Education and training Energy Financial assistance Industrial cooperation Mining Nuclear safety Public administration Regional cooperation Small and medium enter-prises Statistics Taxation	(e) Non-economic policies	Environmental laws Audio visual Cultural cooperation Health Human rights Illicit drugs Money laundering Political dialogue Terrorism

Source: Limão (2016)

measures and the behind-the-border policies (BBPs) affect market access and hence are the factors to characterize the depth of cooperation. Other policies (OPs), such as regional, industrial, and agricultural cooperation and financial assistance, may also affect market access. Limão (2016) proposes that the depth of RTAs is measured by four categories of fields in the WTO+ and WTO-X groups: (a) import tariffs, (b) non-tariff barriers (NTBs), (c) BBPs, and (d) OPs. Field (a) comprises two policy areas, field (b) consists of six policy areas, field (c) consists of five policy areas, and field (d) comprises 16 policy areas (see Table 2.2).

Alternatively, the breadth of RTAs measures how wide the coverage of policy areas is. The classification is made by (i) the type of trade (goods/services), (ii) technology (innovation/spillovers/IPR), and (iii) factors of production (capital/labor).

Then, Limão (2016) proposes that the breadth of RTAs is measured by five fields: (a) services, (b) technology, (c) investment/capital, (d) labor, and (e) non-economic policies (NEPs). Field (a) comprises one policy area, field (b) six policy areas, field (c) three policy areas, field (d) four policy areas, and field (e) nine policy areas (see Table 2.2).

In Sect. 2.5, we use the depth and breadth measures to illustrate the current state of deep RTAs in the world and in the Asia-Pacific region.

2.4 Data on the Content of Deep Trade Agreements

In this section, we explain the data that enable us to analyze deep RTAs.

2.4.1 Content of the Deep Trade Agreements Database

The first dataset on deep RTAs was provided by Horn et al. (2010). The coverage of their dataset was restricted to RTAs signed by the United States and those by European countries. The number of covered RTAs was 100.

Hofmann et al. (2019) substantially extend the coverage of RTAs in the dataset presented by Horn et al. (2010) to 279. The extended dataset, which covers 1958–2015, is called "Deep Trade Agreements database 1.0 (horizontal depth)." It is provided on the World Bank's website.[2]

This dataset includes information on 14 WTO+ policy areas and 38 WTO-X policy areas for agreement and country-pair levels. The dataset consists of the AC and LE indexes for each policy area. We can use the dataset to measure the depth and breadth of RTAs.

2.4.2 Deep Trade Agreements Database 2.0

A new dataset of the content of deep trade agreements, which is called the "Deep Trade Agreements database 2.0 (vertical depth)", was released by the World Bank in 2020 (Mattoo et al. 2020). This dataset includes more detailed information on the provisions in each policy area.[3] The policy areas covered by this new dataset include (1) preferential tariffs, (2) export restrictions, (3) services, (4) investment, (5) movement of capital, (6) IPR, (7) visa and asylum, (8) rules of origin, (9) trade facilitation and customs, (10) anti-dumping, (11) countervailing duties, (12) technical barriers to trade (TBT), (13) sanitary and phytosanitary (SPS) measures, (14) public

---

[2] https://datacatalog.worldbank.org/dataset/content-deep-trade-agreements.

[3] https://datacatalog.worldbank.org/dataset/content-deep-trade-agreements.

procurement, (15) subsidies, (16) state-owned enterprises, (17) competition policy, (18) environmental laws, and (19) labor market regulations. In each of these policy areas, many indexes are constructed to measure the degree of coverage in detail.

The detailed information on this dataset is provided by Mattoo et al. (2020). This dataset is the outcome of a collaborative project of the World Bank's team with a number of academic researchers and other international organizations such as the International Trade Centre, the Organization for Economic Co-operation and Development (OECD), and the World Trade Organization (WTO).

2.4.3 DESTA Dataset

An alternative database of the contents of RTAs called DESTA (Design of Trade Agreements) was created by Dür et al. (2014). It originally covered 587 trade agreements for 1945–2009. This database has now been updated and extended to more than 710 trade agreements.[4] The period has also been extended to 2019. Although only 22 policy areas (15 trade and seven non-trade areas) are covered by the DESTA, each policy area is evaluated in detail by multiple variables.

Its trade-related areas include (1) market access, (2) services, (3) global value chains, (4) investments, (5) temporary entry of business persons, (6) IPRs, (7) public procurement, (8) competition, (9) TBT, (10) SPS measures, (11) regulatory co-operation and transparency, (12) trade defense instruments, (13) e-commerce, (14) data flows, and (15) capital movement and exchange rates. Non-trade areas include (i) corruption, (ii) labor standards, (iii) environmental protection, (iv) human rights, (v) democracy, (vi) security, and (vii) others.

The DESTA project is ongoing. The latest version of the DESTA is likely to include more data.

2.5 The State of Deep Regional Integration

2.5.1 The State of Deep RTAs in the World

Using the Content of Trade Agreement (TA) dataset by the World Bank, which was described in the previous section, Jinji (2021) illustrates the state of deep RTAs in the world.

Figures 2.2a, b show the average number of WTO+ and WTO-X policy areas included in RTAs by signatory group and their year of entry, respectively. The signatory groups are the United States, European countries, Association of South-East Asian Nations (ASEAN) members, Japan, China, Russia, and other countries. The

[4] The DESTA dataset can be found at www.designoftradeagreements.org/.

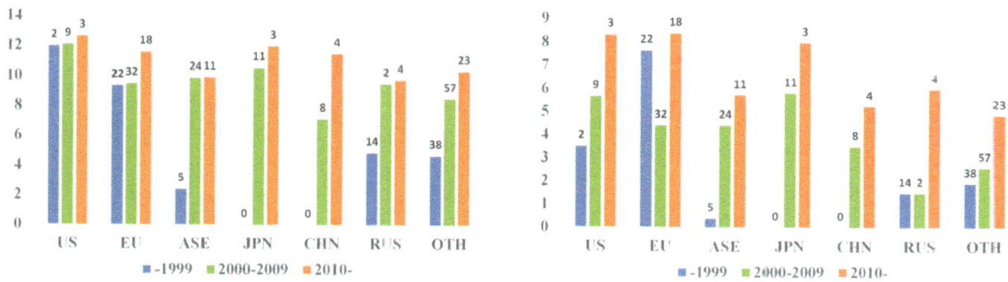

(a) WTO+ LE policy areas (LE=1 or 2) (b) WTO-X LE policy areas (LE=1 or 2)

Fig. 2.2 Average number of WTO+ and WTO-X LE policy areas by RTA signatory group and year of entry. *Note*: Abbreviations in the figure: US = United States, EU = European countries, ASE = ASEAN countries, JPN = Japan, CHN = China, RUS = Russia, and OTH = other countries. Numbers in the graph indicate the number of RTAs entered into force by signatory group and period. *Source*: Fig. 1 in Jinji (2021)

observation period is divided into three: until 1999, from 2000 to 2009, and from 2010 to 2015. For example, as shown in Fig. 2.2a, the RTAs signed by the United States before 2000 include, on average, 12 WTO+ policy areas (of the 14 WTO+ policy areas) with the LE index being either 1 or 2; those in 2000–2009 include, on average, 12.1 WTO+ policy areas with $LE \geq 1$; and those in 2010–2015 include, on average, 12.7 WTO+ policy areas with $LE \geq 1$. The numbers placed above the bars indicate the number of RTAs signed by the signatory country/group that entered into force in each period. For example, the United States signed two RTAs before 2000, nine RTAs during 2000–2009, and three RTAs during 2010–2015.

This figure indicates that the RTAs signed by the United States cover most of the WTO+ policy areas with at least some legal enforceability even before 2000. On average, more than 12 out of the 14 policy areas are covered and legally enforceable. The RTAs signed by the EU include fewer than 10 WTO+ policy areas, on average, until 2009 but more (11.6 on average) in 2010–2015. Although the RTAs formed by ASEAN countries and Russia before 2000 include a small number of WTO+ policy areas (2.4 and 4.9 on average, respectively), those in the 2000s include more WTO+ policy areas (about 10 policy areas on average). As for Japan and China, the number of legally enforceable WTO+ policy areas in RTAs increased in 2010–2015: 12 (Japan) and 11.6 (China) policy areas on average.[5] The number of legally enforceable WTO+ policy areas included in the RTAs signed by other countries has steadily increased.

By contrast, panel (b) of Fig. 2.2 shows the average number of WTO-X policy areas included in RTAs with the LE index taking the value of $LE \geq 1$. There are 38 WTO-X policy areas, but the average number included in RTAs with at least some legal enforceability is fewer than nine for all countries, even in 2010–2015. In general, recent RTAs include more legally enforceable WTO-X policy areas for all countries; however, the highest average is still around eight policy areas in the 2010s (8.3 for the United States, 8.4 for the EU, and 8.0 for Japan).

[5] Neither Japan nor China signed RTAs before 2000.

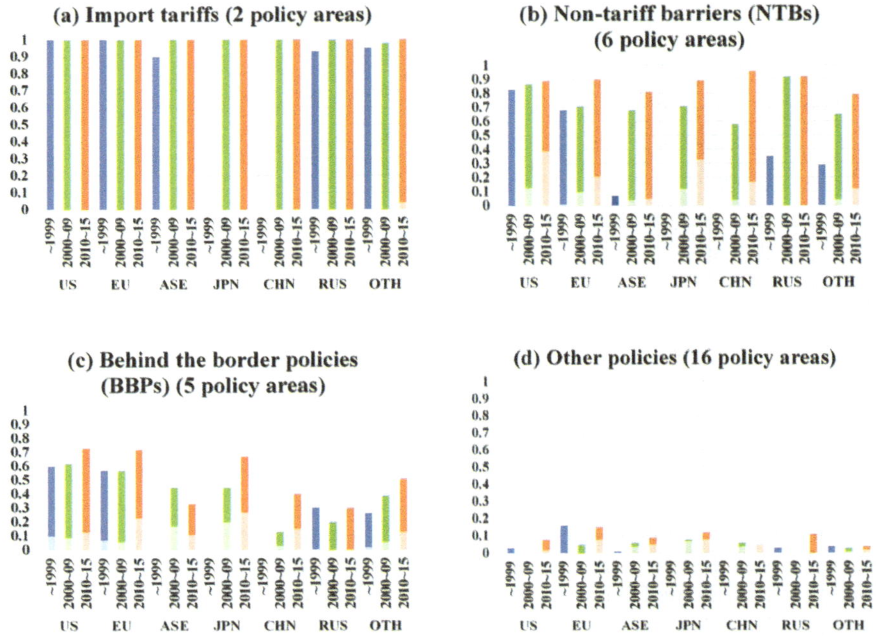

Fig. 2.3 Depth of RTAs by signatory group and period. *Note*: Each bar indicates the shares of $LE = 1$ (light color) and $LE = 2$ (dark color) policy areas included in each field in all the RTAs signed by each country/group that entered into force in each period. *Source*: Fig. 2 in Jinji (2021)

Jinji (2021) also illustrates the state of world RTAs in terms of depth and breadth, as explained in Sect. 2.3.2.

Figure 2.3 shows the depth of RTAs by signatory group and year of entry. Each bar indicates the shares of $LE = 1$ (light color) and $LE = 2$ (dark color) policy areas included in each category in all the RTAs signed by each country/group that entered into force in each period. As shown in panel (a) of Fig. 2.3, most RTAs, particularly those that entered into force in the 2000s, fully cover both policy areas in the category of import tariffs with $LE = 2$. The coverage of policy areas in the NTBs category is relatively high. More than 80% of the RTAs signed by the United States before 2000 cover the policy areas of NTBs with $LE = 2$. In 2010–2015, about 90% of the RTAs signed by the United States cover those policy areas, but about 40% are with $LE = 1$. The RTAs signed by the EU, Japan, and Russia in 2010–15 cover about 90% of the policy areas in this category. The coverage of the RTAs signed by China in 2010–2015 is much higher and close to 1. The coverage of the policy areas in the BBPs category is rather low. Even the highest level of coverage is about 0.7 for the RTAs signed by the United States and the EU in 2010–2015. The coverage of the policy areas in this category by the RTAs signed by ASEAN countries, China, and Russia is less than 0.5. Moreover, the coverage of the policy areas in the category of OPs is much lower. The coverage is below 0.2 for all RTAs in all periods.

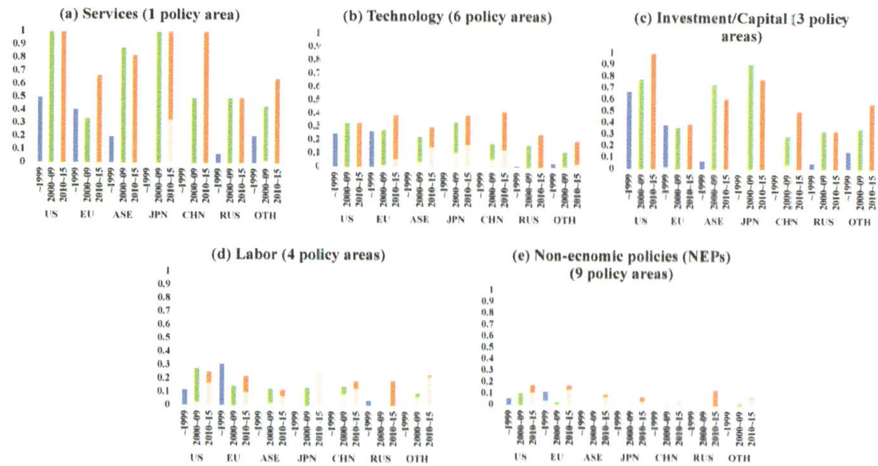

Fig. 2.4 Breadth of RTAs by signatory group and period. *Note*: Each bar indicates the shares of $LE = 1$ (light color) and $LE = 2$ (dark color) policy areas included in each field in all the RTAs signed by each country/group that entered into force in each period. *Source*: Fig. 3 in Jinji (2021)

Figure 2.4 shows the breadth of RTAs by signatory country/group and year of entry. As in Fig. 2.3, each bar indicates the shares of $LE = 1$ (light color) and $LE = 2$ (dark color) policy areas included in each category in all the RTAs signed by each country/group that entered into force in each period.

The fields for which the coverage of policy areas is relatively high are (a) services and (c) investment/capital. However, the coverage depends on the signatory country. The RTAs signed by the United States, Japan, and ASEAN countries in the 2000s cover fields (a) and (c) at relatively high shares. The coverage of the service area in the RTAs signed by China in 2010–2015 is 100%. By contrast, the RTAs signed by the EU and Russia only cover policy areas in fields (a) and (c) at low shares. The coverage of other fields ((b), (d), and (e)) tends to be low for all RTAs. In particular, the coverage of (e) (NEPs) is less than 0.2 for all RTAs.

2.5.2 *The State of Deep RTAs in the Asia-Pacific Region*

We next examine the state of deep RTAs in the Asia-Pacific region using the depth and breadth indexes.

We create the following index for each field of the depth measure by signatory group. Let $N^c(LE \geq 1)_{ikt}$ be the number of policy areas with the LE index taking the value of one or two in field c of the depth measure included in RTA k signed by country i and entered into force in period t. The depth measure consists of fields $c \in \{Tariff, NTB, BBP, OP\}$. We set $t = \{1, 2, 3\}$, where $t = 1$ indicates years until 1999, $t = 2$ indicates years from 2000 to 2009, and $t = 3$ indicates years from 2010 to 2015. Then, we calculate the following index:

$$Av\_Depth\_index_{it}^{c} = \frac{1}{L_{it}} \sum_{k \in S_{it}} \frac{N^{c}(LE \geq 1)_{ikt}}{M^{c}}, \tag{2.1}$$

where L_{it} is the number of RTAs signed by country i and entered into force in period t, S_{it} is the set of RTAs signed by country i and entered into force in period t, and M^c is the number of policy areas in field c of the depth measure. For each field of the depth measure, M^c is two for $Tariff$, six for NTB, five for BBP, and 16 for OP. Thus, $Av\_Depth\_index_{it}^{c}$ is the average share of the policy areas with $LE \geq 1$ in all policy areas in field c of the depth measure of RTAs signed by country i and entered into force in period t.

Figure 2.5 shows the values of $Av\_Depth\_index_{it}^{c}$ for ASEAN, Japan, and China. As a reference, we also show $Av\_Depth\_index_{it}^{c}$ for the United States and the members of the EU.

As is seen in the figure, all countries have the value of the index in the tariff field almost one. However, deep RTAs should include policy areas in the fields of NTBs, BBPs, and OPs. RTAs signed by ASEAN countries show an improvement in the NTB index in 2000–2009 and a further improvement in 2010–2015. However, an improvement in the BBP and OP indexes in the 2000s is small or almost negligible. RTAs signed by Japan in 2010–2015 show almost the same level of the NTB and BBP indexes as those by the United States and European countries. However, the value of

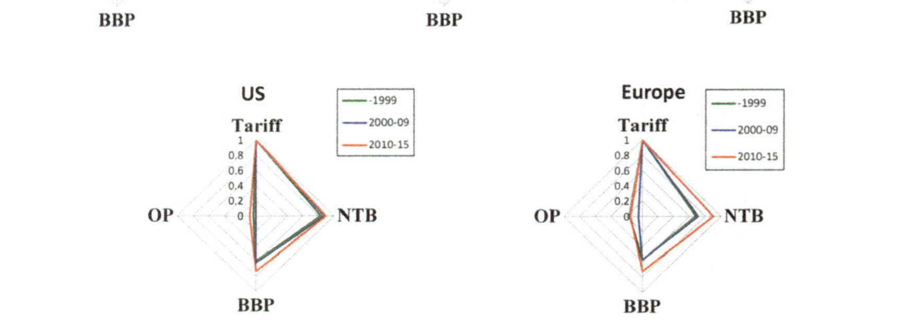

Fig. 2.5 Depth indexes of RTAs by signatory group. *Note*: The average share of $LE \geq 1$ policy areas included in each field in the RTAs signed by each country/group that entered into force in each period is calculated. *Source*: Authors' creation from the World Bank's database

the BBP index in 2010–2015 is still lower than 0.8 for all of Japan, the United States, and European countries. With regard to the RTAs signed by China, an improvement in the NTB and BBP indexes from 2000–2009 to 2010–2015 is large, but the level of the BBP index is still low even in 2010–2015, compared with Japan, the United States, and European countries. Moreover, progress in the inclusion of legally enforceable OP policy areas gets very slow even in 2010–2015 for all countries shown in this figure.

Next, similar to the depth measure, we create the following index for each field of the breadth measure by signatory group:

$$Av\_Breadth\_index_{it}^{c} = \frac{1}{L_{it}} \sum_{k \in S_{it}} \frac{N^{c}(LE \geq 1)_{ikt}}{M^{c}}, \tag{2.2}$$

where the notations are the same as those in Eq. (2.1). Thus, $Av\_Breadth\_index_{it}^{c}$ is the average share of the policy areas with $LE \geq 1$ in all policy areas in field c of the breadth measure of RTAs signed by country i and entered into force in period t. The breadth measure consists of fields $c \in \{GATS$ (Services), $Tech$ (Technology), Inv/Cap (Investment/capital), Lab (Labor), NEP (NEPs)$\}$. For each field of the breadth measure, M^{c} is one for $GATS$, six for $Tech$, three for Inv/Cap, four for Lab, and nine for NEP.

The values of $Av\_Breadth\_index_{it}^{c}$ for ASEAN, Japan, China, the United States, and the members of the EU are shown in Fig. 2.6.

In Fig. 2.6 there are interesting differences in the patterns of the breadth indexes across countries. RTAs signed by ASEAN countries and Japan demonstrate the pat-

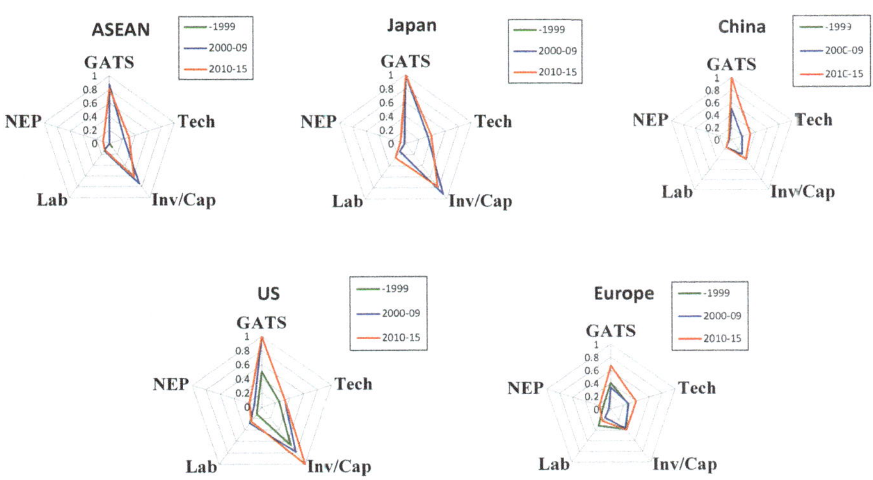

Fig. 2.6 Breadth indexes of RTAs by signatory group. *Note*: The average share of $LE \geq 1$ policy areas included in each field in the RTAs signed by each country/group that entered into force in each period is calculated. *Source*: Authors' creation from the World Bank's database

tern that is similar to that of the RTAs signed by the United States: the value of the GATS index is very high (close to one) and that of the Inv/Cap index is also high. Although the Tech index is lower than the GATS and Inv/Cap indexes, it is relatively higher than the Lab and NEP indexes. By contrast, RTAs signed by China indicate a quite different pattern, compared with other countries. That is, only the GATS index in 2010–2015 is high. Although the level of the Tech index in 2010–2015 is comparable to that of ASEAN and Japan, the level of the Inv/Cap index is much lower than ASEAN and Japan even in 2010–2015. With regard to the Lab index, the level is almost the same among these three signatory groups (i.e., ASEAN, China, and Japan) in 2000–2009, but the Lab index becomes higher for Japan, compared with ASEAN and China, in 2010–2015. RTAs signed by European countries also show distinct patterns. The levels of the breadth indexes are generally low. In particular, the levels of the GATS index and the Inv/Cap index are much lower than those of Japan and the United States.

In summary, the content of RTAs signed by ASEAN countries, China, and Japan is quite different in the depth and breadth measures. Specifically, the differences are significant in the NTB and BBP policy areas in the depth measure and Investment/Capital and Labor policy areas in the breadth measure. The shares of including legally enforceable OP policy areas and NEP policy areas are very low for all of ASEAN countries, China, and Japan. Thus, the degree of deep RTAs in the Asia-Pacific region is still not so high both in the OPs in the depth measure and in the NEPs in the breadth measure.

2.6 The Impact of Deep Regional Integration

Lawrence (1996) points out that deep integration could be better or worse than shallow integration. He argues that deep integration could "take the form of imposing measures on countries that are inappropriate for their stage of development, such as excessively stringent environmental standards, or which reduce economic efficiency" (p. 8). Therefore, we cannot expect a priori that deep integration ensures higher economic welfare than shallow integration. It is important to consider the effects of deep integration on various economic activities and economic welfare of RTA's signatories and non-signatories.

2.6.1 Deep Regional Integration and Global Firms

As argued above, the main driving force for countries to sign deep RTAs is, in the terminology of Baldwin (2016a), the trade–investment–services–intellectual property nexus for global production and supply of goods and services by MNEs. Thus, it is important and interesting to examine how deep regional integration actually affects global activities of firms.

Osnago et al. (2017, 2019) analyze the relationship between deep RTAs and vertical FDI. Osnago et al. (2019) use a simplified version of the model developed by Antràs and Helpman (2004, 2008) and examine theoretically how differences in contractibility across production processes and across countries affect a final good producer's choice over the location (either North or South) of sourcing components and over engaging in vertical FDI or FO. Based on the theoretical analysis, they predict that deep RTAs with provisions improving the contractibility of components (e.g., TBT provision) increase the share of firms engaging in vertical FDI, whereas deep RTAs with those improving the contractibility of headquarters services (e.g., IPR and investment provisions) decrease the share of firms engaging in vertical FDI and raise the share of firms engaging in FO. Using firm-level data, Osnago et al. (2017, 2019) measure vertical FDI from country i to country j in sector k by the aggregate revenue of all the subsidiaries owned by firms in country i that produce inputs for sector k in country j. Osnago et al. (2017) address the endogeneity issue of deep RTAs using the instrumental variable approach and find that deep RTAs have significantly positive effects on vertical FDI. Moreover, Osnago et al. (2019) conduct empirical tests of their theoretical predictions and provide evidence to support both theoretical predictions.

A number of studies have investigated the impact of deep RTAs on global value chains (GVCs) and production networks (Boffa et al. 2019; Laget et al. 2020; Orefice and Rocha 2014). Augmented structural gravity models are extensively employed in the empirical analysis of this issue. Boffa et al. (2019) focus on the different impacts of deep RTAs and bilateral investment treaties (BITs) on various trade in value added indicators, or GVC trade. They find that although both deep RTAs and BITs increase GVC trade, their transmission channels differ. Specifically, backward linkages are stimulated through both deep RTAs and BITs, but only deep RTAs affect forward linkages. Based on this finding, they argue that negotiating a deep RTA with investment provisions has a larger impact on value-added trade than signing a shallow RTA and a separate BIT.

Laget et al. (2020) analyze the impact of deep RTAs on GVC participation. They find that deep RTAs increase the domestic and foreign value-added content of exports. According to their estimates, each additional policy area increases the domestic value-added of intermediate goods and services exports by 0.48% through forward GVC linkages, whereas an additional provision increases the foreign value-added of those exports by 0.38% through backward GVC linkages.

Orefice and Rocha (2014) estimate the relationship between deep RTAs and production networks trade. They capture production networks trade by import values in parts and components. Their finding is that signing deep RTAs increases production networks trade among members by about 12% points. Furthermore, they analyze whether higher levels of production networks trade increase the likelihood of forming deep RTAs. After taking other RTA determinants into account, a 10% point increase in the share of production networks trade over total trade increases the depth of an agreement by about 6% points.

Apart from GVCs and production networks, Jinji et al. (2021) investigate the impact of shallow and deep RTAs on cross-border licensing. They first derive a micro-founded gravity equation for cross-border licensing from the heterogeneous firm trade model by Helpman et al. (2004). Jinji et al. (2021) add licensing as a supply mode to the foreign market, so that firms choose licensing, export, or FDI. Under certain assumptions, low productivity firms engage in cross-border licensing, while high productivity firms serve the foreign market either by export or FDI. Based on comparative statics analyses, they show that deep RTAs as a whole and deep RTAs with IPR provisions in particular increase cross-border licensing. By contrast, shallow RTAs may not enhance cross-border licensing. These theoretical predictions are fairly supported by the empirical evidence obtained through estimating a structural gravity model.

2.6.2 Deep Regional Integration and Technology Spillovers

We turn to the studies on the impact of deep regional integration on knowledge diffusion or technology spillovers. Nowadays, it is an important issue whether signing deep RTAs facilitates knowledge diffusion and enhance technology spillovers among countries. However, compared with the studies on the relationship between deep RTAs and global activities of firms, research on this issue is much scarcer.

To the best of our knowledge, Peri (2005) is the first study to investigate the effects of RTAs on technology spillovers. He uses patent citation data as a proxy of technology spillovers. This approach was pioneered by Jaffe et al. (1993) and has been employed in a number of studies (e.g., Hall et al. 2001; Jaffe and Trajtenberg 1999; Maurseth and Verspagen 2002).[6] Peri (2005) uses a sample of 18 countries with 147 subnational regions in Western Europe and North America from 1975 to 1996. He estimates a gravity-like model to examine the effects of several resistance factors, such as trade blocs as well as regional, national, and linguistic borders, on technology spillovers measured by patent citations. "Trade blocs" correspond to RTAs. The estimated results indicate that while regional, national, and linguistic borders have a negative effect on technology spillovers, the impact of the trade blocs is insignificant, which implies that RTAs do not enhance technology spillovers. Only the European Economic Community (EEC)/the European Community (EC)/the European Union (EU) and North American Free Trade Agreement (NAFTA) are included as RTAs, so that the estimation of the impact of RTAs in his study is quite limited.

Jinji et al. (2013) extend the previous analysis to a sample of 103 countries for the period 1990–1999 using patent citation data. Unlike Peri (2005), they find a positive and significant effect of RTAs on technology spillovers. Their study is also limited because only nine RTAs are included in the analysis. Moreover, neither Peri (2005) nor Jinji et al. (2013) take the depth nature of RTAs into account.

---

[6] Patent citations are references to existing patents included in patent documents. The advantage of using patent citations as a proxy of technology spillovers is that it is a direct measure of knowledge flows (Hall et al. 2001).

Jinji et al. (2019a) is the first study to examine whether deep RTAs enhance international technology spillovers. They measure international technology spillovers by cross-country patent citations and employ panel data on 114 countries/regions for the period 1991–2007. They argue that since international trade in goods is a major channel of technology spillovers and trade liberalization by RTAs increases trade among members, both shallow and deep RTAs facilitate international technology spillovers. However, RTAs and technology spillovers are linked more directly through the inclusion of provisions that stimulate technology spillovers. For example, some RTAs actually include provisions to encourage collaborative research projects and transfer of technology between firms in member countries. As a result, it is expected that deep RTAs enhance technology spillovers more strongly than shallow RTAs. Jinji et al. (2019a) actually find that deep RTAs enhance technology spillovers. Moreover, they analyze which provisions increase technology spillovers more. Interestingly, they find that a deep integration in a broad sense has a greater impact on technology spillovers than RTAs with provisions that are more directly related to technology.

Chapter 7 extends the analysis of Jinji et al. (2019a) and further investigates the issue of the impact of deep RTAs on international technology spillovers.

2.7 Conclusion

It is said that recent RTAs tend to be deeper than old RTAs. In this chapter, we discussed how we can distinguish shallow and deep regional integration. Then, using the classification of the policy areas included in RTAs by the WTO+ and WTO-X groups and the depth and breadth measures, we examined in what sense RTAs that have recently entered into force are actually deeper than those signed before 2000. We also explored the state of deep regional integration in the Asia-Pacific region. After that, we reviewed existing studies on deep regional integration. Our focus was on the effects of deep regional integration on global activities of firms and on the impact of deep regional integration on technology spillovers. In this way, we looked at how deep regional integration, global firms, and technology spillovers are related with each other.

Global firms are the main topic of Chaps. 3 and 4. Chapters 5 and 6 address the issue of technology spillovers. In particular, Chap. 5 focuses on the relationship between international trade and technology spillovers, and Chap. 6 examines how foreign direct investment affects technology spillovers. Then, in Chap. 7, we investigate the impact of deep regional integration on technology spillovers.

Chapter 3
Which Aspect of Firm Performance is Important for the Choice of Globalization Mode?

3.1 Introduction

The relationship between firm performance and the choice of globalization mode, such as exports, foreign direct investment (FDI), and foreign outsourcing (FO), has been extensively investigated. For example, Melitz (2003) theoretically predicts a premium in productivity for firms engaging in exporting goods, relative to those supplying goods only to their domestic markets. Helpman et al. (2004) predict a further productivity premium for multinational enterprises (MNEs). Empirically, the superior performance of exporting firms relative to non-globalized firms has been confirmed by a number of studies (e.g., Bernard and Jensen 1995, 1999; Clerides et al. 1998; Mayer and Ottaviano 2007). Moreover, the productivity advantage of MNEs relative to non-MNE exporters has been documented (e.g., Head and Ries 2003; Helpman et al. 2004; Kimura and Kiyota 2006; Wakasugi 2014).[1]

On the other hand, Antràs and Helpman (2004) theoretically demonstrate that the productivity ordering (from the highest to the lowest) emerges from MNEs, foreign outsourcers, and non-globalized firms. Their prediction is supported by Tomiura (2007), Federico (2010), and Kohler and Smolka (2012) but partially unsupported by Defever and Toubal (2013). As for the choice between FDI and FO, Chen et al. (2012) predict that a high Tobin's q tends to motivate firms to choose FDI rather than FO. Jinji et al. (2019b) find empirical support for their prediction.

In this chapter, we attempt to compare the effects of firm performance on firms' globalization activity through various measures. We use detailed Japanese firm-level data covering the period 1994–1999 for empirical analysis. Our dataset includes information on sales, employment, capital, research and development (R&D) expenditure, direct exports, and costs of domestic and foreign outsourcing of the companies headquartered in Japan, and sales of their foreign affiliates. Data on corporate

[1] For a survey of the literature, see Greenaway and Kneller (2007), Helpman (2006), and Wagner (2007, 2012).

N. Jinji et al., *Deep Integration, Global Firms, and Technology Spillovers*, Advances in Japanese Business and Economics 26,
https://doi.org/10.1007/978-981-16-5210-3_3

balance sheets and patent applications are also included. Then, we capture the degree of engagement in each mode of globalization by calculating the ratio of a mode of globalization activity (export, FDI, or FO) to the domestic sales of headquarters companies. We also capture the relative choice of globalization mode by taking the ratio of the volume of direct export by the headquarters companies to FDI (i.e., sales of foreign affiliates) and their ratio of costs of FO to FDI.

As for the measures of firm performance, we use three variables. First, as a measure of productivity, we use labor productivity (LP), defined by value-added per worker. LP is among the most frequently used measures in the literature, to measure productivity. Second, we employ two different measures to capture the importance of knowledge-capital intensity, discussed in Chen et al. (2012). One measure is Tobin's q (Tobin 1969). We estimate Tobin's q by a simple approximation version proposed by DaDalt et al. (2003). Another one is intangible asset intensity, which is the ratio of intangible to tangible assets. In general, intangible assets include patents, copyrights, trademarks, trade names, goodwill, and other items that lack physical substance but provide long-term benefits to the company. In this chapter, we use the stock of patent applications as a direct measure of intangible assets.

Then, we regress the indexes of firm choice of globalization mode on these variables. We employ a quantile regression in order to incorporate a strong negatively skewed distribution of our indexes of globalization activity. Unlike traditional estimation techniques such as the linear regression model, the quantile regression can provide estimates of parameters at different points in the conditional distribution of the dependent variable. Thus, it incorporates heterogeneity among firms and allows outliers in the sample.[2] In our estimation, we control for capital intensity (capital–labor ratio) and R&D intensity (the ratio of R&D stock to labor).

The main findings are as follows. Our quantile regression estimation indicates that LP plays an important role in the choice between exporting and FDI but Tobin's q does not. In contrast, Tobin's q has a significant effect on the choice between FDI and FO, but LP does not. Interestingly, the intangible asset intensity favors FDI over both exporting and FO. Finally, our estimation result indicates that firms with higher physical capital intensity tend to engage in more FDI and less FO.

The remainder of the chapter is organized as follows. Section 3.2 describes the data employed in this chapter and explains variables used in our analysis. Section 3.3 explains our estimation strategy. Section 3.4 provides empirical results and discusses implications arising from those results. Section 3.5 concludes.

[2] Koenker and Bassett (1978) introduce quantile regressions. See Koenker (2005) and Hao and Naiman (2007) for technical details. In the trade literature, studies of employing quantile regressions include Dufrenot et al. (2010), Figueiredo et al. (2016), Liu and Ma (2021), and Wagner (2006).

3.2 Data and Variables

3.2.1 Data

We first collect firm-level data on Japanese companies from two sources: the Basic Survey of Japanese Business Structure and Activities (BSJBSA) or *Kigyo Katsudo Kihon Chosa*, and the Basic Survey of Overseas Business Activities (BSOBA) or *Kaigai Jigyo Katsudo Kihon Chosa*. These are annual surveys implemented by the Ministry of Economy, Trade and Industry (METI) and include data on the business activities of companies headquartered in Japan and their affiliates, such as sales, employment, capital, R&D expenditure, and direct exports of the headquarters, and sales of their foreign affiliates. The BSJBSA also includes information on outsourcing—i.e., the number of domestic and foreign firms to which a headquarters company contracted out its manufacturing or processing tasks and the cost involved in contracting out business activities during 1994–1999.

We obtain data on corporate balance sheets from the Nikkei Economic Electronic Database Systems (NEEDS) Company Financial Reports, which covers about 4,000 publicly traded firms on the Japanese stock market. All publicly traded firms are identified by two codes—a Nikkei company code defined by Nikkei Inc. and a security code defined by the Japanese Securities Identification Code Committee. Since firm codes in the BSJBSA and BSOBA surveys differ from those in NEEDS, we use the Nikkei company code to link the three datasets. By matching the full names and addresses of companies among the three datasets we were able to identify approximately 1,100 headquarters companies for each year during the period 1994–1999.

Moreover, we collect data on patent applications by companies headquartered in Japan made to the Japanese Patent Office (JPO) during 1990–1999 from the database released by the Institute of Intellectual Property (IIP).[3]

3.2.2 Measures of Globalization Activity

The globalization activity of our sampled companies is indicated by providing the number of firms engaging in each globalization mode in Table 3.1. We identify FDI firms, outsourcing firms, and export firms by acquiring information on foreign affiliates' sales reported in the BSOBA survey in year t and on the costs of FO and export reported in the BSJBSA survey in year t. Among these headquarters companies, about two-thirds reported implementing at least one globalization activity from 1994 to 1999. The share of the companies involved in globalization activities in our sample is overwhelming, contrary to the findings in Tomiura (2007) that about 90% of the firms are "domestic" for Japanese companies. This may be because the publicly traded companies are usually sizable and competitive compared with firms that

[3] See Goto and Motohashi (2007) for the details of the IIP dataset.

Table 3.1 Globalization choice of Japanese companies

Year	No. of firms	Export (X) only	FDI (I) only	FO (O) only	$X+I$	$I+O$	$X+O$	All ($X+I+O$)
1994	1006	325	32	13	315	101	131	89
1995	1280	277	51	6	503	141	167	135
1996	1388	234	68	9	555	167	195	160
1997	1323	193	77	5	569	157	173	149
1998	1334	222	67	9	551	153	186	146
1999	1380	248	71	13	552	157	188	151
Total	7711	1499	366	55	3045	876	1040	830

Source: Authors' calculation from BSJBSA and BSOBA for 1994–1999

Table 3.2 Descriptive statistics

	No. Obs.	Mean	Std. Dev.	Percentiles				
				10%	25%	50%	75%	90%
RXI	3707	32.44	719.43	0.00	0.27	0.84	2.16	7.13
ROI	3707	997.16	28608.99	0.00	0.00	0.00	0.02	19.52
$TobinQ$	7105	1.29	0.61	0.80	0.98	1.18	1.44	1.78
$LnPatK$	5691	− 5.17	1.86	−7.76	−6.31	−4.86	−3.81	−3.02
$LnLP$	7084	2.25	0.72	1.36	1.81	2.26	2.71	3.13
$LnKL$	7104	2.48	0.82	1.54	2.02	2.48	2.95	3.45
$LnRL$	5691	−12.17	1.99	−14.68	−13.34	−11.92	−10.79	−9.94

Source: Authors' calculation from BSJBSA, BSOBA, NEEDS, and IIP for 1994–1999

are not publicly traded. Therefore, the publicly traded companies may have greater ability to enter international markets. Among our sampled companies, over 66% undertake FDI (including companies that also engage in export and/or FO). About 83% of our sampled firms export and 36% outsource. Compared with the number of firms engaged in FDI and exporting, the number of FO firms is quite limited.

To capture the degree of engagement in globalization modes, we construct indexes to measure the relative choice of globalization modes. RXI is the ratio of export sales (denoted X) to FDI, which is measured by sales by foreign affiliates (denoted I). ROI is the ratio of outsourcing costs (denoted O) to foreign affiliate sales (I). The former measures the relative choice of exporting over FDI, and the latter measures the relative choice of FO over FDI.

Descriptive statistics are summarized in Table 3.2. The statistics of the percentiles and mean show that the distributions of the indexes have a strong negative skew. There are some outliers among firms that engage in globalization activities, reflecting that some leading MNEs mainly produce abroad rather than domestically.

3.2.3 Measures of Firm Performance

In this subsection, we explain our measures of firm performance. We begin with LP. Following Tomiura (2007), LP ($LnLP$) is measured in logarithms as

$$LnLP = \log[(Sales - COGS)/L],$$

where L and $Sales$ denote the number of regular employees and total sales, respectively, and $COGS$ refers to the cost of goods sold. Tomiura (2007) argues that this measure is preferable to gross output per worker because deducting costs from sales is important, especially when the manufacturing process involves outsourcing.

Tobin's q (Tobin 1969) is measured as the ratio of the firm's market value to its tangible assets. Corporate finance scholars have developed complex estimations of Tobin's q that rely on the estimated market value of the firm (Abel and Blanchard 1986; Perfect and Wiles 1994). As indicated by DaDalt et al. (2003), these approaches to Tobin's q produce more precise estimations but are computationally costly. Moreover, these approaches may be subject to a larger selection bias. They suggest that a simple approach is preferable unless extreme precision of the q estimates is paramount and the sample selection bias is unlikely to be significant. We attempt to use a simpler approximation version as discussed in DaDalt et al. (2003), who propose the following simple approximation of Tobin's q:

$$\text{Tobin's } q = \frac{MVE + PS + LTDEBT + CL + BVINV - CA}{TA},$$

where MVE is the year-end value of common stock and PS is the liquidation value of preferred stock. $LTDEBT$, CL, $BVINV$, CA, and TA denote the book values of long-term debt, current liabilities, inventory, current assets, and total assets, respectively. We exclude PS in our measure for Tobin's q because the data are unavailable.

As a measure of intangible assets, we use patent stock, Pat. We construct a patent stock at period t from the data on patent applications by using the perpetual inventory method as follows:

$$Pat_t = I_t + (1 - \delta)Pat_{t-1}, \tag{3.1}$$

where Pat_t is the stock of patent applications at the end of period t, I_t is the number of patent applications during period t, and δ is the depreciation rate. Following the convention in the literature, we resort to the traditional 15% depreciation rate (see Hall et al. 2005). We use the number of patent applications in 1990 as the benchmark value for Pat. Since our data on patent applications begin from 1990 and our sample period begins in 1994, there are four years between the benchmark year and the first year of the sample period. Thus, the value of Pat in 1994 estimated by the perpetual inventory method is influenced little by the initial value of Pat in the benchmark year. We then compute the logarithm of the ratio of patent stock to tangible fixed capital, denoted as $LnPatK$, as a measure of the ratio of intangible to tangible assets.

Table 3.3 Correlations of variables

	$LnLP$	$TobinQ$	$LnPatK$	$LnKL$	$LnRL$	RXI	ROI
$LnLP$	1						
$TobinQ$	0.18	1					
$LnPatK$	−0.17	0.15	1				
$LnKL$	0.35	−0.03	−0.26	1			
$LnRL$	−0.21	0.06	0.80	−0.32	1		
RXI	−0.02	0.01	0.01	−0.02	0.01	1	
ROI	0.00	−0.01	0.00	−0.02	0.02	0.09	1

Moreover, as shown in Helpman et al. (2004), we control for capital intensity and R&D intensity. The former is measured by the logarithm of the ratio of tangible fixed capital to regular employees in the headquarters company, denoted as $LnKL$. The latter is measured by the logarithm of the ratio of R&D stock to employees, denoted as $LnRL$. R&D stock, denoted as RD, is computed in the same manner as patent stock. That is, in Eq. (3.1), Pat_t and Pat_{t-1} are replaced by RD_t and RD_{t-1}, respectively, and I_t is interpreted as the R&D expenditure in the period of t. In calculating R&D stock we use $\delta = 0.15$. Similar to the case of patent stock, R&D expenditure in 1990 is used as the benchmark value, and R&D stock in 1994 is estimated by the perpetual inventory method.

Descriptive statistics for these measures of firm performance are presented in Table 3.2 and correlations of the variables are shown in Table 3.3. As shown, the mean and median values of Tobin's q are 1.29 and 1.18, respectively, both of which are very close to those reported in Hall et al. (2005) for the US firms and slightly below those in Fukuda et al. (1999) for Japanese firms in the period 1985–1996.

3.3 Estimation Strategy

As discussed in the previous section, the globalization indexes in our sample have a strong negatively skewed distribution, which indicates that the heterogeneity across firms may be substantial. Thus, the relationships between the globalization indexes and firm characteristics may also differ across firms. It may be important to provide information about the relationship at different points in the conditional distribution of the indexes.

Quantile regressions are a useful tool to address this issue.[4] The major advantage of a quantile regression estimator is that it can provide information about the relationship at different points in the conditional distribution of the globalization indexes. In contrast, traditional regression techniques, such as ordinary least squares (OLS), can only summarize the average relationship between the globalization indexes and the

[4] See Koenker 2005 and Hao and Naiman 2007 for details on quantile regression estimation.

set of regressors. A key underlying assumption of these traditional techniques is that the effects of the regressors on the dependent variable are best represented at the conditional mean of the dependent variable. This is not the case in the presence of a skewed distribution.

Here, we use an algorithm known as least absolute deviations (LAD) to provide quantile estimates, where estimation is implemented by solving linear-programming problems.[5]

3.4 Empirical Results

In this section, we report our empirical results. We examine the effects of LP, Tobin's q, and the intensity of intangible assets on the relative choice between two globalization modes, RXI and ROI. Following Helpman et al. (2004), we use a linearized version of regression equations and consider a specification that controls for the firm's capital intensity ($LnKL$) and R&D intensity ($LnRL$).

Tables 3.4, 3.5 and 3.6 summarize quantile regressions of $LnLP$, $TobinQ$, and $LnPatK$ on globalization choices RXI and ROI. For RXI, the estimated coefficients of $LnLP$ in Table 3.4 are negatively significant at two higher quantiles of the 50th and 75th percentiles. This result implies that an increase in LP tends to motivate a firm to choose more FDI and less exporting. However, all coefficients of $LnLP$ fail the null hypothesis for ROI. In Table 3.5, the coefficients of $TobinQ$ are significantly negative for ROI at the 25th and 75th percentiles, whereas we find no significant effects of $TobinQ$ on RXI. Thus, an increase in Tobin's q tends to

Table 3.4 Quantile estimates of productivity on globalization choices

Variables	RXI			ROI		
	QR_{25}	QR_{50}	QR_{75}	QR_{25}	QR_{50}	QR_{75}
$LnLP$	−0.02	−0.15***	−0.31***	0.25	0.15	−1.13
	(0.027)	(0.040)	(0.12)	(0.19)	(0.97)	(2.51)
$LnKL$	0.07***	0.13***	0.46***	−1.55***	−5.24***	−15.96***
	(0.019)	(0.039)	(0.12)	(0.26)	(1.33)	(3.52)
$LnRL$	0.04***	0.10***	0.32***	0.56***	3.32***	4.05***
	(0.0087)	(0.016)	(0.047)	(0.12)	(0.58)	(1.53)
No. of Obs.	3034	3034	3034	868	858	868

Notes: (a) ***, **, and * indicate significance at the 1%, 5%, and 10% levels, respectively. (b) The values in the parentheses are standard errors. (c) QR_X refers to quantile regression at X th percentile. (d) A constant term and industrial and year dummies are included in the estimations. (e) Quantile regression is based on the least-absolute value (LAV) model

[5] See Cameron and Trivedi (2009) for the detailed Stata command for the quantile estimation.

Table 3.5 Quantile estimates of Tobin's q on globalization choices

Variables	RXI			ROI		
	QR_{25}	QR_{50}	QR_{75}	QR_{25}	QR_{50}	QR_{75}
$TobinQ$	0.01	−0.01	0.00	−0.40**	−1.47	−5.99**
	(0.014)	(0.045)	(0.002)	(0.18)	(0.94)	(3.00)
$LnKL$	0.06***	0.05	0.30***	−1.40***	−5.57***	−16.07***
	(0.018)	(0.038)	(0.11)	(0.26)	(1.17)	(3.42)
$LnRL$	0.04***	0.09***	0.29***	0.44***	3.08***	3.71**
	(0.0088)	(0.018)	(0.048)	(0.13)	(0.53)	(1.58)
No. of Obs.	3042	3042	3042	871	871	871

Notes: (a) ***, **, and * indicate significance at the 1%, 5%, and 10% levels, respectively. (b) The values in the parentheses are standard errors. (c) QR_X refers to quantile regression at X th percentile. (d) A constant term and industrial and year dummies are included in the estimations. (e) Quantile regression is based on the LAV model

Table 3.6 Quantile estimates of intangible asset intensity on globalization choices

Variables	RXI			ROI		
	QR_{25}	QR_{50}	QR_{75}	QR_{25}	QR_{50}	QR_{75}
$LnPatK$	−0.04***	−0.20***	−0.40***	−1.81***	−4.43***	−16.87***
	(0.011)	(0.017)	(0.064)	(0.17)	(0.41)	(1.28)
$LnKL$	0.06***	0.06**	0.36***	−1.80***	−5.79***	−26.90***
	(0.016)	(0.025)	(0.10)	(0.33)	(0.73)	(2.10)
$LnRL$	0.06***	0.19***	0.50***	0.92***	4.51***	6.34***
	(0.009)	(0.016)	(0.058)	(0.17)	(0.37)	(1.19)
No. of Obs.	3042	3042	3042	871	871	871

Notes: (a) ***, **, and * indicate significance at the 1%, 5%, and 10% levels, respectively. (b) The values in the parentheses are standard errors. (c) QR_X refers to quantile regression at X th percentile. (d) A constant term and industrial and year dummies are included in the estimations. (e) Quantile regression is based on the LAV model

motivate a firm to choose more FDI and less FO, but it does not affect the choice between exporting and FDI.

In Table 3.6, on the other hand, all quantile estimates of $LnPatK$ are significantly negative for both RXI and ROI. This result implies that headquarters companies with relatively higher intangible assets tend to favor FDI over exporting and outsourcing. In short, the effects of intangible asset intensity on firms' choices of globalization mode are not the same as those of Tobin's q.

In Tables 3.4, 3.5 and 3.6, all coefficients of $LnKL$ are significantly negative in the regressions for ROI: an increase in capital intensity leads a firm to choose more FDI and less FO. This result seems consistent with the finding of Tomiura (2007) and confirms the prediction by Antràs (2003). In contrast, the coefficients of $LnKL$ in the regressions for RXI are significantly positive in most cases. This suggests that an increase in capital intensity prompts a firm to choose more exporting and less FDI. This contradicts the result shown by Helpman et al. (2004), who find that firms in more capital-intensive sectors tend to export less relative to FDI.[6] However, to our knowledge, there are no definitive theoretical predictions regarding the relationship between capital intensity and the choice between exporting and FDI.

Moreover, all coefficients of $LnRL$ are significantly positive. Thus, an increase in R&D intensity causes a firm to export and outsource more relative to an engagement in FDI. One might regard this result as inconsistent with the conventional wisdom. However, Helpman et al. (2004) show that R&D intensity is not a useful predictor of exports versus FDI. Norbäck (2001) finds that firms with higher R&D intensity tend to export rather than engage in FDI if the costs of technology transfer are high, while the opposite is true if its costs are low. Theoretically, there is no definitive relationship between R&D intensity and the choice of globalization mode. Our empirical results suggest that the relationship between R&D intensity and the choice of the globalization mode should be investigated further theoretically and empirically.

3.5 Conclusion

By using firm-level data on Japanese firms, in this chapter it has been investigated empirically which measure of performance is important for a firm to choose various modes of globalization activity. Using quantile regressions, we found that a difference in LP is important in the choice between exporting and FDI but not important in the choice between FDI and FO. In contrast, a difference in Tobin's q is important in the choice between FDI and FO but not in the choice between exporting and FDI. Interestingly, a difference in the intangible asset intensity is important in the choice between exporting and FDI as well as in the choice between FDI and FO. Thus, our analysis revealed the differences among various measures of firm performance in the effects of globalization activity.

Our findings have important policy implications. Although existing empirical studies have primarily focused on the relationship between a firm's productivity and its choice of globalization mode, our findings illuminate the potential importance of Tobin's q on firms' globalization activities. In particular, we found that a difference in Tobin's q affects the choice between FDI and FO, whereas that in productivity is relatively less important for the choice between those two activities. Firms with lower Tobin's q are relatively more active in FO than in FDI. Thus, policies to facilitate FO will benefit the domestic economy, because FO contributes to improving the competitiveness of outsourcers by reducing their production costs. Since relatively lower values of Tobin's q imply that these firms do not effectively utilize their capital, deregulation and expansion of supportive services to small and medium enterprises may be helpful. Providing information on regulations in foreign countries and helping to find potential partner companies for outsourcing may also enhance gains from FO

[6] Tomiura (2007) also finds that MNEs tend to be more capital intensive than exporters.

by reducing the fixed costs of outsourcing. On the other hand, firms with lower Tobin's q may be reluctant to enhance FDI because they have difficulties in financing the costs of investment, as indicated by the low value of Tobin's q. Thus, policies to create a financing mechanism for FDI will help those firms facilitate outward FDI.

There are a few caveats with respect to our analysis. First, we captured firms' globalization activities in the relative size measured by sales of foreign affiliates, such as the ratio of exports to sales of foreign affiliates and the ratio of costs of FO to sales of foreign affiliates, because many globalized firms engage in more than one globalization mode. In the theoretical models of Helpman et al. (2004) and Chen et al. (2012), by contrast, individual firms do not engage in multiple modes of globalization, although we observe multiple modes at the aggregated industry level. Second, we cannot fully explain our estimation results regarding the effects of capital intensity and R&D intensity on the choice of globalization mode. Further theoretical and empirical studies on this issue are required.

Chapter 4
Does Tobin's *q* Matter for a Firm's Choice of Globalization Mode?

4.1 Introduction

For the last two decades, sorting of firms by productivity into different modes of globalization has been well documented both theoretically and empirically in the trade literature.[1] Melitz (2003) presents a model in which the most productive firms export goods to foreign markets, whereas less productive firms supply goods only to their domestic market. Helpman et al. (2004) extend the framework in Melitz (2003) to incorporate the possibility that firms serve foreign markets through foreign direct investment (FDI). They predict that only the most productive firms find it profitable to serve foreign markets via FDI and that medium-productivity firms serve foreign markets through exports. A large empirical literature confirms these sorting patterns (e.g., Bernard and Jensen 1995, 1999; Head and Ries 2003; Helpman et al. 2004; Kimura and Kiyota 2006; Mayer and Ottaviano 2007). On the other hand, an offshored production may be conducted via FDI or outsourced to a local firm. In such a situation, Antràs and Helpman (2004) predict that relatively more productive firms conduct FDI, whereas relatively less productive firms choose foreign outsourcing (FO). Because of data limitations, only a few studies have reported firm-level evidence on this issue. Using Japanese data, Tomiura (2007) observes that firms engaging only in FO tend to be less productive than those engaging in FDI. Federico (2010) and Kohler and Smolka (2012) find similar patterns for Italian and Spanish firms, respectively. In contrast, Defever and Toubal (2013) report a reverse ordering of firm productivity due to the higher fixed costs of outsourcing for French firms.

In the previous chapter we investigated the effects of the various aspects of firms' performance on their globalization activities. We measured firm performance by productivity, Tobin's q, and intangible asset intensity. In this chapter we focus more

[1] Helpman (2006), Greenaway and Kneller (2007), and Wagner (2007, 2012) provide useful surveys of the literature.

N. Jinji et al., *Deep Integration, Global Firms, and Technology Spillovers*, Advances in Japanese Business and Economics 26,
https://doi.org/10.1007/978-981-16-5210-3_4

on Tobin's q (Tobin 1969). Specifically, we attempt to sort firms into different modes of globalization by Tobin's q. Our study is motivated by a theoretical analysis by Chen et al. (2012). Combining the property-rights approach (Grossman and Hart 1986; Hart and Moore 1990) and the knowledge-capital model (Horstmann and Markusen 1987; Markusen 1984, 2002), they examine how the relative importance of knowledge capital over physical capital affects a firm's choice between FDI and FO for the offshored production. They show that firms with a higher physical-capital intensity tend to choose FO, whereas firms with a higher knowledge-capital intensity tend to conduct FDI. An interesting testable hypothesis is obtained from this result: firms with a high Tobin's q (i.e., the ratio of firm's market value to the replacement value of book equity) tend to conduct FDI, whereas those with a low Tobin's q tend to choose FO. Because the firm's market value reflects both knowledge-based and physical assets, and given that the book value of capital reflects only physical assets, a firm with a higher knowledge-capital intensity will have a higher Tobin's q. Thus, the above hypothesis follows. Moreover, although the knowledge-capital model predicts that firms with a high Tobin's q tend to prefer FDI to exports to serve the foreign market, this relationship is not so robust as the imperfect contractibility of knowledge capital and the costly transfer of knowledge capital tend to make FDI less attractive to knowledge-capital intensive firms.

In our empirical study, we employ detailed Japanese firm-level data covering the period 1994–1999. Our dataset includes information on sales, employment, capital, research and development (R&D) expenditure, direct exports, the values of domestic and foreign outsourcing of the companies headquartered in Japan, and the sales of their foreign affiliates. Moreover, corporate balance sheet data are included. Our dataset enables us to identify not only whether a firm engages in a particular globalization activity (i.e., exports, FDI, and FO) but also the extent to which it is involved in that activity. We utilize this feature of our dataset to construct indexes to measure the relative choice of globalization mode by calculating the ratio of the values of FO (i.e., total expenditure on outsourcing to foreign contracting firms) to the total FDI (i.e., total sales of foreign affiliates) and the ratio of the volume of direct exports by the headquarters company to *horizontal* FDI (i.e., sales of foreign affiliates, excluding exports to Japan). Thereafter, we regress these indexes of globalization activity on Tobin's q. Our measurement of Tobin's q is based on the simple approximation proposed by DaDalt et al. (2003). Furthermore, we regress the indexes of globalization activity on the total factor productivity (TFP) of individual firms to demonstrate the manner in which sorting patterns by Tobin's q differ from those by the firm's productivity. We employ the method developed by Olley and Pakes (1996) to compute TFP. Our analysis mainly focuses on firms engaging in multiple globalization modes and attempts to reveal whether a difference in Tobin's q (and TFP) motivates these firms to select more or less FDI relative to FO or exports.[2] In addition, we verify the robustness of results by including firms choosing a single globalization mode in estimations.

[2] We also estimate the relationship between Tobin's q (and TFP) and each globalization activity by constructing indexes to measure the degree of engagement in each globalization mode.

We need to address two important econometric issues in our analysis. First, the globalization indexes in our sample exhibit strong negative skewness and include outliers. As is well known, the presence of outliers may distort the classical least squares estimator (Wooldridge 2010). Thus, we employ several estimation methods to cope with this issue, namely, the median regression (or quantile regression) estimators, Huber M-estimators, and the MM-estimators (Huber 1981; Rousseeuw and Yohai 1984; Verardi and Croux 2009; Wooldridge 2010). The second econometric issue is endogeneity. Endogeneity potentially arises when factors that simultaneously influence the choice of globalization mode and Tobin's q exist. Except for this the problems of omitted variables may involve endogeneity. To control for possible endogeneity, we employ the endogenous quantile regression (QRIV) techniques proposed by Lee (2007), using two sets of instrumental variables (IVs). We discuss our estimation strategy in detail in Sect. 4.4.

The main findings of this chapter are as follows. First, we find that Tobin's q is negatively (positively) and significantly correlated with the ratio of FO to the total FDI (the ratio of total FDI to FO), which strongly supports the hypothesis that a higher Tobin's q is associated with a higher FDI engagement relative to FO by multinational enterprises (MNEs). In contrast, little evidence exists on a definite relationship between Tobin's q and the ratio of exports to horizontal FDI (or the ratio of horizontal FDI to exports). This result seems to imply that the imperfect contractibility of knowledge capital and a higher technology transfer cost actually matter for knowledge-capital intensive firms to choose between exports and FDI, because these factors weaken the positive relationship between Tobin's q and the ratio of FDI to exports. These findings are quite robust even when we include firms engaging in a single globalization mode in estimations. Moreover, we find that the relationship between Tobin's q and the firm's choice of globalization mode fairly differs from that of TFP. When we regress our globalization indexes on TFP, we find that TFP is negatively (positively) and significantly correlated with the ratio of exports to horizontal FDI (the ratio of horizontal FDI to exports), whereas no significant relationship exists between TFP and the ratio of FO to the total FDI (or the ratio of total FDI to FO). The former result is consistent with the theoretical prediction of Helpman et al. (2004) and a large number of existing empirical studies (Head and Ries 2003; Helpman et al. 2004; Kimura and Kiyota 2006; Mayer and Ottaviano 2007; Yeaple 2009).[3] However, the latter result differs from the prediction and findings of Antràs and Helpman (2004) in a limited number of existing studies (Federico 2010; Kohler and Smolka 2012; Tomiura 2007).

This chapter extends the empirical analysis of Jinji et al. (2019b) in three ways. First, we employ different estimation techniques from theirs to examine the impact of Tobin's q on the firm's choice between FO and FDI. In this respect, we provide evidence consistent with their findings. Second, we analyze the relationship between Tobin's q and another choice of globalization mode, namely, the choice between export and FDI. Third, we extend the analysis to the impact of productivity (i.e.,

[3] Greenaway and Kneller (2007) and Hayakawa et al. (2012) provide useful surveys of the literature.

TFP) on the firm's choice of globalization mode. The second and the third issues are not investigated by Jinji et al. (2019b)

The remainder of the chapter proceeds as follows. The next section discusses our empirical hypotheses. Section 4.3 describes the data and variables employed in the analysis. Section 4.4 explains our estimation strategy. Section 4.5 reports the estimation results. Section 4.6 concludes the chapter.

4.2 Theory and Hypotheses

This section briefly discusses our empirical hypotheses and theory behind them. We mainly focus on the relationship between the firm's value of Tobin's q and its mode choice for globalization strategy. As a straightforward extension of the q investment theory to the case of FDI (i.e., investment abroad), one may simply expect a positive relationship between Tobin's q and FDI. In the presence of an alternative mode of globalization, however, we need to consider the relationship between Tobin's q and a shift of the firm's activities between FDI and an alternative mode in each of the following two different situations: offshoring of production and the supply of goods to foreign markets. As we argue below, the relationship between Tobin's q and FDI will differ in these two situations. A key in our argument below is that, besides its role in the investment theory, Tobin's q indicates a firm's knowledge-capital intensity (relative to physical capital).

We first consider the situation in which production is offshored to a foreign country. A firm has two options: to produce goods at a foreign subsidiary (i.e., FDI) or to outsource production to a local firm (i.e., FO). In this situation, we expect that Tobin's q is positively related to the ratio of FDI to FO. Our argument is based on the theoretical analysis by Chen et al. (2012) and Jinji et al. (2019b). Chen et al. (2012) demonstrate that knowledge-capital (relative to physical capital) intensity rather than physical capital (relative to labor) intensity is an important factor for the firm's choice between FDI and FO. The reason is as follows. The owner of physical capital can relatively easily control the use of the physical capital. In contrast, it is relatively difficult for the owner of knowledge capital to specify and completely control the use of the knowledge capital. This is mainly because knowledge capital is partly non-excludable in nature and hence its use is not fully contractible.

Let us consider the case in which production in foreign country requires both physical and knowledge capital along with non-contractible effort by a local agent. The local agent is a manager if production occurs at a subsidiary and a licensee if it is outsourced to an independent local firm. An MNE that owns knowledge capital produces a good in two periods. Under FO, the agent who owns the physical capital makes an efficient effort to utilize its capital in period 1. Under FDI, in contrast, as the MNE owns the physical capital, the agent has no incentive to make an effort under the incomplete-contracting environment. On the other hand, under FO, the MNE transfers only an insufficient amount of the knowledge capital to the agent to prevent the agent from using knowledge absorbed in period 1 together with the physical capital for outside uses in period 2. Under FDI, as the agent who does not own the physical capital cannot use the absorbed knowledge for outside uses in period 2, the MNE transfers the full amount of the knowledge capital to the agent in period 1. The more important knowledge capital is in production, the smaller is the loss for the MNE from the agent's inefficient effort in period 1 under FDI and the larger is the loss for the MNE from an insufficient transfer of the knowledge capital to the agent under FO. Thus, the MNE prefers FDI to FO. If the physical capital is more important, the opposite is true and hence the MNE prefers FO.

We can easily extend the above model by Chen et al. (2012) to the case in which a final good is produced by assembling many intermediate goods. The whole production process is offshored to a foreign country. Intermediate goods vary in their knowledge-capital intensity. An MNE decides whether to outsource production for each intermediate good. Then, as the average knowledge-capital intensity of the MNE is higher, a smaller fraction of intermediate goods is outsourced. As argued in Sect. 4.1, a higher knowledge-capital intensity implies a higher value of Tobin's q. Given this, the above argument yields our first empirical hypothesis that Tobin's q is positively related to an FDI engagement relative to FO by MNEs.

We next consider the situation in which a firm supplies its goods to a foreign market. The firm can do so either via exports or horizontal FDI. There are two types of fixed costs: firm-specific fixed costs that mainly reflect knowledge-based assets and plant-specific fixed costs that mainly reflect physical assets. The knowledge-capital models of horizontal FDI (Horstmann and Markusen 1992; Markusen 1984, 2002) reveal that the jointness property of knowledge capital leads to multi-plant economies of scale. Hence, a firm with a higher intensity of knowledge capital tends to prefer FDI to exports. However, this tendency will be weakened as the degree of contractibility of knowledge capital is lower. This is because a wage premium is required when a manager of the foreign subsidiary, who absorbs knowledge capital, moves to a local competing firm (Fosfuri et al. 2001). In addition, the use of knowledge capital in foreign production incurs technology transfer costs that are increasing in technological complexity (Keller and Yeaple 2013). A higher intensity of knowledge capital generally implies higher technology transfer costs. This factor functions against the tendency mentioned above. Overall, whether a higher intensity of knowledge capital is associated with a lower ratio of exports to FDI depends on the relative strengths of the three factors mentioned above. Thus, our second empirical hypothesis is that there is no clear-cut relationship between Tobin's q and an MNE's ratio of exports to FDI.

4.3 Data and Variables

4.3.1 Data

We primarily collect data from three datasets of Japanese companies: the Basic Survey of Japanese Business Structure and Activities (BSJBSA) or *Kigyo Katsudo Kihon Chosa*, the Basic Survey on Overseas Business Activities (BSOBA) or *Kaigai Jigyo Katsudo Kihon Chosa*, and the Nikkei Economic Electronic Database Systems (NEEDS) Company Financial Reports.

BSJBSA and BSOBA are annual surveys by the Ministry of Economy, Trade, and Industry (METI).[4] BSJBSA is a mandatory survey for all firms with 50 or more employees and paid-up capital or investment funds exceeding 30 million yen. It covers mining, manufacturing, wholesale/retail trade, and service industries, and approximately 26,000 firms responded to the survey in 1999. On the other hand, BSOBA is an approved-type survey for Japanese corporations which (as of the end of March) own or previously have owned overseas affiliates. BSOBA lists two types of overseas affiliates: (1) those with at least 10% of their capital held by a Japanese parent company; and (2) those with at least 50% of their capital held by a foreign subsidiary that in turn has at least 50% of its capital held by a Japanese parent company. However, BSOBA excludes foreign affiliates in the financial, insurance, and real estate industries. Approximately 2,200 Japanese parent companies and 14,000 overseas affiliates responded to the survey in 1999. The data from BSJBSA and BSOBA include sales, employment, capital, R&D expenditures, headquarters' direct exports, and their foreign affiliates' sales. BSJBSA for the period 1994–1999 also includes information on outsourcing, that is, the number of domestic and foreign firms to which a headquarters company has contracted manufacturing and/or processing tasks and the total expenditures on the contracting out of business activities. Unfortunately, detailed data on outsourcing are unavailable after 2000. Because of this data limitation, our sample is restricted to the period of 1994–1999.

The corporate balance sheet data that we use to calculate Tobin's q and TFP are extracted from NEEDS, which incorporates approximately 4,000 publicly traded firms on the Japanese stock market, and covers the period from 1975 to the present. All publicly traded Japanese firms are identifiable using two codes—a Nikkei company code defined by Nikkei, Inc., and a security code defined by the Japanese Securities Identification Code Committee. Given that firm codes in BSJBSA and BSOBA differ from those in NEEDS, we use the Nikkei company code to link the three datasets. In addition, we identify approximately 1,000 to 1,300 headquarters companies for each year during the period 1994–1999 by matching full names and addresses of

[4] See METI's websites for details on these surveys (BSJBSA: www.meti.go.jp/english/statistics/tyo/kikatu/index.html; and BSOBA: www.meti.go.jp/english/statistics/tyo/kaigaizi/index.html).

companies in the three datasets.[5] In our sample, each headquarters company engages in at least one globalization activity (exports, FDI, or FO).[6]

4.3.2 Indexes of Globalization Activity

As shown by Table 3.1 in Chap. 3, many firms engage in multiple globalization modes rather than a single mode. For example, more than 550 firms engaged in both exports and FDI in 1999. This is more than double the number of firms engaged only in exports in 1999. This evidence is important when we select our preferred empirical framework.

Moreover, our dataset contains unique information regarding other dimensions of firms' globalization activities, including sales of foreign affiliates, the value of exports from the headquarters in Japan, and the value of FO. We utilize the information available in our dataset to measure the extent of engagement in each globalization mode by taking the ratio of the size of a particular activity (exports, FDI, or FO) to the domestic sales of headquarters companies. Moreover, we can measure the firm's relative choice of globalization mode by calculating the ratio of two variables representing its globalization activity. First, we denote domestic sales by headquarters companies in Japan as D, the total sales of foreign affiliates as I, the value of exports from the headquarters companies as X, and the total expenditure on outsourcing to companies abroad as O. Note that we can measure the size of the total FDI by I. Thereafter, we construct an additional measure of FDI denoted as I^h (where the superscript h refers to the horizontal type) by excluding exports to Japan from the sales of foreign affiliates, which measures the size of *horizontal* FDI. We employ these variables to calculate the ratio of each globalization activity (i.e., X, I, I^h, and O) to D, denoted as RXD, RID, RI^hD, and ROD, respectively. Moreover, we calculate the ratio of O to I, denoted as ROI, to capture the relative choice between FO and FDI, and the ratio of X to I^h, denoted as RXI^h, to capture the relative choice between exports and horizontal FDI. In the index for the relative choice of exports over FDI, we use I^h as the measure of FDI because, as Helpman et al. (2004) reveal, horizontal FDI matters to firms when choosing between export and FDI. Conversely, ROI measures the relative choice of FO over FDI. In this index, we consider that the total sales of foreign affiliates, including exports to the source country, are an appropriate measure of FDI. Note that by specifying the total sales of foreign affiliates as a measure of FDI, our analysis is consistent with that of Chen et al. (2012), who consider only the case where production occurs in the foreign country and a domestic firm chooses either FDI or outsourcing. In their model, FDI can be horizontal or vertical.

---

[5] Note that even among those identified companies, many do not answer every item in the surveys each year during the sample period.

[6] In the sample of headquarters companies in the BSOBA and BSJBSA surveys, approximately two-thirds of them report implementing at least one globalization activity during 1994–1999.

Table 4.1 Definition of variables

Variable	Definition
D	The value of domestic sales by a headquarters company in Japan (million yen)
X	The value of exports from a headquarters company in Japan (million yen)
I	The value of total sales of overseas affiliates held by a Japanese headquarters company (million yen)
I^h	I minus the value of total exports to Japan from overseas affiliates (million yen)
O	The total expenditure on outsourcing to companies abroad by a headquarters company (million yen)
RXD	The ratio of X to D
RID	The ratio of I to D
RI^hD	The ratio of I^h to D
ROD	The ratio of O to D
RXI^h	The ratio of X to I^h
RI^hX	The ratio of I^h to X
ROI	The ratio of O to I
RIO	The ratio of I to O

Table 4.1 summarizes the definition of variables that measure the firm's globalization activities.

4.3.3 *Tobin's q and TFP*

We measure Tobin's q (Tobin 1969) using the ratio of the firm's market value to its tangible assets. We follow DaDalt et al. (2003) and specify the following simple approximation of Tobin's q[7]:

$$\text{Tobin's } q = \frac{MVE + PS + LTDEBT + CL + BVINV - NCA}{TA},$$

where MVE denotes the year-end value of a common stock, PS denotes the liquidation value of a preferred stock, and $LTDEBT$, CL, $BVINV$, CA, and TA denote the book values of long-term debt, current liabilities, inventory, current assets, and

[7] Several studies significantly incorporate more complex estimations of Tobin's q, which rely on the estimated market value of the firm (Abel and Blanchard 1986; Perfect and Wiles 1994). However, as argued by DaDalt et al. (2003), although the approaches to Tobin's q produce more precise estimations, they are computationally costly. Moreover, these approaches may be subject to greater selection bias. DaDalt et al. (2003) suggest that a simple approach is then preferable unless the extreme precision of the q estimates is paramount and the sample selection bias is not likely to be significant.

total assets, respectively. We exclude PS in our measure of Tobin's q because the requisite data are unavailable.

We estimate TFP following Olley and Pakes (1996) and Keller and Yeaple (2009). We first define value-added and capital stock. The value-added of firm i at time t Y_{it} is measured as follows:

$$Y_{it} = SA_{it} - COGS_{it} - SGA_{it} + OR_{it} + PE_{it} + DE_{it} + ST_{it},$$

where SA, $COGS$, SGA, OR, PE, DE, and ST denote total sales, cost of goods sold, selling, general and administrative expenses, office rents, payroll expenses, depreciation expenses, and sundry taxes of firm i at time t, respectively. All values are converted into real measures using the GDP deflator released by METI.

The capital stock K_{it} is estimated by the perpetual inventory method:

$$K_{it} = I_{it} + (1 - \delta)K_{it-1}, \tag{4.1}$$

where K_{it} is the stock of equipment of firm i at the end of period t, I_{it} is the real investment of equipment of firm i during period t, and δ is the depreciation rate. Real investment I_{it} includes three types of investment involved in firm production: buildings and structures, machinery, and transportation machinery and tools. Following Hayashi and Inoue (1991), we apply depreciation rates of 5.2%, 9.5%, and 3.8% to buildings and structures, machinery, and transportation machinery and tools, respectively. We estimate each type of investment using Eq. (4.1) first and then aggregate them into K_{it}.

Then, let y_{it} be the logarithm of the value added of firm i at time t, and k_{it} and l_{it} be the logarithm of the firm's capital and labor, respectively. We consider the following production function:

$$y_{it} = \beta_0 + \beta_k k_{it} + \beta_l l_{it} + \omega_{it} + \eta_{it}, \tag{4.2}$$

where y_{it} is the logarithm of value-added $\ln Y$ in firm i at time t, k_{it} is the logarithm of the capital input $\ln K$, l_{it} is the logarithm of the number of full-time employees $\ln L$, ω_{it} is productivity, and η_{it} is either the measurement error or a shock to production. Both ω and η are not observed. Olley and Pakes (1996) argue that the endogeneity of input demand and self-selection induced by the exit behavior bias the OLS estimates of Eq. (4.2). In general, endogeneity arises because input choices are determined by the firm's beliefs regarding ω_{it} when these inputs are used.

Following Olley and Pakes (1996), we assume that labor l is the only variable factor whose choice can be affected by the current value of ω and that capital k is a fixed factor only affected by the distribution of ω_{it}, conditional on the information available at time $t - 1$ and past values of ω. The investment demand function is then given by $i_{it} = i(\omega_{it}, k_{it})$. Provided $i_{it} > 0$, the equation is strictly increasing in ω for any k, so that the investment demand function can be inverted to yield $\omega_{it} = h(i_{it}, k_{it})$. Substituting this result into Eq. (4.2) gives

$$y_{it} = \beta_l l_{it} + \phi(i_{it}, k_{it}) + \eta_{it}, \tag{4.3}$$

where $\phi(i_{it}, k_{it}) = \beta_0 + \beta_k k_{it} + h(i_{it}, k_{it})$. Because $\phi(\cdot)$ contains the productivity term ω, which is the source of the simultaneity bias, we can estimate Eq. (4.3) to obtain consistent estimates for β_l.[8] We use a fourth-order polynomial with interaction terms in investment and capital to identify the unknown function $\phi(\cdot)$. As the investment demand function (and hence $\phi(\cdot)$) should differ across industries, we estimate different polynomials for each of 10 main sectors: (i) food, textiles/apparel, and wood/paper products; (ii) chemicals, pharmaceuticals, and refined petroleum products; (iii) non-metallic products, basic metals, and fabricated metal products; (iv) machinery and precision instruments; (v) electrical and electronic equipment; (vi) transportation equipment; (vii) construction; (viii) trading; (ix) wholesale trade; and (x) other service activities.

A firm maximizes its expected value of both current and future profits and evolves according to an exogenous Markov process. In every period, the firm decides whether to continue an operation along with decisions on its labor input l and investment i, conditional on staying in the market. With consistent estimates of β_l, we use estimates of the survival probabilities to identify β_k. The survival probabilities Pr_{it} are obtained using a probit regression on a fourth-order polynomial with the interaction terms for capital and investment with a one-period lag. The final step to estimate β_k is as follows:

$$y_{it} - \hat{\beta}_l l_{it} = \beta_k k_{it} + g(\hat{\phi}_{it-1} - \beta_k k_{it-1}, \widehat{Pr}_{it}) + \eta_{it}, \tag{4.4}$$

where variables with a hat ($\hat{}$) indicate estimators of these variables. In Eq. (4.4), we also estimate the unknown function $g(\cdot)$ using a fourth-order polynomial with interaction terms for $\hat{\phi}_{it-1} - \beta_k k_{it-1}$ and $\widehat{Pr}_{it}$ with non-linear regression on β_k. Using consistent estimates of β_l and β_k, we estimate TFP as

$$TFP_{it} = y_{it} - \hat{\beta}_l l_{it} - \hat{\beta}_k k_{it}.$$

Table 4.2 provides descriptive statistics for variables in our analysis. As shown, the percentiles and means suggest that the distributions of these indexes are extremely negatively skewed.

Table 4.3 reports the correlations of the variables. In our data, it turns out that the correlation between Tobin's q and *TFP* is positive but weak. The correlation coefficient is 0.013.[9]

---

[8] Equation (4.3) is referred to as the "partially linear" model, which identifies β_l but not the coefficient of capital β_k in the production function.

[9] The relationship between firm productivity and Tobin's q is not obvious. In theory, there may or may not be a positive relationship between them (Dwyer 2001). In the presence of *ex ante* uncertainty with respect to the outcome of investment, and given that firms with successful investments will have high productivity and market value relative to the replacement cost of assets, a positive relationship exists between productivity and Tobin's q (Hopenhayn 1992; Jovanovic 1982; Melitz 2003). In contrast, if physical capital embodies any productivity differential, the relationship between them is not necessarily positive (Cooley et al. 1997). Some studies in the corporate finance literature find

Table 4.2 Descriptive statistics

	No. of obs.	Mean	Std. Dev.	Percentiles						
				5%	10%	25%	50%	75%	90%	95%
Tobin's q	5221	1.177	0.723	0.441	0.577	0.840	1.106	1.390	1.714	1.986
TFP	5148	1.260	0.587	0.464	0.607	0.863	1.254	1.635	1.963	2.186
RXD	4884	0.132	0.550	0.000	0.000	0.009	0.048	0.154	0.326	0.459
RID	4035	0.469	2.593	0.000	0.000	0.004	0.073	0.303	0.850	1.623
RI^hD	2461	0.359	1.632	0.000	0.001	0.018	0.086	0.280	0.696	1.272
ROD	4792	0.014	0.082	0.000	0.000	0.000	0.000	0.000	0.016	0.057
RXI^h	2436	21.008	459.833	0.000	0.000	0.081	0.388	1.399	4.921	13.259
RI^hX	2162	26.132	363.223	0.000	0.020	0.321	1.305	4.526	14.185	31.304
ROI	3402	8.722	292.082	0.000	0.000	0.000	0.000	0.001	0.151	0.506
RIO	940	160.636	818.611	0.000	0.000	1.629	9.425	47.427	181.589	584.900
CF	7432	3424.8	11313.1	−528.0	19.0	286.5	773.5	2356.5	6930.0	14646.0
LnK	6798	10.677	1.685	8.040	8.690	9.647	10.609	11.643	12.971	13.639
LnT^B	5187	3.927	0.324	3.258	3.555	3.829	3.932	4.111	4.344	4.382

Source: Authors' calculation from BSJBSA, BSOBA, and NEEDS for 1994–1999

Table 4.3 Correlations of variables

	LnQ	TFP	RXD	RID	RI^hD	ROD	RXI^h	RI^hX
LnQ	1.000							
TFP	0.013	1.000						
RXD	−0.019	0.007	1.000					
RID	0.010	0.035	0.576	1.000				
RI^hD	−0.016	0.082	0.455	0.854	1.000			
ROD	−0.082	−0.050	0.669	0.563	0.434	1.000		
RXI^h	0.094	0.015	0.019	0.099	−0.034	−0.005	1.000	
RI^hX	−0.010	0.060	−0.045	0.013	0.054	−0.016	−0.007	1.000
ROI	−0.071	0.047	−0.075	−0.138	−0.144	0.120	−0.002	−0.034
RIO	0.055	−0.195	0.005	−0.019	−0.037	−0.083	0.045	0.084
CF	0.134	0.145	0.028	0.113	0.109	−0.067	0.132	0.001
LnK	0.227	−0.213	0.063	0.159	0.153	−0.048	0.057	0.008
LnT^B	−0.006	−0.057	−0.029	0.118	0.107	0.044	0.031	−0.020
	ROI	RIO	CF	LnK	LnT^B			
ROI	1.000							
RIO	−0.107	1.000						
CF	−0.107	0.058	1.000					
LnK	−0.214	0.115	0.476	1.000				
LnT^B	−0.037	−0.072	0.061	0.353	1.000			

4.4 Estimation Strategy

In this section, we explain our empirical strategy. First, when we estimate the relationship of Tobin's q or TFP to our globalization indexes RXD, RID, RI^hD, and ROD, we need to address the censoring problem in the data because only a small proportion of the sampled firms engage in all three globalization activities. Thus, we implement Tobit regression, in addition to the ordinary least squares (OLS) estimation.

Second, as discussed in the previous section, the relative globalization indexes (i.e., ROI and RXI^h) in our sample have a strong negatively skewed distribution, indicating that heterogeneity across firms may be substantial, and outliers may exist in the dataset. As is well known, the presence of outliers can strongly distort the OLS estimator, leading to unreliable results. Thus, in addition to the OLS method, we employ several robust regression methods to cope with these issues, as robust OLS estimator, median regression estimator, Huber M-estimator, and MM-estimator. The robust OLS (ROLS) is an OLS regression with robust variance estimates (Huber 1981). The *median regression estimator*, or *quantile regression* (QR) estimator, deals with the heterogeneity across firms and the presence of outliers (Wooldridge 2010). Although the QR estimators are resistant to the existence of *vertical outliers* (i.e., outliers in the y dimension without outlying in the x dimension), they behave poorly in the presence of *bad leverage points* (i.e., points associated with outlying values in the x dimension that locate far away from the true regression line) (Verardi and Croux 2009). In addition, their efficiency is low at a normal distribution (Huber 1981). The *Huber M-estimator* generalizes the QR estimators by considering a loss function other than the absolute values of the residuals, which increases the efficiency, keeping robustness with respect to vertical outliers (Verardi and Croux 2009). However, the M-estimators are not robust with respect to bad leverage points (Rousseeuw and Yohai 1984). Finally, the *MM-estimator* introduced by Yohai (1987) performs well in both high efficiency and a high breakdown point. A breakdown point is the smallest fraction of contamination (i.e., very bad outliers) in the sample that can cause an estimator to take on values arbitrarily far from the true values (Rousseeuw and Leroy 1987). Thus, a higher breakdown point means that the estimator is more resistant to outliers.[10]

In addition to the issue of outliers, endogeneity is another important issue to be addressed in our estimation. Endogeneity potentially arises because factors that simultaneously influence the choice of globalization mode and Tobin's q may exist. The problem of omitted variables may also involve endogeneity. For example, previous studies in the investment literature have shown that the presence of adjustment costs or financial frictions causes Tobin's q to diverge from the marginal value of installed capital, or "marginal q" (Abel and Eberly 1994; Hennessy 2004). More recently, Abel and Eberly (2011) have demonstrated that investment is positively

---

a positive relationship between the firm's productivity and Tobin's q even after controlling other factors that affect the firm's market value (Dwyer 2001; Palia and Lichtenberg 1999).

[10] For example, the OLS has a 0% breakdown point. In contrast, Yohai (1987) shows that the MM-estimator guarantees a 50% breakdown point, which is the best that can be expected.

related to both Tobin's q and cash flow even in the absence of adjustment costs or financial frictions. Moreover, Gala and Julio (2012) suggest that, in addition to Tobin's q and cash flow, firm size may play an important role in explaining investment. Therefore, our regression of the globalization indexes on Tobin's q may suffer from omitted variable bias if these variables are not controlled for.

We employ the QRIV technique proposed by Lee (2007) to control for possible endogeneity with the potential presence of outliers. The estimation procedure comprises two steps: the first step is to estimate the residuals of the reduced-form equation for the endogenous explanatory variable (i.e., Tobin's q); and the second step is to use the reduced-form residual as an additional explanatory variable to estimate the primary equation, which describes the relationship between the choice of globalization mode and Tobin's q.

In our QRIV estimations, we employ IVs that are assumed to be related to the omitted variable problem in measuring firm performance, which are suggested in the literature (Abel and Eberly 2011; Gala and Julio 2012). Among others, we employ two sets of IVs to verify the robustness of our estimation results. The first set includes the cash flow CF_{it-1} and the years in business T_{it}^{B} for the headquarters company i, where CF_{it-1} stands for the beginning-of-year cash flow for the headquarters company i in year $t-1$.[11] We denote the QRIV with the first set of IVs as QRIV(1). The second set of IVs comprises CF_{it-1}/K_{it-1}, LnK_{it-1}, and LnT_{it}^{B}, which denote the ratio of cash flow to capital stock, the natural logarithm of capital stock, and the natural logarithm of years in business for the headquarters company, respectively. Now K_{it-1} is the beginning-of-year capital stock for the headquarters company i in year $t-1$. We use LnK as a measurement of firm size, as suggested by Gala and Julio (2012). We denote the QRIV with the second set of IVs as QRIV(2). We assume that if changes in these IVs are not controlled, they will be part of the error, accounting for inconsistent estimates as long as they are correlated with the performance of the headquarters companies, such as Tobin's q.[12]

4.5 Empirical Results

4.5.1 *The Relationships of Tobin's q and TFP to the Degree of the Firm's Engagement in Globalization Modes*

We first analyze the relationship between Tobin's q or TFP and the degree of the firm's engagement in a particular globalization mode by regressing each of RXD, RID, $RI^{h}D$, and ROD on Tobin's q or TFP. Results are reported in Table 4.4.

[11] Cash flow CF_{it} is calculated by $CF_{it} = DE_{it} + PF_{it} - ST_{it}$, where PF denotes profits.

[12] As shown in Table 4.3, our IVs are fairly correlated with Tobin's q, while they have no evident correlation with the indexes of globalization activity.

Table 4.4 OLS and Tobit estimates

	OLS				Tobit			
	RXD	RID	RI^hD	ROD	RXD	RID	RI^hD	ROD
LnQ	0.050***	0.326***	0.064	0.005***	0.056***	0.492***	0.069	0.038***
	(0.019)	(0.11)	(0.058)	(0.0014)	(0.018)	(0.10)	(0.078)	(0.0087)
No. of obs.	4870	4024	2455	4778	4870	4024	2455	4778
R^2	0.0208	0.0174	0.0139	0.0345				
Pseudo R^2					0.0224	0.0057	0.0040	0.1512
TFP	0.033	−0.063	0.140	0.003	0.050**	−0.063	0.156*	0.027***
	(0.025)	(0.19)	(0.13)	(0.0019)	(0.0020)	(0.11)	(0.087)	(0.0097)
No. of obs.	4870	4024	2455	4778	4870	4024	2455	4778
R^2	0.0199	0.0137	0.0146	0.0342				
Pseudo R^2					0.0225	0.0043	0.0042	0.1443

Notes: (a) A constant term and industrial and year dummies are included in the estimations. (b) Values in the parentheses are standard errors. (c) ***, **, and * indicate statistical significance at the 1%, 5%, and 10% levels, respectively

The upper panel of Table 4.4 shows the results of OLS and Tobit regression of the globalization indexes (i.e., RXD, RID, RI^hD, and ROD) on the logarithm of Tobin's q, denoted as LnQ. The estimation results for TFP are summarized in the lower panel of Table 4.4. The OLS and Tobit estimates of LnQ are both statistically significant and positive except for the case of RI^hD. In contrast, the OLS estimates of TFP fail against the null hypothesis for all of the globalization indexes. After we control for censoring problems by adopting Tobit regression censored at zero, the estimates of TFP are positively significant for RXD, RI^hD, and ROD.

Our results indicate the positive relationship between Tobin's q and the globalization indexes. In addition, the results for TFP are consistent with Tomiura (2007) for the most part. That is, highly productive firms tend to engage in more globalization activity (FDI, exporting, or FO). However, the results for RID suggest that higher-productivity firms do not necessarily have a higher ratio of foreign affiliate sales to domestic sales of the headquarters company. This may be because FDI in RID includes both the horizontal and vertical types of FDI, and vertical FDI may not be implemented by high-productivity firms.

Table 4.5 Estimation results (explanatory variable: $Ln\,Q$)

Regression technique	Dependent Variable			
	ROI	RIO	RXI^h	RI^hX
(1) OLS	44.078	75.197	23.169	−7.615
	(30.86)	(53.73)	(14.81)	(8.40)
(2) ROLS	−0.025**	−0.050	2.460	−0.069
	(0.011)	(0.035)	(1.97)	(0.11)
(3) QR	−0.064**	8.160***	−0.004	0.011
	(0.027)	(2.96)	(0.024)	(0.092)
(4) Huber M-estimators	−0.056***	7.228**	0.093	−0.185
	(0.021)	(3.59)	(0.058)	(0.18)
(5) MM-estimators	−0.022*	2.373**	−0.057*	−0.079
	(0.0012)	(1.05)	(0.034)	(0.070)
No. of Observations	858	828	2095	1964

Notes: (a) ROLS, QR, Huber M-estimation, and MM-estimation are implemented in Stata's command `rreg`, `qreg`, `mregress`, and `mmregress`. (b) Chamberlain's bandwidth and triangle kernel function are used to measure robust VCE for `qreg`. (c) A constant term and industrial and year dummies are included in the estimations. (d) Values in parentheses are robust standard errors for (1), (3), and (5) and standard errors for (2) and (4). (e) Robust variance calculation is used in the variance estimator for OLS regression. (f) ***, **, and * indicate statistical significance at the 1%, 5%, and 10% levels, respectively

4.5.2 *Tobin's q and the Relative Choice of Globalization Modes*

We next regress the indexes of the relative choice of globalization modes on Tobin's q. As we calculate the ratios of the two globalization modes and their multiplicative inverses (i.e., FO to the total FDI for ROI, exports to horizontal FDI for RXI^h, and their multiplicative inverses, RIO and RI^hX), we exclude the observations that have zero values for at least one of the two modes.[13] We check the robustness of our estimation results by including the observations with zero values in Sect. 4.5.3.

Table 4.5 summarizes the results of regressing the four globalization indexes on the logarithm of Tobin's q, denoted as $Ln\,Q$. We first estimate the model by the OLS. As shown in row (1) of Table 4.5, the OLS estimates of the coefficients of $Ln\,Q$ are all insignificant, and the magnitude of the estimated coefficients is relatively large, suggesting that the presence of outliers seriously affects the regression coefficients.

[13] Multi-nationality may possibly increase a firm's Tobin's q. As we restrict our sample to MNEs, we do not have to address this issue. Morck and Yeung (1991) report that multi-nationality itself does not significantly impact Tobin's q.

Thereafter, we run the ROLS with robust variance estimates.[14] As reported in row (2), the magnitude of the estimated coefficients becomes modest by employing ROLS, and the coefficient of ROI is negative at the 5% significance level.

We next run the robust regression with QR, Huber M-estimators, and MM-estimators.[15] Estimated results are reported in rows (3), (4), and (5) in Table 4.5, respectively. As shown in the table, the three types of estimates are all significant and negative for ROI and positive for RIO, indicating that Tobin's q is positively correlated with a motive of a firm toward more FDI and away from FO. Unlike ROI and RIO, the estimates of RXI^h and RI^hX are statistically insignificant, except for the MM-estimate of RXI^h, which is negative at the 10% significance level. Thus, we cannot find any evident relationship of Tobin's q to the choice of globalization mode between horizontal FDI and exports.

Furthermore, we employ a QRIV technique using two sets of IVs, as explained in the previous section, to account for the possible endogeneity.[16] Table 4.6 reports the estimated results from the QRIV median estimates. It indicates that the results are quite consistent between the two sets of IVs. That is, the estimated coefficient of LnQ is negative and statistically significant for ROI and positive for RIO, whereas the estimated coefficients are all insignificant for RXI^h and RI^hX. These results suggest that our findings reported in Table 4.5 can be supported even after controlling for possible endogeneity in our estimations.

As the globalization indexes in our sample have a strong negatively skewed distribution, the relationships between the globalization indexes and firm characteristics may substantially differ at different points in the conditional distribution of the globalization indexes. We estimate the coefficients of LnQ for ROI and RXI^h at various quantiles between 10% and 90% using QRIV(2) to check heterogeneity between globalization indexes and firm characteristics. We report the results in Fig. 4.1. In this figure, we plot point and interval estimates from QRIV(2) for LnQ. In each panel in Fig. 4.1, the horizontal axis measures the quantile, and the vertical axis measures the value of estimates. Moreover, the thick black lines depict the point estimates at various quantiles, and dashed lines indicate the lower and upper bounds of a 95% confidence interval.

Panel (1) shows that the confidence interval for the estimated coefficient of LnQ in the regression of ROI lies below zero at all quantiles between 10% and 90%. In

[14] The ROLS estimations are implemented using Stata's command `rreg`.

[15] The QR estimators, Huber M-estimators, and MM-estimators are obtained by using Stata's command `qreg`, `mregress`, and `mmregress`. For the `qreg`, the robust VCE is used with Chamberlain's bandwidth and triangle kernel function.

[16] The estimation is implemented using Stata's command `cqiv`. The Stata code for `cqiv` is released and introduced by Chernozhukov et al. (2015). We employ an endogenous quantile estimation involved in `cqiv` without censoring, which is developed on the basis of Lee (2007). The information required to build pointwise confidence intervals is obtained by 500 bootstrap replications. The value of t-statistics is measured using the bootstrap mean and the lower and upper bounds of a 95% confidence interval. To check the robustness of the estimated results by QRIV, we employ an alternative approach of QRIV proposed by Chernozhukov and Hansen (2008), using Stata's command `ivqreg` produced by Kwak (2010). The results, which are available from the corresponding author upon request, are fairly consistent with those in Table 4.6.

Table 4.6 Endogenous quantile regression (explanatory variable: LnQ)

Regression technique	Dependent variable			
	ROI	RIO	RXI^h	RI^hX
QRIV(1)	−0.228**	59.013*	0.017	1.693
	(0.10)	(34.11)	(0.85)	(3.26)
QRIV(2)	−0.356***	55.569**	0.034	1.116
	(0.11)	(27.37)	(0.85)	(3.02)
No. of Observations	869	835	2105	1973

Notes: (a) QRIV(1) and QRIV(2) estimations are implemented using Stata's command `cqiv` with 500 bootstrap replications. (b) A constant term and industrial and year dummies are included in the estimations. (c) Values in parentheses are standard errors measured by bootstrap. (d) An endogenous variable estimator is LnQ. QRIV(1) includes CF_{t-1} and T^B, and QRIV(2) includes CF_{t-1}/K_{t-1}, LnK_{t-1}, and LnT^B as IVs. (e) ***, **, and * indicate statistical significance at the 1%, 5%, and 10% levels, respectively

contrast, panel (2) shows that the 95% confidence interval in the regression of RXI^h includes zero at all quantiles. As a result, Fig. 4.1 suggests that the estimated results reported in Table 4.6 hold at all quantiles between 10% and 90%.

4.5.3 Robustness of the Results

In the analysis in the previous subsection, we focused on firms engaging in multiple globalization modes. However, firms may choose a single mode rather than multiple modes, as suggested by theoretical models such as that in Chen et al. (2012). Thus, we check whether our results in the previous subsection are robust even when we include firms that engage only in a single mode in our estimation.

The globalization indexes we used in the previous subsection are ROI and RIO for the choice between FO and FDI, and RXI^h and RI^hX for the choice between exports and horizontal FDI. Here, we include observations with zero values for the numerator of each index. For example, in the case of RIO, all firms in the sample for estimation engage in FO but some of them do not conduct FDI.

Besides the estimation techniques we employed in the previous subsection, we estimate the model using a censored quantile regression (CQR) technique to address the censoring problem in the data.[17] As shown in Table 3.2, the value of ROI is zero even at the 0.70 quantile because only a small fraction of firms that conduct FDI also engage in FO. Consequently, we cannot obtain technically sound quantile estimates, such as a median estimate, for ROI. Therefore, we omit the estimated results for ROI.

[17] We use the Stata's command `cqiv`, which implements the estimator proposed by Chernozhukov and Hong (2002) for CQR.

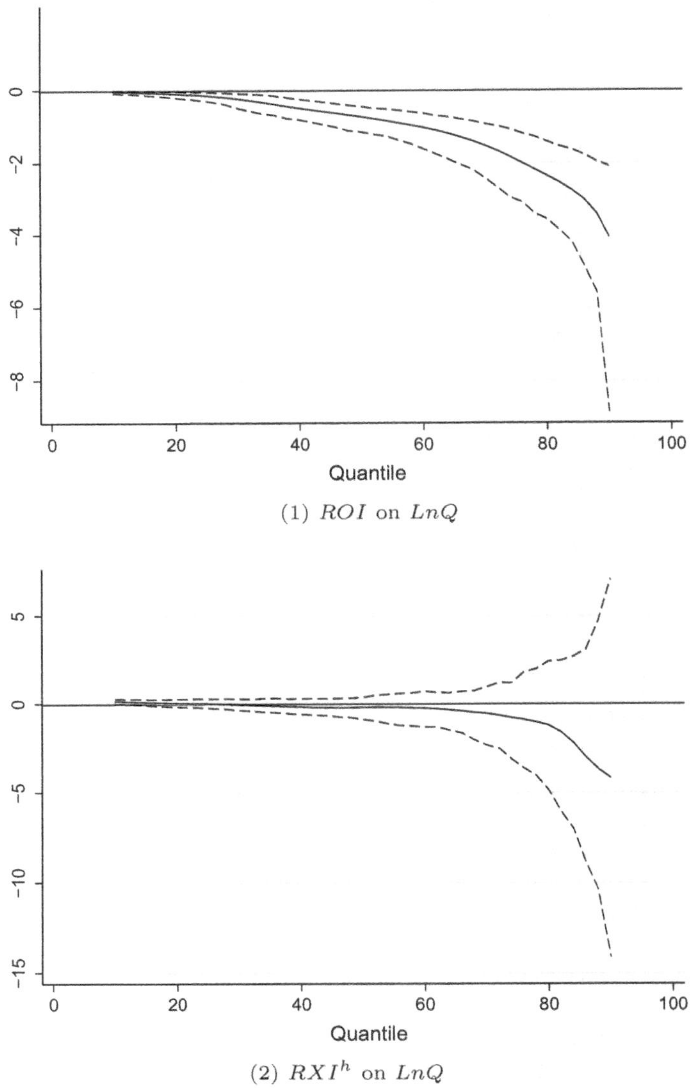

Fig. 4.1 Estimates and confidence intervals for LnQ by QRIV(2)

Table 4.7 Robustness check by including single-mode firms (explanatory variable: $Ln Q$)

Dependent variable	ROLS	Huber M-estimator	MM-estimator	QR	CQR	No. of Obs.
RIO	1.724	4.806*	1.110	5.076**	5.785*	920
	(1.33)	(2.75)	(0.77)	(2.43)	(3.27)	
RXI^h	−0.038	0.090*	−0.009	0.037	0.042	2402
	(0.027)	(0.047)	(0.021)	(0.033)	(0.060)	
RI^hX	−0.062	−0.143	−0.106*	−0.051	−0.044	2134
	(0.092)	(0.15)	(0.062)	(0.090)	(0.15)	

Notes: (a) Values in parentheses are standard errors. (b) The coefficients of QR and CQR are estimated at median quartile. CQR is implemented using Stata's command `cqiv` with 500 bootstrap replications. (c) ***, **, and * indicate statistical significance at the 1%, 5%, and 10% levels, respectively. (d) A constant term and industrial and year dummies are included in the estimations

The estimated results with zero values in the numerator of the globalization index are reported in Table 4.7. The Huber M-estimator, QR, and CQR provide positive and statistically significant estimates of the coefficient of $Ln Q$ in the regression of RIO. In contrast, in the regression of RXI^h, statistically insignificant estimates are obtained for $Ln Q$, except for the Huber M-estimator. Similarly, for RI^hX, insignificant estimates of $Ln Q$ are provided, except for the MM-estimator. These findings are quite consistent with those in the previous subsection.

Thus, from the analysis in this subsection we conclude that our findings in Sect. 4.5.2 are quite robust even when we include firms engaging in a single mode in the estimation.

4.5.4 *TFP and the Relative Choice of Globalization Modes*

We next regress the indexes of globalization modes on TFP using the same estimation methods as those employed in Sect. 4.5.2 to investigate any possible differences between Tobin's q and productivity in the firm's choice of globalization mode. Table 4.8 reports the estimated results.

As shown in the table, the estimates of ROI and RIO are insignificant for all estimators. We cannot find any significant relationship of TFP to the choice of globalization mode between FDI and FO.[18] On the other hand, as for its relationship with the choice between horizontal FDI and exports, the results indicate that the estimates of RI^hX are positive and statistically significant, except for OLS, and that

[18] This finding may appear to be inconsistent with the prediction of Antràs and Helpman (2004). However, as Grossman et al. (2005) and Defever and Toubal (2013) show, the productivity ordering in the model of Antràs and Helpman (2004) depends crucially on the relative size of fixed costs associated to FDI and FO. That is, their prediction concerning the productivity ordering is not robust. Our estimates reveal that there is actually no evident relationship between TFP and the choice of FDI versus FO.

Table 4.8 Estimation results (explanatory variable: TFP)

Regression technique	Dependent Variable			
	ROI	RIO	RXI^h	RI^hX
(1) OLS	139.478	−43.532	20.376	−8.680
	(101.47)	(47.11)	(15.91)	(16.84)
(2) ROLS	0.012	0.027	−0.449	0.225**
	(0.0094)	(0.035)	(1.68)	(0.11)
(3) QR	0.007	−1.979	−0.110*	0.293**
	(0.020)	(3.16)	(0.066)	(0.15)
(4) Huber M-estimators	−0.014	3.445	−0.095*	0.312*
	(0.017)	(3.04)	(0.057)	(0.17)
(5) MM-estimators	−0.002	−1.063	0.021	0.126*
	(0.0054)	(1.10)	(0.022)	(0.076)
No. of Observations	862	832	2104	1973

Notes: (a) ROLS, QR, Huber M-estimation, and MM-estimation are implemented using Stata's command `rreg`, `qreg`, `mregress`, and `mmregress`. (b) Chamberlain's bandwidth and triangle kernel function are used to measure robust VCE for `qreg`. (c) A constant term and industrial and year dummies are included in the estimations. (d) Values in parentheses are robust standard errors for (1) and (3) and standard errors for (2), (4), and (5). (e) Robust variance calculation is used in the variance estimator for OLS. (f) ***, **, and * indicate statistical significance at the 1%, 5%, and 10% levels, respectively

the estimates of RXI^h are negative and significant by QR and Huber M-estimators. This suggests a positive relationship between TFP and a motive of a firm toward a greater horizontal FDI and less export, which is consistent with the findings in the large empirical literature.

It is then apparent from a comparison between Tables 4.5 and 4.8 that the relationships of Tobin's q with the relative choice of globalization modes clearly differ from those of TFP.

4.6 Conclusion

Using Japanese firm-level data, we empirically investigated the manner in which the firm's choice of globalization mode differs according to the value of Tobin's q. Our empirical results indicated that Tobin's q is negatively related to the ratio of FO to FDI by Japanese MNEs. This finding implies that the knowledge-capital intensity plays an important role in the choice between FDI and FO, as Chen et al. (2012) demonstrate. This finding is consistent with that of Jinji et al. (2019b). In contrast, we could not find a definite relationship between Tobin's q and the ratio of exports to horizontal FDI. This may be explained by the dominance of a higher technology transfer cost for knowledge capital and/or the imperfect contractibility of knowledge capital over multi-plant economies of scale of knowledge capital. Moreover, we found that the relationship between Tobin's q and an MNE's mode choice for globalized activity fairly differs from the relationship between productivity and an MNE's choice of the mode for globalized activity. Our estimated results revealed that TFP is negatively correlated with the ratio of exports to horizontal FDI but has only an insignificant relationship with the outsourcing decision. The former evidence supports the prediction by Helpman et al. (2004) and is consistent with the findings of existing empirical studies.

Chapter 5
Trade Patterns and International Technology Spillovers: Theory and Evidence from Japanese and European Patent Citations

5.1 Introduction

International diffusion of knowledge is important to both the speed of the world's technology frontier expansion and income convergence across countries. For example, Eaton and Kortum (1996) estimate innovation and technology diffusion among 19 Organization for Economic Co-operation and Development (OECD) countries to test predictions from a quality ladders model of endogenous growth with patenting. They find that each OECD country other than the United States obtains more than half of its productivity growth from technological knowledge originated abroad. They also find that more than half of the growth in every OECD country is derived from innovation in the United States, Japan, and Germany. Eaton and Kortum (1999) fit a similar model to research employment, productivity, and international patenting among the five leading research economies, i.e., the United States, Japan, Germany, the United Kingdom, and France. They find that research performed abroad is about two-thirds as influential as domestic research. In particular, technological knowledge from Japan and Germany diffuses most rapidly, while France and Germany are the quickest to exploit knowledge. They also show that the United States and Japan together contribute to over 65% of the growth in each of the five countries.

Previous studies have identified international trade as a major channel of international diffusion of knowledge.[1] Coe and Helpman (1995) examine international

[1] Trade works as a channel of international diffusion of knowledge because, for example, firms can obtain information on advanced technology by reverse engineering of imported goods. International trade also provides channels of cross-border communication that facilitates learning of production and organizational methods and market conditions (Grossman and Helpman 1991). Another major channel is foreign direct investment (FDI). Productivity spillovers through FDI are empirically confirmed by a number of studies (Branstetter 2006; Haskel et al. 2007; Javorcik 2004; Keller and Yeaple 2009), while some studies do not find significant spillovers (Aitken and Harrison 1999; Haddad and Harrison 1993).

N. Jinji et al., *Deep Integration, Global Firms, and Technology Spillovers*,
Advances in Japanese Business and Economics 26,
https://doi.org/10.1007/978-981-16-5210-3_5

productivity spillovers among OECD countries and find large spillover effects from foreign research and development (R&D) capital stocks to domestic productivity that is measured by total factor productivity (TFP). They also show that countries exhibit higher productivity levels by importing goods from countries with high levels of technological knowledge, which supports the existence of trade-related international productivity spillovers. However, Keller (1998) provides a finding that casts doubt on Coe and Helpman's result by employing a Monte-Carlo-based robustness test. He finds that estimated international productivity spillovers among randomly matched trade partners turn out to be large (and even larger than those among actual trade partners). Xu and Wang (1999) estimate that about half of the returns on R&D investment in seven OECD countries spilled over to other OECD countries and that trade in capital goods is a significant channel of productivity spillovers. Acharya and Keller (2009) find that the diffusion of technological knowledge is strongly varying across country-pairs. They show that imports are crucial for technology diffusion from Germany, France, and the United Kingdom, while non-trade channels are relatively more important for the United States, Japan, and Canada.

Although a number of studies have investigated international diffusion of technological knowledge through trade, none of the existing studies have paid attention to the relationship between bilateral trade patterns and technology spillovers. The only exception is Jinji et al. (2015). They empirically examine the relationship between the bilateral trade structure and technology spillovers. In this chapter, we complement Jinji et al. (2015) by both analyzing theoretically the relationship between the bilateral trade structure and technology spillovers and providing further evidence on such a relationship based on Japanese and European patent data. We follow Jinji et al. (2015) to categorize bilateral trade flows into one way trade (OWT), or inter-industry trade, and two-way trade, or intra-industry trade (IIT). IIT is further decomposed into horizontal intra-industry trade (HIIT) and vertical intra-industry trade (VIIT) (e.g., Fontagné and Freudenberg 1997; Fukao et al. 2003; Greenaway et al. 1995). The difference between HIIT and VIIT reflects differences in the quality of products in the same category traded between two countries. In HIIT, horizontally differentiated products (i.e., products with similar quality but different varieties) are traded, whereas vertically differentiated products (i.e., products with different qualities) are traded in VIIT.[2] As for data, HIIT and VIIT can be distinguished by using unit values (i.e., total value of import or export in one product category divided by the quantity of import or export in that product category) under the assumption that unit values are increasing in product quality.

The theoretical literature on IIT has been separated into two branches for a long period. As is well known, trade models with monopolistic competition could explain HIIT (e.g., Eaton and Kierzkowski 1984; Helpman 1981; Krugman 1979, 1980). However, in these models, product varieties are symmetric and not differentiated in

[2] Note that in the literature the terms of HIIT and VIIT are sometimes used in different meanings. In an alternative definition, HIIT means trade of final goods in the same industry across countries, while VIIT involves trade of intermediate goods with final goods in the same industry (Yomogida 2004). Since we do not consider the distinction between intermediate goods and final goods in this chapter, this alternative definition of HIIT and VIIT is not applicable.

quality. Trade models with vertical differentiation, on the other hand, could explain VIIT but could not explain HIIT (e.g., Falvey 1981; Falvey and Kierzkowski 1987; Flam and Helpman 1987; Herguera and Lutz 1998; Lambertini 1997; Motta et al. 1997; Shaked and Sutton 1984). Given the fact that HIIT and VIIT arise in continuous phenomena, this divergence in the theory would not be acceptable. More recently, a number of studies have attempted to introduce quality differentiation into the monopolistically competitive trade model. Some studies use a quality-augmented type of Dixit–Stiglitz demand specification (Dixit and Stiglitz 1977) in the framework of Melitz (2003)[3] with the assumption that higher quality is associated with higher marginal cost (Baldwin and Harrigan 2011; Gervais 2015; Helble and Okubo 2008; Johnson 2012; Kugler and Verhoogen 2012; Mandel 2010). On the other hand, Antoniades (2015) introduces quality differentiation into the quasi-linear utility with a quadratic subutility specification in the framework of Melitz and Ottaviano (2008) and considers endogenous quality upgrading by heterogeneous firms. He shows that firms with higher productivity choose higher qualities and charge higher prices. However, his model has some limitations when it is extended to the case of two-country trade. In this chapter, we also introduce quality differentiation into the framework of Melitz and Ottaviano (2008). We employ a different approach from Antoniades (2015). We assume that firms randomly draw their product quality so that firms with identical productivity are heterogeneous in product quality. This reflects the stochastic nature of product R&D. This formulation of quality differentiation turns out to be tractable. Then, we show that our model can explain OWT, HIIT, and VIIT in one unified framework. Using this framework, we examine how international technology spillovers are associated with bilateral trade structure.

For empirical analysis of international technology spillovers, we use data on patent citations as a proxy for spillovers of technological knowledge. There are a number of empirical studies on knowledge flow based on patent citations (e.g., Haruna et al. 2010; Hu and Jaffe 2003; Jaffe and Trajtenberg 1999; Jaffe et al. 1993; MacGarvie 2006; Mancusi 2008).[4] In the literature, patent citation data are used as a direct measure of technology spillovers (Hall et al. 2007). Hu and Jaffe (2003) use data on patents granted in the United States and examine patent citations by inventors residing in Korea, Japan, Taiwan, and the United States to infer the pattern of technological knowledge flows from the United States and Japan to Korea and Taiwan. They find that Korean patents are much more likely to cite Japanese patents than US patents, while Taiwanese patents cite both Japanese and US patents evenly. Mancusi (2008) estimates technological knowledge diffusion within and across sectors and countries by using European patents and citations for 14 OECD countries. She finds that international knowledge diffusion is effective in increasing innovative productivity in technologically laggard countries, while technological leaders (the United States,

[3] Originally, Melitz (2003) mentions that differences in productivity may be interpreted as those in product quality at equal cost.

[4] However, Jaffe et al. (1993) admit that patent citations are a coarse and noisy measure of knowledge flow, because not all inventions are patented and not all knowledge flows can be captured by patent citations. Based on a survey of inventors, Jaffe et al. (2000) suggest the validity of patent citations as indicators of technology spillovers, despite the presence of noise.

Japan, and Germany) are a source rather than a destination of knowledge flows. Using French firms' patent citations and firm-level trade data, MacGarvie (2006) finds that the patents of importing firms are significantly more likely to be influenced by technology in the exporting country than are the patents of firms that do not import. In contrast, she finds no significant evidence of exporting firms' citing more patents from their destination countries. Moreover, Haruna et al. (2010) investigate whether the trade structure plays an important role as a channel of technological knowledge diffusion between Asian economies (Korea, Taiwan, China, and India) and G7 countries including the United States and Japan. In that paper, they use a modified version of the Balassa's index of Revealed Comparative Advantage (RCA), which represents the share of country i in sector j relative to the country's export (or import) share for all sectors. Then, they find that trade specialization, especially import specialization, has a direct effect on knowledge diffusion.

In this chapter, we take our study one step further and investigate in more detail the relationship between bilateral trade patterns and international knowledge flow. In order to accomplish this task, we develop a two-country model of monopolistic competition with quality differentiation, in which inter- and (horizontal and vertical) intra-industry trade patterns endogenously arise, depending on the conditions of trading countries. Our model is an extension of the model developed by Melitz and Ottaviano (2008), and firms are heterogeneous in product quality rather than in productivity. Then, after deriving hypotheses from the model, we test them by using data on bilateral trade among 44 countries/economies and patent citations at the European and Japanese patent offices.

The main results are as follows. Our model predicts that the bilateral trade pattern is HIIT when the two countries have access to a similar level of technology, while it is VIIT when there is technological difference between them. Moreover, if the technological difference is sufficiently large, the bilateral trade pattern becomes OWT. Our model also predicts that technology spillovers are highest when the bilateral trade pattern is HIIT, followed by VIIT and OWT. Our estimation results basically confirm the predictions of the model. We find that an increase in the share of intra-industry trade in the bilateral trade has a positive effect on the number of patent citations between the two countries. HIIT has a larger effect than VIIT. On the other hand, the effects of OWT on the number of citations are much weaker than those of IIT. These findings for Japanese and European patents are generally consistent with that of Jinji et al. (2015) for the US patents.

The remainder of the chapter is organized in the following way. Section 5.2 sets up a closed-economy model of monopolistic competition with quality differentiation. Section 5.3 extends the model to the case of two-country trade and derives testable implications from the theoretical model. Section 5.4 conducts an empirical analysis. Section 5.5 concludes this chapter.

5.2 The Basic Model

In this section, we describe the basic structure of the model in a closed economy. Consider country d that has two sectors: a homogenous numeraire sector and a differentiated manufacturing sector.[5] We introduce quality differentiation in a quasi-linear (instantaneous) utility with a quadratic subutility, developed by Ottaviano et al. (2002) and Melitz and Ottaviano (2008).[6] There are L^d consumers, which is constant over time. Preferences are identical across consumers and defined over a continuum of differentiated varieties indexed by $i \in \Omega^d$, where Ω^d is a set of varieties available in the market, and a homogeneous numeraire good. The infinitely lived representative consumer maximizes an additively separable intertemporal utility:

$$U = \int_0^{\infty} u(t)e^{-\rho t}\mathrm{d}t, \tag{5.1}$$

where ρ is the common subjective discount rate and $u(t)$ is the instantaneous utility given by

$$u(t) = q_{0t} + \int_{i\in\Omega_t^d} \alpha_{it}q_{it}\mathrm{d}i - \frac{1}{2}\gamma\int_{i\in\Omega_t^d}(q_{it})^2\mathrm{d}i - \frac{1}{2}\eta\left(\int_{i\in\Omega_t^d} q_{it}\mathrm{d}i\right)^2, \tag{5.2}$$

where q_{0t} and q_{it} are the individual consumption levels of the numeraire and variety i, and $\alpha_{it} > 0$ measures the product quality of variety i at time t.[7] The parameter $\gamma > 0$ measures the degree of horizontal differentiation, and the parameter $\eta > 0$ captures the degree of substitution between the differentiated varieties and the numeraire.

We assume that consumers have positive demands for the numeraire. The inverse demand for variety i is then given by

$$p_{it}^d = \alpha_{it} - \gamma q_{it} - \eta Q_t, \tag{5.3}$$

where p_{it}^d is the price of variety i, and $Q_t = \int_{i\in\Omega_t^d} q_{it}\mathrm{d}i$ is the total consumption level over all varieties. Let $\Omega_t^{d*} \subset \Omega_t^d$ be the subset of varieties that are actually consumed. From Eq. (5.3), the market demand for variety $i \in \Omega_t^{d*}$ is

---

[5] In this section, we develop a simple two-sector model. The analysis can be easily extended to a model with many differentiated manufacturing sectors, similar to that in Eckel and Neary (2010). However, such an extension will not qualitatively change the main results.

[6] The formulation proposed by Antoniades (2015) is different from ours. In his model, more productive firms choose higher qualities and charge higher prices. Another approach is to use a quality-augmented Dixit–Stiglitz demand specification (Dixit and Stiglitz 1977) in the framework of Melitz (2003), which assumes that higher quality is associated with higher marginal cost (Baldwin and Harrigan 2011; Johnson 2012; Kugler and Verhoogen 2012).

[7] Häckner (2000) provides this treatment of product quality in a discrete version of quadratic utility.

$$q_{it}^d \equiv L^d q_{it} = \frac{L^d}{\gamma}\alpha_{it} - \frac{\eta L^d N_t^d}{\gamma(\eta N_t^d + \gamma)}\bar{\alpha}_t^d - \frac{L^d}{\gamma}p_{it}^d + \frac{\eta L^d N_t^d}{\gamma(\eta N_t^d + \gamma)}\bar{p}_t^d, \tag{5.4}$$

where N_t^d is the measure of consumed varieties in Ω_t^{d*}, and $\bar{\alpha}_t^d = (1/N_t^d)\int_{i\in\Omega_t^{d*}} \alpha_{it}\mathrm{d}i$ and $\bar{p}_t^d = (1/N_t^d)\int_{i\in\Omega_t^{d*}} p_{it}^d\mathrm{d}i$ are their average quality and price.

In both sectors, labor, which is inelastically supplied in the competitive labor market, is the only production factor. One unit of labor is required to produce one unit of the numeraire, yielding that the wage rate w is equal to one.

In the differentiated manufacturing sector, each firm produces a different variety. Every product variety has generations (or versions) depending on the date of development. For simplicity, we assume that each product generation loses its consumption value after one period. Thus, each firm must engage in product R&D to develop a new generation of variety in every period. While the cost of product R&D, f (measured in units of labor), is identical for all manufacturing firms, the outcome of product R&D, α_{it}, is stochastic.[8] Since R&D in practice has an uncertain outcome, it is quite natural to model R&D as a stochastic process. Let α_{Mt}^d be the maximum possible product quality with the current technology. For firm i the degree of successfulness of R&D, a_{it}, is randomly given from a time-invariant common (and known) probability density function $g(a)$ with support on $[\underline{a}, 1]$, where $\underline{a} \in (0, 1)$. Assume that $g'(a) < 0$. Then, firm i's product quality is given by $\alpha_{it} = a_{it}\alpha_{Mt}^d$. This implies that the product R&D can be equivalently expressed as a random draw from a cumulative distribution function $G_t^d(\alpha)$ with support on $[\underline{\alpha}_t^d, \alpha_{Mt}^d]$, where $\underline{\alpha}_t^d = \underline{a}\alpha_{Mt}^d$. As is explained below, $G_t^d(\alpha)$ shifts as time passes. Let us normalize $\alpha_{M0}^d = 1$.

In the manufacturing sector, firms compete in a three-stage game. In stage one, all potential entrants decide whether to engage in product R&D. In stage two, the firms that chose to conduct R&D observe the outcome of the R&D and then decide whether to stay in the market. In stage three, the firms that chose to stay in the market select prices to maximize their own profits.

A variety of the manufactured goods is produced under the constant returns to scale technology at unit labor requirement c. Given $w = 1$, c is the (constant) marginal cost. Since the R&D costs are sunk costs, firms able to cover their marginal production costs survive and supply goods to the market. Surviving firms maximize their profits in each period by taking the average quality level $\bar{\alpha}^d$, the average price level $\bar{p}^d$ and the number of firms N^d in that period as given. Hereafter, we omit the time index unless it is necessary. Given the market demand for variety i (Eq. (5.4)), it is easily seen that the price elasticity of demand, $\varepsilon_i \equiv -(\partial q_i^d/\partial p_i^d)(p_i^d/q_i^d)$, does not tend to infinity as N^d goes to infinity. Thus, the manufacturing sector is characterized by monopolistic competition. Let $p_{\max}^d(\alpha)$ be the price at which demand for a variety with quality α is driven to 0. Equation (5.4) yields

[8] The cost of product R&D serves as a fixed entry cost. Since firms pay a fixed entry cost and are randomly given their productivity parameter in Melitz (2003) and Melitz and Ottaviano (2008), they engage in stochastic *process* R&D. In our model, however, firms engage in stochastic *product* R&D.

$$p_{\max}^{d}(\alpha) \equiv \alpha - \frac{\eta N^{d}}{\eta N^{d} + \gamma}(\bar{\alpha}^{d} - \bar{p}^{d}). \tag{5.5}$$

Then, any $i \in \Omega^{d*}$ satisfies $p_i^d \leq p_{\max}^d(\alpha_i)$. Given Eq. (5.4), firm i's gross profit from domestic sales is $\pi_i^d = p_i^d q_i^d - c q_i^d$. From the first-order condition for profit maximization, we obtain

$$q_D^d(\alpha) = \frac{L^d}{\gamma}[p_D^d(\alpha) - c], \tag{5.6}$$

where $q_D^d(\alpha)$ and $p_D^d(\alpha)$ are profit-maximizing output and price for domestic sales of the product with quality α and the subscript D indicates variables for domestic sales. Let α_D^d be the quality level for the firm that earns zero profit from domestic sales due to $p_D^d(\alpha_D^d) = p_{\max}^d(\alpha_D^d) = c$. Equation (5.5) yields

$$\alpha_D^d = \frac{\eta N^d}{\eta N^d + \gamma}(\bar{\alpha}^d - \bar{p}^d) + c. \tag{5.7}$$

Then, substitute Eq. (5.4) into Eq. (5.6) and use Eq. (5.7) to obtain

$$p^d(\alpha) = \frac{\alpha - \alpha_D^d}{2} + c.$$

This implies that firms with positive demands charge prices above the marginal cost and the prices increase with product quality. The average price $\bar{p}^d$ is given by

$$\bar{p}^d = \frac{\bar{\alpha}^d - \alpha_D^d}{2} + c. \tag{5.8}$$

Equations (5.7) and (5.8) yield the mass of surviving firms:

$$N^d = \frac{2\gamma(\alpha_D^d - c)}{\eta(\bar{\alpha}^d - \alpha_D^d)}. \tag{5.9}$$

Note that the average product quality of the surviving firms, $\bar{\alpha}^d$, is expressed as $\bar{\alpha}^d = [\int_{\alpha_D^d}^{\alpha_M^d} \alpha \mathrm{d}G_t^d(\alpha)]/[1 - G_t^d(\alpha_D^d)]$ and the mass of entrants in country d is given by $N_E^d = N^d/[1 - G_t^d(\alpha_D^d)]$.

We assume the following condition:

Assumption 5.1 $0 < \mathrm{d}\bar{\alpha}^d/\mathrm{d}\alpha_D^d < 1$.

This condition means that an increase in the cut-off quality increases the average quality of products supplied in the market, but the extent of the increase in the average quality of the products is smaller than that of the increase in α_D^d. This condition restricts the shape of the distribution $G_t^d(\alpha)$.

Let $\mu_D^d(\alpha) = p_D^d(\alpha) - c$ and $\pi_D^d(\alpha) = p_D^d(\alpha)q_D^d(\alpha) - q_D^d(\alpha)c$ be the absolute mark-up and the profit of a firm that produces a product with quality α, respectively. It holds that

$$\mu_D^d(\alpha) = \frac{\alpha - \alpha_D^d}{2} \quad \text{and} \quad \pi_D^d(\alpha) = \frac{L^d}{4\gamma}(\alpha - \alpha_D^d)^2. \tag{5.10}$$

Since the expected profit prior to entry at time t is given by $\int_{\alpha_D^d}^{\alpha_M^d} \pi_D^d(\alpha)\mathrm{d}G_t^d(\alpha) - f$ from Eq. (5.10), the free-entry equilibrium condition is given by

$$\int_{\alpha_D^d}^{\alpha_M^d} \pi_D^d(\alpha)\mathrm{d}G_t^d(\alpha) = \frac{L^d}{4\gamma}\int_{\alpha_D^d}^{\alpha_M^d} (\alpha - \alpha_D^d)^2\mathrm{d}G_t^d(\alpha) = f. \tag{5.11}$$

From Eqs. (5.9) and (5.11), we obtain

Lemma 5.1 *(i) Given $G_t^d(\alpha)$, α_D^d and $\bar{\alpha}^d$ are both decreasing in f (R&D cost) and γ (the degree of horizontal differentiation) and increasing in L^d (the market size). (ii) Under Assumption 5.1, for a given $G_t^d(\alpha)$, a higher α_D^d results in a higher N^d (more varieties) and a higher N_E^d (more entrants).*

Proof Part (i) is directly obtained from Eq. (5.11). For part (ii), differentiate Eq. (5.9) with respect to α_D^d to yield

$$\frac{\mathrm{d}N^d}{\mathrm{d}\alpha_D^d} = \frac{2\gamma}{\eta(\bar{\alpha}^d - \alpha_D^d)} - \frac{2\gamma(\alpha_D^d - c)}{\eta(\bar{\alpha}^d - \alpha_D^d)^2}\frac{\mathrm{d}(\bar{\alpha}^d - \alpha_D^d)}{\mathrm{d}\alpha_D^d} > 0.$$

Assumption 5.1 ensures that the right-hand side of the above equation is positive. Then, since $N_E^d = N^d/[1 - G_t^d(\alpha_D^d)]$, a higher α_D^d and a higher N^d result in a higher N_E^d. *Q.E.D.*

We consider a shift of the distribution $G^d(\alpha)$ to the right with keeping its shape.

Lemma 5.2 *An upward shift of $G^d(\alpha)$ leaves $\mu_D^d(\alpha)$ and $\pi_D^d(\alpha)$ unchanged, but increases N^d and N_E^d.*

Proof Let $G^{d0}(\alpha^0)$ and $G^{d1}(\alpha^1)$ be the distributions before and after the change, respectively. Let α_M^{d0} and α_M^{d1} be the upper bounds of $G^{d0}(\alpha^0)$ and $G^{d1}(\alpha^1)$, and set $\alpha_M^{d1} = \alpha_M^{d0} + k$ with $k > 0$. Then, since $\alpha^1 = \alpha^0 + k$ holds for any α^0 and α^1 that take the same relative position in each distribution, Eq. (5.11) for $G^{d0}(\alpha^0)$ can be transformed to that of $G^{d1}(\alpha^1)$. Thus, Eq. (5.10) is unchanged. However, since $\bar{\alpha}^d - \alpha_D^d$ is unchanged and $\alpha_D^{d1} = \alpha_D^{d0} + k$, Eq. (5.9) yields a higher N^d and hence a higher N_E^d. *Q.E.D.*

This lemma implies that as long as all firms have equal access to general knowledge, technology improvement, in the sense of an upward shift of $G^d(\alpha)$, increases the absolute levels of product quality for all varieties, but the relative positions of the firms in the industry remain unchanged. Besides, Lemma 5.2 implies that there are more varieties in an economy with advanced technology than in an economy with less advanced technology.

5.3 Trade Between Two Countries

5.3.1 A Two-Country Setting

Now, we consider two countries, Home (H) and Foreign (F), with L^d consumers in country d $(= H, F)$. Consumers in both countries share the same preferences given by Eqs. (5.1) and (5.2). We assume that the markets in the two countries are segmented, while firms can produce in one location and supply their products to the market in the other country by incurring a per-unit trade cost.

Manufacturing firms in the two countries have the same marginal cost c and draw product quality α^d from their domestic distributions $G_t^d(\alpha)$ with support on $[\underline{\alpha}_t^d, \alpha_{Mt}^d]$.

Following Melitz and Ottaviano (2008), we assume that firms in country s $(\neq d, s = H, F)$ must incur the unit cost of $\tau^d c$ with $\tau^d > 1$ to deliver one unit of their products to the market in country d. We also assume that the homogeneous numeraire good is always produced in each country after opening up to trade, such that the wage rate is equal to one in both countries.

The price threshold for positive demand in market d is given by Eq. (5.5), but N^d denotes the mass of firms selling in country d, which includes both domestic firms in country d and exporters from country s, and $\bar{\alpha}^d$ and $\bar{p}^d$ are average quality and average price of both local and exporting firms in country d. Let N_D^d and N_X^d denote the masses of firms producing in country d that supply products to the domestic market and the other country's market, respectively. Then, $N^d = N_D^d + N_X^s$ holds.

Firms maximize their profits earned from local and export sales independently (due to the assumptions of segmented markets and constant returns to scale technology). The quality level for a firm producing in country d that earns zero profits from local sales, α_D^d, is still given by Eq. (5.7). Similarly, let α_X^d be the quality level for the firm producing in country d that earns zero profits from export sales. From $p(\alpha_X^d) = p_{\max}^s(\alpha_D^s) = \tau^s c$, we obtain

$$\alpha_X^d = \frac{\eta N^s}{\eta N^s + \gamma}(\bar{\alpha}^s - \bar{p}^s) + \tau^s c. \tag{5.12}$$

From Eqs. (5.7) and (5.12), it holds that

$$\alpha_X^s = \alpha_D^d + (\tau^d - 1)c. \tag{5.13}$$

Let $\pi_X^d(\alpha) = [p_X^d(\alpha) - \tau^s c]q_X^d(\alpha)$ be the maximized value of profits for a firm with quality α producing in country d from export sales, where $p_X^d(\alpha)$ is the profit-maximizing price for export sales and $q_X^d(\alpha)$ is the corresponding quantity. From the first-order condition, it holds that $q_X^d(\alpha) = (L^s/\gamma)[p_X^d(\alpha) - \tau^s c]$. Then, the optimal price and output for export sales are respectively given by

$$p_X^d(\alpha) = \frac{\alpha - \alpha_X^d}{2} + \tau^s c, \quad q_X^d(\alpha) = \frac{L^s(\alpha - \alpha_X^d)}{2\gamma}.$$

The maximized profits from export sales are given by

$$\pi_X^d(\alpha) = \frac{L^s}{4\gamma}(\alpha - \alpha_X^d)^2. \tag{5.14}$$

Note that the maximized profits from domestic sales, $\pi_D^d(\alpha)$, are still given by Eq. (5.10).

In the case of the open economy, the free-entry equilibrium condition in country d at t is given by

$$\int_{\alpha_{Dt}^d}^{\alpha_{Mt}^d} \pi_D^d(\alpha) \mathrm{d}G_t^d(\alpha) + \int_{\alpha_{Xt}^d}^{\alpha_{Mt}^d} \pi_X^d(\alpha) \mathrm{d}G_t^d(\alpha) = f.$$

Substitute Eqs. (5.10), (5.13), and (5.14) into this to yield the two free-entry equilibrium conditions for countries H and F:

$$\begin{aligned} &L^H \int_{\alpha_{Dt}^H}^{\alpha_{Mt}^H} \left(\alpha - \alpha_{Dt}^H\right)^2 \mathrm{d}G_t^H(\alpha) \\ &+L^F \int_{\alpha_{Dt}^F+(\tau^F-1)c}^{\alpha_{Mt}^H} \left[\alpha - \alpha_{Dt}^F - (\tau^F - 1)c\right]^2 \mathrm{d}G_t^H(\alpha) = 4\gamma f, \end{aligned} \tag{5.15}$$

$$\begin{aligned} &L^F \int_{\alpha_{Dt}^F}^{\alpha_{Mt}^F} \left(\alpha - \alpha_{Dt}^F\right)^2 \mathrm{d}G_t^F(\alpha) \\ &+L^H \int_{\alpha_{Dt}^H+(\tau^H-1)c}^{\alpha_{Mt}^F} \left[\alpha - \alpha_{Dt}^H - (\tau^H - 1)c\right]^2 \mathrm{d}G_t^F(\alpha) = 4\gamma f, \end{aligned} \tag{5.16}$$

which jointly determine the cut-off qualities for domestic sales in countries H and F at time t, α_{Dt}^H and α_{Dt}^F. We then assume the following:

Assumption 5.2 $\int_{\underline{\alpha}_t^d}^{\alpha_{Mt}^d} \pi_D^d(\alpha) \mathrm{d}G_t^d(\alpha) + \int_{\underline{\alpha}_t^d}^{\alpha_{Mt}^d} \pi_X^d(\alpha) \mathrm{d}G_t^d(\alpha) > f.$

Assumption 5.2 ensures that the range of possible product qualities is wide enough to yield the interior cut-off for country d, that is, $\alpha_{Dt}^d > \underline{\alpha}_t^d$, even in the latter case. This assumption implies that there are always some firms that exit the market in country d even if no firm enters the market in country s.

The mass of firms selling in country d at time t is still determined by Eq. (5.9), but $\bar{\alpha}_t^d$ is now given by

$$\bar{\alpha}_t^d = \frac{\int_{\alpha_{Dt}^d}^{\alpha_{Mt}^d} \alpha \, \mathrm{d}G_t^d(\alpha) + \int_{\alpha_{Dt}^d+(\tau^d-1)c}^{\alpha_{Mt}^s} \alpha \, \mathrm{d}G_t^s(\alpha)}{2 - G_t^d(\alpha_{Dt}^d) - G_t^s(\alpha_{Dt}^d + (\tau^d - 1)c)}, \qquad d \neq s.$$

The mass of entrants producing in country d at time t, N_{Et}^d, is now determined by

$$[1 - G_t^H(\alpha_{Dt}^H)]N_{Et}^H + [1 - G_t^F(\alpha_{Xt}^F)]N_{Et}^F = N_t^H,$$
$$[1 - G_t^F(\alpha_{Dt}^F)]N_{Et}^F + [1 - G_t^H(\alpha_{Xt}^H)]N_{Et}^H = N_t^F,$$

where $[1 - G_t^d(\alpha_{Dt}^d)]N_{Et}^d = N_{Dt}^d$ and $[1 - G_t^d(\alpha_{Xt}^d)]N_{Et}^d = N_{Xt}^d$, for $d = H, F$. The free-entry equilibrium conditions (5.15) and (5.16) hold so long as there is a positive mass of entrants $N_{Et}^s > 0$ in country s at time t. Otherwise, $N_{Et}^s = 0$ and country s specializes in the production of the numeraire good.

5.3.2 Technology Spillovers

In the manufacturing sector, an individual firm's technological knowledge spills over to other firms irrespective of whether or not its spillovers are deliberate. In the spirit of Romer (1990) and Grossman and Helpman (1990, 1991), we assume that technological knowledge has a public-good nature. That is, each individual firm's R&D output contributes to "knowledge" in the country, and all firms in the same country have equal access to the general knowledge of the country without any added cost. We capture technology spillovers by the expansion of the technology frontier, α_{Mt}. More specifically, we assume that α_{Mt}^d changes in the following way:

$$\dot{\alpha}_{Mt}^d = \lambda K_t^d \alpha_{Mt}^d, \quad d = H, F, \tag{5.17}$$

where $\lambda > 0$ and K_t^d is the knowledge flow at time t. Assuming that the knowledge flow is proportional to the number of varieties supplied in the country and knowledge spillover is perfect within a country but imperfect across countries, we have

$$K_t^d = N_{Dt}^d + \phi^d(\alpha_{Mt}^d, \alpha_{Mt}^s)N_{Xt}^s, \quad d, s = H, F, \ s \neq d, \tag{5.18}$$

where

$$\phi^d(\alpha_{Mt}^d, \alpha_{Mt}^s) \begin{cases} = 1, & \text{if } \alpha_{Mt}^d = \alpha_{Mt}^s, \\ \in (0, 1), & \text{otherwise}, \end{cases} \tag{5.19}$$

which controls the degree of international knowledge spillovers, depending on the technology gap between the two countries. We assume $\partial\phi^d/\partial\alpha^d_{Mt} > 0$ for $\alpha^d_{Mt} < \alpha^s_{Mt}$.

In Eq. (5.18), our primary interest is in technology spillovers from countries s to d at time t, S_{dst}:

$$S_{dst} = \phi^d(\alpha^d_{Mt}, \alpha^s_{Mt})N^s_{Xt}. \tag{5.20}$$

We assume that technology spillovers are proportional to the number of varieties actually imported. However, the degree of technology spillovers is reduced unless the two countries share the same technology level: when country d is more technologically advanced than country s, knowledge spillovers from s to d are reduced because a technologically advanced country benefits less from an inferior technology, and when country d is technologically less advanced than country s, knowledge spillovers from s to d may also be reduced as a technologically less advanced country has a lower capacity to absorb knowledge.

5.3.3 *Trade Patterns and Technology Spillovers*

We now investigate the relationship between trade patterns and international technology spillovers. First consider a case in which two countries share the same technology at a given time t, that is, $\alpha^H_{Mt} = \alpha^F_{Mt}$. If the size of the market and the trade barriers are symmetric (i.e., $L^H = L^F$ and $\tau^H = \tau^F$), then the countries have the same average quality and the same average price of export goods. Then the two countries have an HIIT trade pattern. As a result, technology spillovers occur in both directions in the same degree (i.e., $S_{HFt} = S_{FHt}$) because $\phi^H = \phi^L = 1$ and $N^H_{Xt} = N^F_{Xt}$.

We next consider cases in which there is a technology gap between the two countries. Without loss of generality, we assume that the home country is technologically superior to the foreign country at a given time. We continue to assume that $L^H = L^F$.

It is useful to consider both a symmetric case, $\alpha^H_{Mt} = \alpha^F_{Mt}$, and an asymmetric case, $\alpha^H_{Mt} > \alpha^F_{Mt}$. Let us label the symmetric case as "case 0" and the asymmetric case as "case 1". Assume that $\alpha^{H0}_{Mt} = \alpha^{H1}_{Mt} = \alpha^{F0}_{Mt} > \alpha^{F1}_{Mt}$ holds, where the numerical superscript (0 or 1) indicates the symmetric or asymmetric case. It follows from this assumption that $G^{H0}_t(\alpha) = G^{H1}_t(\alpha) = G^{F0}_t(\alpha)$ holds for all α , and $G^{F0}_t(\alpha)$ first-order stochastically dominates $G^{F1}_t(\alpha)$, i.e., $G^{F1}_t(\alpha) \geq G^{F0}_t(\alpha)$ for any α. Then, from Lemmas 5.1 (ii) and 5.2, both $\alpha^{d0}_{Dt} > \alpha^{d1}_{Dt}$ and $N^{d0}_t > N^{d1}_t$ hold, and then $N^{d0}_{Et} > N^{d1}_{Et}$ holds ($d = H, F$). Moreover, from Eq. (5.13), $\alpha^{d0}_{Dt} > \alpha^{d1}_{Dt}$ implies $\alpha^{d0}_{Xt} > \alpha^{d1}_{Xt}$, and hence $N^{d0}_{Xt} > N^{d1}_{Xt}$ holds for the free-entry equilibrium conditions.

In case 0, due to transport costs, competition must be more intensive in the home market than in the foreign market unless τ^F is sufficiently higher than τ^H, so that both $\alpha^{H1}_{Dt} > \alpha^{F1}_{Dt}$ and $\alpha^{H1}_{Xt} < \alpha^{F1}_{Xt}$ hold.[9] The average quality and price of goods exported from country d are given by

[9] Note that if $\tau^H = \tau^F = 1$, then the cut-off quality has to be identical in the two markets.

$$\bar{\alpha}_{Xt}^d = \frac{\int_{\alpha_{Xt}^d}^{\alpha_{Mt}^d} \alpha \, dG_t^d(\alpha)}{1 - G_t^d(\alpha_{Xt}^d)}, \qquad \text{and} \qquad \bar{p}_{Xt}^d = \frac{\bar{\alpha}_{Xt}^d - \alpha_{Xt}^d}{2} + \tau^s c.$$

In case 1, $\alpha_{Mt}^{H1} > \alpha_{Mt}^{F1}$ holds, and this difference is larger than that between α_{Xt}^{F1} and α_{Xt}^{H1} unless the transport costs are highly asymmetric. Consequently, $\bar{\alpha}_{Xt}^{H1} > \bar{\alpha}_{Xt}^{F1}$ and $\bar{p}_{Xt}^{H1} > \bar{p}_{Xt}^{F1}$ hold. On average, the home country exports varieties with a higher quality at a higher price.

Recall that the size of technology spillovers from countries s to d is measured by Eq. (5.20), which consists of the degree of technology spillovers, ϕ^d, and the mass of varieties actually imported, N_{Xt}^s. As for technology spillovers under VIIT, ϕ^H and ϕ^F are both smaller in case 1 than in case 0, and N_{Xt}^H and N_{Xt}^F are both smaller in case 1 than in case 0. In other words, when countries engage in VIIT, both the degree of technology spillovers and the mass of varieties actually imported are smaller in either direction, compared to the case of HIIT. Therefore, we obtain

Result 5.1 The size of technology spillovers is lower in either direction when the trade pattern is VIIT than when it is HIIT.

This result implies that two countries with similar levels of technologies benefit more from technology spillovers than those with different levels of technologies.

In which direction is the size of technology spillovers larger when countries engage in VIIT? Since $\alpha_{Dt}^{H1} > \alpha_{Dt}^{F1}$ and $\bar{\alpha}_{Xt}^{H1} > \bar{\alpha}_{Xt}^{F1}$, it yields $N_{Xt}^{H1} > N_{Xt}^{F1}$. However, this does not necessarily imply that the size of technology spillovers from countries H to F is larger than in the opposite direction. The reason is that $\phi^H > \phi^F$ may hold and may cause $S_{HF} > S_{FH}$ to hold. Thus, we obtain

Result 5.2 When the trade pattern is VIIT, the relative size of technology spillovers from the home country to the foreign country and those in the opposite direction is ambiguous.

The intuition is the following: the country exporting varieties with higher average quality exports more varieties than the other exporting country. However, the country importing varieties with higher average quality may not necessarily benefit more from technology spillovers because its absorptive capacity of technology is lower and a difference in the absorptive capacity may dominate the effect of a larger mass of varieties in imports.

We next consider a case where the technology gap between the two countries is widened further, such that either (i) $\alpha_{Mt}^F < \alpha_{Xt}^F$ holds or (ii) the free-entry equilibrium condition in country F (Eq. (5.16)) becomes

$$L^F \int_{\alpha_{Dt}^F}^{\alpha_{Mt}^F} (\alpha - \alpha_{Dt}^F)^2 \, dG_t^F(\alpha)$$
$$+ L^H \int_{\alpha_{Dt}^H + (\tau^H - 1)c}^{\alpha_{Mt}^F} \left[\alpha - \alpha_{Dt}^H - (\tau^H - 1)c\right]^2 dG_t^F(\alpha) < 4\gamma f.$$

In the former case, some foreign firms may still enter the manufacturing sector but no foreign firms can export goods to country H. In the latter case, $N_{Et}^F = 0$ holds and country F is specialized in the numeraire. In either case, the trade pattern is characterized by pure OWT. Technology spillovers still occur from countries H to F but no spillovers occur in the opposite direction. As is evident from the above discussion of the VIIT trade pattern, a widened technology gap causes α_{Dt}^H and α_{Dt}^F to be smaller under OWT than under VIIT. Then, α_{Xt}^H is also smaller when there is OWT than when there is VIIT, which implies that the mass of varieties exported from country H (i.e., N_{Xt}^H) is smaller when there is OWT. Moreover, since the gap between α_{Mt}^H and α_{Mt}^F is greater, ϕ^F becomes smaller.

Result 5.3 The size of technology spillovers is lower in the OWT case than in the VIIT case.

As will be argued in the next section, OWT does not necessarily mean that the trade pattern is *completely* inter-industry. In the empirical analysis, a small amount of intra-industry trade that is below some critical value is categorized into OWT. Thus, the direction of technology spillovers in the case of OWT is not necessarily one way.

One may presume that the technology gap between two countries rather than trade patterns is the primary factor determining international technology spillovers. This may not hold true because the technology gap itself does not induce technology spillovers if there is no trade between two countries.

From the theoretical investigation, we obtained three testable hypotheses (i.e., Results 5.1, 5.2, and 5.3) on the relationship between trade patterns and international technology spillovers. In the next section, we empirically test these three hypotheses.

5.4 Empirical Analysis

In the previous section, we have shown that technology spillovers across countries may be related to the patterns of bilateral trade. In this section, we empirically test the predictions of the theoretical model by using bilateral trade data and patent citation data.

5.4.1 Estimation Framework

We first explain the method of categorizing bilateral trade flows. In the previous studies, trade patterns are usually categorized into three types, namely, OWT, HIIT, and VIIT (e.g., Fontagné and Freudenberg 1997; Fukao et al. 2003; Greenaway et al. 1995). The standard method of categorization is given by Fontagné and Freudenberg (1997), which is based on the assumption that the gap between the unit values of imports and exports for each commodity reflects the qualitative differences of the products exported and imported between two countries.[10] We extend the standard method to take the direction of trade into account and categorize bilateral trade flows into five types.

Let X_{ijk} and M_{ijk} be the values of country i's exports to and imports from country j of product k, respectively. Then, the trade pattern in industry k is *one-way trade with importing* (OWT_M) if

$$\frac{\min(X_{ijk}, M_{ijk})}{\max(X_{ijk}, M_{ijk})} \leq \theta \quad \text{and} \quad X_{ijk} < M_{ijk}$$

hold, where θ is set at some value, and *one-way trade with exporting* (OWT_X) if

$$\frac{\min(X_{ijk}, M_{ijk})}{\max(X_{ijk}, M_{ijk})} \leq \theta \quad \text{and} \quad X_{ijk} > M_{ijk}$$

hold. The trade pattern in industry k is *two-way trade* or *intra*-industry trade (IIT) if

$$\frac{\min(X_{ijk}, M_{ijk})}{\max(X_{ijk}, M_{ijk})} > \theta$$

holds. IIT is further divided into three types. Let UV_{ijk}^X and UV_{ijk}^M be unit values of country i's exports to and imports from country j of product k, respectively. Then, the trade pattern in industry k is *horizontal intra-industry trade* (HIIT) if

$$1 - \xi \leq \frac{UV_{ijk}^X}{UV_{ijk}^M} \leq 1 + \xi$$

holds (This condition is the same as that in the standard method), where ξ is set at some value. The trade pattern in industry k is *vertical intra-industry trade with importing higher-quality products* (VIIT_M) if

$$\frac{UV_{ijk}^X}{UV_{ijk}^M} < 1 - \xi$$

[10] There is another method of categorizing trade patterns proposed by Greenaway et al. (1994, 1995), which is based on a decomposition of Grubel–Lloyd index. In their method, intra-industry trade in industry k is measured by

$$IIT_k = 1 - \frac{\sum_n |X_{kn}^z - M_{kn}^z|}{\sum_n (X_{kn}^z + M_{kn}^z)},$$

where n refers to products and z denotes HIIT or VIIT. In order to disentangle total IIT into HIIT and VIIT, they also use the ratio of unit values. Fontagné et al. (2006) investigate the difference between these two methods. They argue that, while the two methods diverge on the definition of IIT, they rely on the same assumption regarding the relationship between unit values and the quality of traded products.

holds, and *vertical intra-industry trade with exporting higher-quality products* ($VIIT_X$) if

$$\frac{UV^X_{ijk}}{UV^M_{ijk}} > 1 + \xi$$

holds. Now the share of each trade pattern is defined by

$$\frac{\sum_k (X^z_{ijk} + M^z_{ijk})}{\sum_k (X_{ijk} + M_{ijk})},$$

where z denotes one of the five trade types, i.e., OWT_M, OWT_X, HIIT, $VIIT_M$, and $VIIT_X$. In the above conditions, the choice of θ and ξ is to a large extent arbitrary. Although Fontagné and Freudenberg (1997) and some other studies use $\xi = 0.15$, Fontagné et al. (2006) report the sensitivity of the relative importance of HIIT to total intra-industry trade and argue that defining θ as 0.1 and ξ as 0.25 is quite reasonable. Fukao et al. (2003) also employ $\theta = 0.1$ and $\xi = 0.25$ and argue that a 25% threshold would be reasonable because of the possible effects of exchange rate fluctuations on the value recorded in trade statistics and noise in the measurements of unit values at a six-digit level of trade statistics. Then we use $\theta = 0.1$ and $\xi = 0.25$ in our analysis.

We use patent citations to measure technology spillovers. The use of patent citations in measuring technology spillovers has been pioneered by Jaffe et al. (1993), in which patent citations are used to measure the extent of technology spillovers within the United States. Every US patent applicant is required to disclose any knowledge of the "prior art" in his or her application. Hall et al. (2001) point out that the presumption for using patent citations as a proxy for learning technology is that the citations to the "prior art" are informative of the causal links between those patented innovations, because citations made may constitute a "paper trail" for diffusion, i.e., the fact that patent B cites patent A may be indicative of knowledge flowing from A to B. This logic is also practicable to the case of the patent citations between countries.

On the other hand, patent citations between two countries may be associated with the past records of patenting in both the cited and the citing countries. The number of patents filed by the citing country is related to the scale of human resource in this country, and reflects the indigenous capacity to absorb foreign technology. The number of patents in the cited country simultaneously implies a potential opportunity of citations for the citing country. Based on the reasoning above, our regression model is defined as follows:

$$\begin{aligned} \ln c^*_{ijt} &= \beta' x_{ijt} + \epsilon_{ijt} \\ &= \beta_1 Share_{ijt}(OWT_M, OWT_X, HIIT, VIIT_M, \text{ or } VIIT_X) \\ &\quad + \beta_2 \ln(P_{it} \times P_{jt}) + u_{ij} + e_{ijt}, \end{aligned}$$

where c^*_{ijt} is the number of patent citations made by patents filed by country i (the citing country) to country j (the cited country) in year t, x_{ijt} is a vector of independent variables, $Share_{ijt}$ is bilateral OWT_M, OWT_X, HIIT, $VIIT_M$, or $VIIT_X$ share between countries i and j in year t, P_{it} and P_{jt} are the number of patent applications filed by countries i and j, respectively, in year t.[11] Thus, we use c^*_{ijt} as a proxy for technology spillovers from countries j to i. The term $P_{it} \times P_{jt}$ is included to control the effects of the citing country's absorptive capacity of technology and the cited country's potential opportunity of citations.

Since some countries rarely cite patents applied by inventors of other countries, there are substantial zero values in c^*_{ijt}. We then use a random-effects panel Tobit model to deal with this issue. In that case, the dependent variable is now a latent variable, where

$$\ln c_{ijt} = \begin{cases} \ln c^*_{ijt}, & \text{if } c^*_{ijt} > 0, \\ 0, & \text{otherwise,} \end{cases}$$

and

$$\epsilon_{ijt} = u_{ij} + e_{ijt}, \quad u \sim NID(0, \sigma_u^2), \quad e \sim NID(0, \sigma_e^2), \quad \rho \equiv \frac{\sigma_u^2}{\sigma_u^2 + \sigma_e^2}.$$

In general, independence between the u and e is assumed. On the other hand, there is neither a convenient test nor an estimation method for the test of random versus fixed-effects of the Tobit model as well as for estimation of a conditional fixed-effects model.[12] In order to assess the robustness of the estimated results by the random-effects panel Tobit model, we try to use a fixed-effects negative binomial model proposed by Hausman et al. (1984) for our same sample.

5.4.2 Data

5.4.2.1 Trade Data

There are several kinds of datasets on empirical analysis of international trade such as International Trade Commodity Statistics (ITCS–SITC) released by the OECD, and Personal Computer Trade Analysis System (PC–TAS) published by the United Nations Statistical Division. As indicated by Gaulier and Zignago (2008), the empirical analysis suffers due to the two different figures for the same trade flow, because the import values are generally reported in CIF (cost, insurance, and freight) and export values in FOB (free on board). To reconcile the two figures, Gaulier and Zignago (2008) develop a procedure to estimate an average CIF rate and remove it from

[11] The stochastic nature of product R&D assumed in our theoretical model is not directly reflected in our estimation framework. As we have shown in the previous sections, however, the average quality and the distribution of quality among actually supplied products in an industry are invariant for a given distribution $G_t(\alpha)$. Since we use the industry average to determine the bilateral trade patterns, our empirical framework is considered to be consistent with the theoretical model in the previous sections.

[12] Honoré (1992) has developed a semiparametric estimator for fixed-effects Tobit models.

the declarations of imports to provide FOB import values for bilateral trade flows drawn on United Nations COMTRADE data. Now we utilize this reconstructed trade dataset, called BACI. The BACI dataset covers more than 200 countries and 5,000 products from 1995.[13] In this chapter we use the BACI data from 1995 to 2004.

5.4.2.2 Patent Citation Data

The data on patents and patent citations used in this chapter consist of two sources, i.e., European Patent Office (EPO) Worldwide Patent Statistical Database (PATSTAT) and the Institute of Intellectual Property (IIP) Dataset. We collect the patent statistics of EPO from the former, and those of the Japanese Patent Office (JPO) from the latter. The two datasets include the dates of patent applications, the International Patent Classification (IPC), the citation information, and the country names of both citing and cited patent applicants.

Unlike the patent applications in the United States Patent and Trademark Office (USPTO), the patent applicants in the JPO have no legal duty to list the patents that he/she cites on the front page of document, although some referenced information provided by the applicants lies scattered across the patent body text. The citations information on the front page is usually added by the examiners in the JPO as well as in the EPO (Hall et al. 2007). According to Goto and Motohashi (2007), since the 1990s about two thirds of JPO citations have been decided by the examiners.

Although the decision on which patents to cite ultimately depends on the patent examiner, implying that the inventors may have been unaware of the cited patents, the presumption that the citations are relevant as the indicator of technology links between the citing and the cited is widely recognized in many empirical studies, such as Jaffe et al. (1993), Jaffe and Trajtenberg (1996, 1999), and Hall et al. (2001) for US patents, and Maurseth and Verspagen (2002), and MacGarvie (2006) for European patents.

5.4.2.3 Sample Selection

We start to select our sample from the top 60 trading countries/economies in 2008, according to the quantity of their import and exports in the world. Because crude oil makes up most of the trade in some top trade countries/economies such as Saudi Arabia, Nigeria, Russia, and Venezuela, we exclude these countries from our sample. At the same time, we exclude countries such as Kazakhstan, Peru, and Vietnam, since they rarely made or received patent citations in the JPO or EPO. As a result, we obtain a sample that covers 44 countries/economies across advanced, emerging, and developing economies in the world. The list of sample countries/economies is presented in Table 5.1.

---

[13] See the CEPII website (www.cepii.fr) for the details of BACI dataset. The existing studies that use BACI dataset include Fontagné et al. (2005, 2006) and Olper and Raimondi (2009).

Table 5.1 Sample countries/economies

No.	Country/Economy	No.	Country/Economy
1	Germany	23	Australia
2	China	24	Norway
3	United States	25	Poland
4	Japan	26	Czech Republic
5	France	27	Ireland
6	Italy	28	Indonesia
7	Netherlands	29	Turkey
8	United Kingdom	30	Denmark
9	Belgium–Luxembourg	31	Hungary
10	Canada	32	Finland
11	Korea	33	South Africa
12	Singapore	34	Chile
13	Mexico	35	Slovak Republic
14	Spain	36	Argentina
15	Taiwan	37	Israel
16	Malaysia	38	Philippines
17	Sweden	39	Portugal
18	Switzerland	40	Ukraine
19	Brazil	41	Romania
20	Austria	42	Colombia
21	Thailand	43	New Zealand
22	India	44	Slovenia

The patent statistics used in this chapter are classified according to the IPC, which is based either on the intrinsic nature of the invention or on the function of the invention. Schmoch et al. (2003) provide a concordance between technical fields and industrial sectors. This concordance table refers to IPC for patents, and international classifications, namely the European Union's Classification of Economic Activities within the European Communities (NACE), the United Nations' International Standard Industrial Cassification (ISIC), and the US Standard Industrial Classification (SIC) with 44 industrial sectors. The empirical analyses in Schmoch et al (2003) show that this concordance with 44 industrial sectors (or technical fields) has a reasonable level of disaggregation, because the economic data on international comparisons are not available in the finer differentiation. Thus, we use their concordance table to allocate the patent statistics into 44 industrial sectors, as shown in Table 5.2. Since the number of citations is very limited in some sectors, especially for products in some light manufacturing sectors such as textiles, wearing, and paint, we focus our analysis on five fields, i.e., non-metal products, metal products, machinery, ICT related equipment, and motor vehicles. The five fields correspond with Sectors 17 and 18, Sector 20, Sectors 21–25, Sectors 28 and 34–38, and Sector 42 in Schmoch et al. (2003).

Table 5.2 Correspondence between technical fields and ISIC industrial classifications

Field No.	Sector	ISIC ver. 3
1	Food	15
2	Tobacco	16
3	Textiles	17
4	Wearing	18
5	Leather	19
6	Wood products	20
7	Paper	21
8	Publishing	22
9	Petroleum	23
10	Basic chemicals	241
11	Pesticides	2421
12	Paint	2422
13	Pharmaceuticals	2423
14	Soaps	2424
15	Other chemicals	2429
16	Man-made fibers	243
17	Plastic products	25
18	Mineral products	26
19	Basic metals	27
20	Metal products	28
21	Energy machinery	2911, 2912, 2913
22	Non-specific machinery	2914, 2915, 2919
23	Agricultural machinery	2921
24	Machine-tools	2922
25	Special machinery	2923, 2924, 2925, 2926, 2929
26	Weapons	2927
27	Domestic appliances	293
28	Computers	30
29	Electrical motors	311
30	Electrical distribution	312, 313
31	Accumulators	314
32	Lightening	314
33	Other electrical	315
34	Electronic components	321
35	Telecommunications	322
36	Television	323
37	Medical equipment	3311
38	Measuring instruments	3312
39	Industrial control	3313
40	Optics	332
41	Watches	333
42	Motor vehicles	34
43	Other transport	35
44	Consumer goods	36

Source: Tables 3–1 and 3–5 in Schmoch et al. (2003)

Table 5.3 Descriptive statistics

Variable	No. of Obs.	Mean	Std. Dev.	Min	Max
$HIIT$	46764	0.05	0.10	0.00	1.00
$VIIT$	46764	0.17	0.19	0.00	1.00
OWT	46764	0.28	0.24	0.00	1.00
JPO citations	47300	14.5	419.0	0	39332
P_i in JPO	47300	2382.7	19395.3	0	279823
P_j in JPO	47300	1527.8	11114.7	0	233511
EPO citations	47300	0.9	18.3	0	1614
P_i in EPO	47300	275.1	1273.5	0	16533
P_j in EPO	47300	275.1	1273.5	0	16533

In order to match the data on trade with patents, we map the six-digit Harmonized System (HS6) and the ISIC rev. 3 according to the industrial concordance table provided by Jon Haveman.[14] Then, we use the method explained above to measure the shares of OWT, HIIT, and VIIT for our sample countries in the five fields discussed above for the periods of 1995–1996, 1997–1998, 1999–2000, 2001–2002, and 2003–2004 (i.e., five periods). The descriptive statistics for the shares of OWT, HIIT, and VIIT, and the number of citations are presented in Table 5.3. On one hand, there are substantial citations between some developed countries, especially between the United States and Japan. For instance, the US patents that belonged to Sector 28 made more than 56,300 citations to Japanese patents during the period of 2003 and 2004. On the other hand, of about four fifths of observations citations are not identified in our sample period.

Table 5.4 describes the shares of OWT, HIIT, and VIIT for some selected sample countries averagely across five fields and five periods. From the table, we find that remarkable bilateral IIT (HIIT+VIIT) intensities are observed among European countries. More than 91% of trade is IIT for the trade between Germany and France, 79% for France and Belgium–Luxembourg, and 92% for Netherlands and Belgium–Luxembourg. These figures largely coincide with those reported by Fontagné et al. (2006) for the same country-pairs (86.2%, 80.4%, and 85.0%, respectively), based on trade statistics for the year 2000.

Table 5.5 presents how patent citations have been made by the patents of some selected countries filed to the USPTO, JPO, and EPO, respectively. Although the scale of citations is different across the patent offices, the patterns of citations between the selected countries are similar across the patent offices. For example, the United States, Japan, and Germany are the largest targets of citations not only for other countries, but also for each other, while citations are to date relatively less received as well as made by Chinese patents.

---

[14] See www.macalester.edu/research/economics/page/haveman/trade.resources/tradedata.html.

Table 5.4 Shares of OWT, HIIT, and VIIT for selected countries

	China	US	Japan	France	Italy	Netherlands	UK	Belgium	Canada	Korea
Germany	0.63	0.25	0.36	0.08	0.19	0.11	0.12	0.16	0.52	0.58
	0.03	0.20	0.21	0.51	0.31	0.48	0.37	0.40	0.09	0.05
	0.25	0.54	0.42	0.41	0.50	0.40	0.51	0.43	0.29	0.29
China		0.63	0.50	0.59	0.53	0.64	0.63	0.50	0.63	0.42
		0.04	0.07	0.04	0.04	0.02	0.03	0.02	0.01	0.12
		0.30	0.39	0.23	0.34	0.19	0.25	0.18	0.16	0.37
US			0.48	0.28	0.41	0.36	0.21	0.44	0.08	0.58
			0.12	0.19	0.08	0.09	0.24	0.12	0.28	0.06
			0.40	0.52	0.51	0.52	0.53	0.41	0.28	0.35
Japan				0.51	0.48	0.57	0.44	0.59	0.67	0.42
				0.15	0.10	0.04	0.13	0.02	0.04	0.06
				0.28	0.33	0.30	0.40	0.22	0.12	0.50
France					0.19	0.20	0.08	0.11	0.34	0.51
					0.37	0.28	0.45	0.42	0.10	0.06
					0.43	0.51	0.47	0.47	0.42	0.26
Italy						0.29	0.26	0.32	0.50	0.53
						0.13	0.26	0.28	0.05	0.07
						0.55	0.47	0.39	0.28	0.21
Netherlands							0.14	0.07	0.37	0.46
							0.25	0.42	0.07	0.03
							0.60	0.50	0.38	0.18
UK								0.20	0.32	0.58
								0.26	0.11	0.03
								0.53	0.51	0.28
Belgium									0.45	0.35
									0.03	0.06
									0.22	0.23
Canada										0.57
										0.02
										0.15

Notes: (a) The upper, middle and lower figures are for OWT, HIIT and VIIT, respectively. (b) The sum of OWT, HIIT and VIIT could be less than 1.0 due to unavailability for the unit value in some cases. (c) Luxembourg is included in Belgium. *Source*: Authors' calculation from the BACI data

5.4.3 *Estimation Results*

Table 5.6 summarizes the results for full fields, estimated based on the patent citations in the JPO and EPO, respectively. We added dummy variables to control for the fields and time periods, and, as we expected, the coefficient estimates of the number of patents held by citing and cited countries are positively significant. To assess the robustness of the estimated results in Table 5.6 at the same time, we also apply an alternative regression technique, namely, a fixed-effects negative binomial model proposed by Hausman et al. (1984), to the same sample. Table 5.7 summarizes the

Table 5.5 Patent citations for selected countries

Citing	Cited Country										
Country	Germany	China	US	Japan	France	Italy	Netherlands	UK	Belgium	Canada	Korea
	Citations in JPO										
Germany		8	5834	63171	835	350	499	578	85	117	317
China	18		127	1550	21	3	3	3	0	6	15
US	3855	21		177390	1729	463	1277	1457	182	400	1369
Japan	32394	173	108506		10506	2939	7545	7001	1296	1870	15195
France	737	0	2371	19458		102	207	213	25	48	162
Italy	322	0	490	4327	152		33	35	2	21	19
Netherlands	451	0	2374	23097	166	58		172	22	23	231
UK	435	1	1560	10452	169	35	108		14	41	56
Belgium	55	0	188	1844	33	5	8	24		8	16
Canada	143	0	483	3608	43	9	27	50	4		21
Korea	457	6	3790	67141	284	84	229	150	18	77	
	Citations in EPO										
Germany		1	2041	2221	323	220	160	295	34	41	39
China	6		48	62	9	0	0	4	0	9	3
US	940	9		4581	513	247	300	538	99	129	178
Japan	1121	10	6809		517	245	474	478	126	109	395
France	247	1	1046	862		68	81	117	11	37	49
Italy	136	0	303	318	58		16	34	5	2	14
Netherlands	76	1	301	314	58	15		23	2	5	17
UK	70	1	381	281	41	12	22		9	7	8
Belgium	40	0	135	138	25	6	16	11		3	3
Canada	20	1	226	117	14	4	9	6	2		9
Korea	77	3	678	1357	59	12	54	35	5	24	

Note: US and UK denote the United States and the United Kingdom, respectively.
Source: Authors' calculation from the JPO and EPO patent citation data

Table 5.6 Random-effects panel Tobit estimates for patent citations

	JPO citations				EPO citations			
	(1)	(2)	(3)	(4)	(5)	(6)	(7)	(8)
$HIIT$	2.615***	2.699***		2.290***	2.434***	2.433***		1.974***
	(0.17)	(0.17)		(0.17)	(0.13)	(0.13)		(0.13)
$VIIT_M$	2.338***	2.420***	2.548***		2.137***	2.100***	2.107***	
	(0.15)	(0.15)	(0.16)		(0.12)	(0.12)	(0.13)	
$VIIT_X$	2.399***	2.466***	2.580***		2.183***	2.195***	2.169***	
	(0.16)	(0.16)	(0.16)		(0.12)	(0.12)	(0.13)	
OWT_M	1.268***		1.600***	1.037***	1.116***		1.205***	0.754***
	(0.13)		(0.14)	(0.13)	(0.10)		(0.11)	(0.10)
OWT_X		1.498***	1.737***	1.180***		1.128***	1.214***	0.781***
		(0.13)	(0.13)	(0.13)		(0.10)	(0.11)	(0.10)
$\ln(P_i \times P_j)$	0.152***	0.151***	0.153***	0.158***	0.076***	0.076***	0.081***	0.081***
	(0.0045)	(0.0045)	(0.0045)	(0.0047)	(0.0031)	(0.0031)	(0.0032)	(0.0032)
$1/\sigma_u$	1.991***	1.992***	2.000***	2.044***	1.379***	1.387***	1.414***	1.443***
	(0.037)	(0.038)	(0.038)	(0.039)	(0.030)	(0.030)	(0.030)	(0.031)
$1/\sigma_e$	1.064***	1.063***	1.066***	1.066***	0.718***	0.715***	0.720***	0.712***
	(0.014)	(0.014)	(0.014)	(0.015)	(0.012)	(0.012)	(0.012)	(0.012)
ρ	0.778	0.778	0.779	0.786	0.787	0.790	0.794	0.804
	(0.97)	(0.97)	(0.97)	(0.98)	(0.98)	(0.99)	(0.99)	(1.01)
No. of obs.	46764	46764	46764	46764	46764	46764	46764	46764
Log likelihood	−13169	−13148	−13201	−13324	−8099	−8099	−8218	−8338
Ward test (Prob4>chi^2)	0.0	0.0	0.0	0.0	0.0	0.0	0.0	0.0
LR test (Prob>chi^2)	0.0	0.0	0.0	0.0	0.0	0.0	0.0	0.0

Notes: (a) The regression is based on full sample and includes a constant term. (b) Period dummies and field dummies are included. (c) ***, **, and * indicate significance at the 1%, 5%, and 10% levels, respectively. (d) The values in the parentheses are standard errors. (e) The likelihood ratio test for RE model versus pooled model

fixed-effects negative binomial estimates, where the number of citations is used as a dependent variable.

In Tables 5.6 and 5.7, we see that most of the coefficient estimates for HIIT and VIIT are significant and positive, implying that intra-industry trade plays a significant role in technology spillovers. The coefficients for HIIT are evidently larger than those for VIIT, when the two variables are used in the same regression for the two different patent statistics. This pattern remains true also in Table 5.7. Compared with the vertical intra-industry trade, the horizontal intra-industry trade shows a dominant effect on technology spillovers.

Unlike the intra-industry trade, the estimations for the relationship between OWT and the number of citations reveal somewhat mixed results. In Table 5.6, the estimated coefficients of OWT are significantly positive, whereas the magnitudes of the coefficients are smaller than those for HIIT and VIIT. In Table 5.7, the estimated coefficients of OWT_M are insignificant in the case of the EPO and even significantly

Table 5.7 Fixed-effects negative binomial estimates for patent citations

	JPO citations				EPO citations			
	(1)	(2)	(3)	(4)	(5)	(6)	(7)	(8)
$HIIT$	0.400***	0.871***	0.343**		0.469**	0.636***		0.234
	(0.15)	(0.15)		(0.14)	(0.20)	(0.20)		(0.17)
$VIIT_M$	0.130	0.609***	0.235*		0.295	0.459**	0.219	
	(0.14)	(0.14)	(0.14)		(0.20)	(0.20)	(0.19)	
$VIIT_X$	0.493***	0.974***	0.598***		0.598***	0.773***	0.518***	
	(0.15)	(0.15)	(0.15)		(0.20)	(0.20)	(0.19)	
OWT_M	−0.259*		−0.110	−0.248*	0.235		0.192	0.052
	(0.14)		(0.15)	(0.13)	(0.20)		(0.20)	(0.18)
OWT_X		0.968***	0.657***	0.514 ***		0.608***	0.407**	0.264
		(0.13)	(0.14)	(0.12)		(0.20)	(0.19)	(0.17)
$\ln(P_i \times P_j)$	0.058***	0.056***	0.058***	0.058***	0.024***	0.024***	0.024***	0.023***
	(0.0048)	(0.0048)	(0.0048)	(0.0048)	(0.0036)	(0.0036)	(0.0036)	(0.0036)
No. of obs.	8900	8900	8900	8900	6110	6110	6110	6110
Log likelihood	−11335	−11311	−11327	−11332	−6216	−6212	−6217	−6220
Ward test (Prob>chi^2)	0.0	0.0	0.0	0.0	0.0	0.0	0.0	0.0

Notes: (a) The regression is based on full sample. (b) Period dummies are included. (c) ***, **, and * denote significance at the 1%, 5%, and 10% levels, respectively. (d) The values in the parentheses are standard errors

negative in the case of the JPO. In contrast, some of the estimated coefficients of OWT_X are comparable to those for HIIT and VIIT. These results imply that the effect of OWT on technology spillovers is much weaker than that of IIT if the country is an importer, whereas that effect may be comparable to that of IIT if the country is an exporter.

5.5 Conclusion

In this chapter, we have examined how technology spillovers across countries would differ according to bilateral trade patterns. We first developed a two-country model of monopolistic competition with quality differentiation by extending the model of Melitz and Ottaviano (2008). In our model, the quality of each product in the manufacturing sector is differentiated and stochastically determined by firms' engaging in product R&D. The structure of our model is similar to that of Melitz and Ottaviano (2008), except for the fact that firms are heterogeneous in product quality rather than in productivity. We then introduced technology spillovers in our model as the process of expanding the technology frontier of the industry. We assumed that, in a given sector, all firms in the same country equally have access to the "general knowledge" without paying any cost. However, technology spillovers are imperfect across countries. In particular, the degree of international technology spillovers falls as the technology gap between the two countries increases. We then showed that in our model the trade pattern is intra-industry when the technology gap between the two countries is small, while it is inter-industry when the technology gap is sufficiently large. Since products are differentiated in quality in our model, both horizontal and vertical intra-industry trade patterns also emerge endogenously.

From the model we derived three testable hypotheses for empirical analysis. The first hypothesis (Result 5.1) was that technology spillovers are larger when the trade pattern between the two countries is HIIT than when it is VIIT. The second hypothesis (Result 5.2) was that when the trade pattern is VIIT, the relative size of technology spillovers from the country exporting high quality products on average to the country exporting low quality products on average and in the opposite direction is ambiguous. The third hypothesis (Result 5.3) was that technology spillovers are lower when the trade pattern is IIT or OWT than when it is VIIT.

We then empirically tested these hypotheses by using bilateral trade data among 44 countries at six-digit level and patent citations data at the EPO and JPO. Following Jaffe et al. (1993) and other recent studies on technology spillovers, we measure international technology spillovers by patent citations among countries.

Our estimation results basically confirmed the predictions of our model. That is, we found that an increase in the shares of HIIT and VIIT has a significantly positive effect on international technology spillovers. Our estimation results showed that HIIT has a larger effect on spillovers than VIIT does. On the other hand, the relative magnitudes of technology spillovers between the country exporting high quality products and the country exporting low quality products on average under VIIT are generally ambiguous. We also found that the effect of OWT on technology spillovers tends to be much weaker than that of other trade patterns. These results from Japanese and European patents are generally consistent with the finding by Jinji et al. (2015) from US patents. Therefore, we conclude that intra-industry trade plays a significant role in technology spillovers.

In this chapter, we primarily focused on technology spillovers through international trade but did not take the effects of FDI into account. As argued in the introduction, however, a number of existing studies have empirically confirmed that FDI is also a major channel of international technology spillovers. In our estimations, we found that an increase in the share of OWT has a significantly positive effect on technology spillovers in some cases, in particular in the cases of the JPO and EPO. The positive effect of OWT with exporting the good in question even exceeds those of HIIT and/or VIIT in some cases in Table 5.7, which contradicts the predictions by our theoretical model. This may be due to FDI. Thus, in the next chapter, we analyze the effects of FDI on technology spillovers.

Chapter 6
Vertical Versus Horizontal Foreign Direct Investment and Technology Spillovers

6.1 Introduction

Foreign direct investment (FDI) and international trade are two major channels of international diffusion of technological knowledge (Keller 2004,2010). While a number of empirical studies confirm significant spillover effects of knowledge through imports, the empirical findings on technology spillover effects through FDI are conflicting. In particular, there is relatively little evidence of spillovers of knowledge from inward FDI to the host country's firms in the same industry. For example, Haskel et al. (2007) examine the situation in the United Kingdom and find significantly positive productivity spillovers from FDI. In addition, Keller and Yeaple (2009) show similar results for the United States. By contrast, Aitken and Harrison (1999) and Haddad and Harrison (1993) find no significant or weak productivity spillovers from FDI for developing countries hosting FDI (the former and the latter obtain results on Venezuela and Morocco, respectively).[1] Addressing the endogenous nature of the FDI decision, Lu et al. (2017) examine the spillover effects of FDI in China and find that the presence of FDI in the same industry has a significantly negative effect on the productivity levels of domestic firms due to the competition effect, while it has no significant effect on the exporting performance and research and development (R&D) investment of domestic firms. Todo (2006) and Todo and Miyamoto (2006) derive that R&D activities play an important role in productivity spillovers from FDI to local firms in the same industry: for example, a positive, statistically significant spillover effect is observed only for R&D-performing foreign firms (in Indonesia) or foreign firms' R&D stock (in Japan). In contrast, a number of studies find significant productivity spillovers from inward FDI to the host country's upstream firms through backward linkages. These studies include Javorcik (2004) for the case of Lithuania, Javorcik and Spatareanu (2008) for that of Romania, Blalock and Gertler (2008) for that of Indonesia, and Newman et al. (2015) for that of Viet-

[1] For example, Aitken and Harrison (1999) find negative spillover effects of FDI on the productivity of domestically owned plants in Venezuela.

N. Jinji et al., *Deep Integration, Global Firms, and Technology Spillovers*, Advances in Japanese Business and Economics 26,
https://doi.org/10.1007/978-981-16-5210-3_6

nam.[2] Moreover, Branstetter (2006) and Singh (2007) find evidence of technology spillovers from outward FDI. That is, firms investing in foreign countries acquire technological knowledge from other firms in the host countries.

When a firm establishes business enterprises in two or more countries through FDI, it becomes a multinational enterprise (MNE). Canonical FDI theory defines two types, namely horizontal and vertical, of FDI and an MNE's activities.[3] Horizontal FDI (HFDI) replicates a subset of the production process in foreign countries to serve local markets (Brainard, 1993, 1997; Helpman et al., 2004; Markusen, 1984, 1995; Markusen and Venables, 1998, 2000). It is often motivated by an intention to reduce transportation costs. In contrast, vertical FDI (VFDI) involves geographical fragmentation of the production process and is often motivated by an intention to take advantage of factor cost differentials (Helpman, 1984, 1985; Helpman and Krugman, 1985; Venables, 1999). However, the actual patterns of FDI and an MNE's activities are much more complex than the simple dichotomy of "horizontal" and "vertical". Yeaple (2003a) constructs a model in which horizontal, vertical, and complex (i.e., both horizontal and vertical) FDI arises endogenously. Grossman et al. (2006) also analyze MNEs' integration strategies that may simultaneously involve horizontal and vertical FDI. Ekholm et al. (2007) propose the type of "export-platform FDI" as another type of FDI. Moreover, utilizing the information on sales and sourcing patterns of foreign affiliates of MNEs, Baldwin and Okubo (2014) support the importance of "networked FDI."

A number of empirical studies provide support to the predictions for HFDI. For example, Brainard (1993, 1997) obtains evidence of HFDI but little evidence of VFDI. Markusen and Maskus (2002) argue that a large proportion of FDI takes place among developed countries and is characterized by the horizontal type of FDI. Looking at the location decisions of MNEs, however, Yeaple (2003b) and Hanson et al. (2005) find evidence consistent with comparative advantage. Moreover, Alfaro and Charlton (2009) point out that the share of VFDI is much higher than previously thought even within developed countries. They argue that a significant amount of VFDI has been misclassified as horizontal in the previous studies and find that a substantial amount of VFDI between developed countries emerges in high-skill sectors, because parent firms own the stages of production proximate to their final production and source raw materials and inputs in low-skill production stages from outside of the firms.

[2] However, Keller (2010) argues that some issues such as a measurement problem in contractual payment between the MNEs and local firms may lead to estimation bias. Besides, Barrios et al. (2011) argue that the measures of backward linkages used in recent studies on spillovers are potentially problematic. Using the standard measures employed in the literature, they fail to find robust evidence for spillovers through backward linkages. On the other hand, they obtain robust evidence for positive FDI backward spillover effects.

[3] See Markusen (1995), Markusen (2002), Markusen and Maskus (2003), and Helpman (2006) for the survey of the literature.

A literature that is separated from studies on FDI has shown the importance of international fragmentation of production and the involvement of firms in international production networks (or global value chains (GVC)).[4]

Depending on the type of FDI or the degree of involvement in GVC, affiliates of MNEs conduct different activities in their host economies, affecting the extent of technology spillovers between MNEs and domestic firms in the host economies. For example, when MNEs conduct VFDI, foreign affiliates engage in intra-firm trade with their parent firms in the source country. On the other hand, in the case of networked FDI, foreign affiliates are involved in GVC and are likely to trade with other affiliates in the same region. Ramondo et al. (2016) document that intra-firm trade is concentrated on a small group of large foreign affiliates of MNEs headquartered in the United States. They find that the median manufacturing foreign affiliate of the US MNEs has no transaction of goods with its parent in the United States. This finding suggests that VFDI is concentrated on large firms and large affiliates.[5] To the best of our knowledge, no existing studies have investigated how the type of FDI or the degree of involvement in GVC affects technology spillovers between MNEs and their host economies.

An empirical work by Branstetter (2006) is closely related to the analysis in this chapter. He defines the term "technology spillovers" as "the process by which one inventor learns from the research outcomes of others' research projects and is able to enhance her own research productivity with this knowledge without fully compensating the other inventors for the value of this learning" (pp. 327–328). In this sense, technology spillovers must be distinguished from the term "productivity spillovers" which measures how productivity of a firm is affected by other firms' one or R&D activities. Then, in the literature with respect to spillovers, patent citation data have been used as a proxy of technology spillovers in the above definition (Jaffe et al. 1993).[6] Branstetter (2006) analyzes firm-level data on Japanese MNEs in the United States and patent citations at the United States Patent and Trademark Office (USPTO) and obtains evidence that FDI facilitates technology spillovers both from investing firms to local firms in the host country and from the local firms to the investing firms. Although he examines whether different types of FDI, such as acquisition, greenfield investment, and R&D facilities, have different effects on spillovers, he does not distinguish various production activities of foreign affiliates.

---

4 See Antràs and Chor (2013), Baldwin and Venables (2013), and Costinot et al. (2013) for theoretical work and Alfaro et al. (2019) and Timmer et al. (2014) for empirical evidence. See Amador and Cabral (2016) for the survey of the literature.

5 The finding by Ramondo et al. (2016) is related to the observation by Atalay et al. (2014) for production chains within the United States. In particular, they show that the ownership of vertically linked affiliates is not related to the transfer of goods within the boundaries of the firm. Ramondo et al. (2016)) argue that the vertical ownership promotes efficient intra-firm transfers of intangible inputs.

6 There are a number of existing empirical studies on technology spillovers based on patent citations (Cappelli and Montobbio, 2020; Haruna et al., 2010; Hu and Jaffe, 2003; Jaffe and Trajtenberg, 1999; Jinji et al., 2013, 2015, 2019a; Li, 2014; MacGarvie, 2006; Mancusi, 2008; Murata et al., 2014; Peri, 2005).

In this chapter, we attempt to identify how the structure of MNEs' activities in terms of horizontal and vertical FDI affects technology spillovers between MNEs and host countries. Then, we combine a comprehensive firm-level dataset of the business activities of Japanese MNEs' foreign affiliates and information on the patent citations between MNEs and their host countries. Following Branstetter (2006), we define "technology spillovers" as the effects on the research productivity from the outcomes of others' research activities without full compensation for the value of research productivity enhancement.[7] Alternatively, we use firm-level data on Japanese firms' FDI and patent citations at the USPTO.[8] Our firm-level dataset includes information on the sales and purchases of the foreign affiliates, classified according to the destination and source countries. We exploit this information to construct new measures of horizontal and vertical FDI based on the shares of the host and home countries in their transactions. Now we define a measure of "pure horizontal FDI" as the extent to which affiliates' purchases of intermediate inputs and sales of final goods are concentrated in the local market. We also define a measure of "pure vertical FDI" as the extent to which their affiliates' purchases of intermediate inputs and sales of final goods are linked to the home country. We, furthermore, define measures of "partially horizontal" and "partially vertical" FDI. We then estimate how different types of FDI affect technology spillovers from Japanese MNEs to the host country and from the host country to Japanese MNEs. As for the empirical methodology, we follow Branstetter (2006). Since the dependent variable (i.e., patent citations) is the count data, we utilize a negative binomial model developed by Hausman et al. (1984). Moreover, to deal with a potential endogeneity problem we employ an endogenous switching model discussed by Miranda and Rabe-Hesketh (2006).

Our main findings are as follows. We find that an increase in the degree of pure VFDI has significantly positive effects on technology spillovers captured by patent citations when technologically advanced economies host Japanese MNEs. Technology spillovers occur in both directions between the MNEs and their host countries. These positive effects of pure VFDI on technology spillovers are robust for different specifications as well. Partially VFDI (i.e., FDI with a higher share of purchase of intermediate inputs in the local market and a higher share of sales of outputs to the home country) also has significantly positive effects on technology spillovers from the (high-income) host countries to the MNEs.[9] By contrast, an increase in the degree of pure HFDI has no significant effect or significantly negative effects on technology spillovers between the MNEs and their host countries. Partially HFDI (i.e., FDI with a higher share of purchases from the home country and a higher share of sales to

[7] Therefore, our definition of technology spillovers is narrower than that used in studies on the productivity change due to FDI or trade. However, it seems that our definition is useful, because it focuses on direct effects and can still capture an important part of the effects in terms of the contribution to the expansion of the world's technology frontier.

[8] We acknowledge that the range of technology spillovers measured in the data may be narrowed, particularly for developing countries, by using patent citations, because many indigenous firms in developing countries are not so active in the application of patents.

[9] The positive effects of partially VFDI are not robust when we employ different specifications, although we do not report the details of the estimated results in this chapter.

the local market) has significantly positive effects on technology spillovers from the MNEs to the (high-income) host countries, but the result is not robust for different estimations. From these results, we conclude that pure VFDI plays a dominant role in technology spillovers in both directions between Japanese MNEs and the high-income host countries.

To explain the mechanism for the observed relationship between the structure of FDI and technology spillovers, we develop a simple partial-equilibrium model of FDI and technology spillovers among developed countries. A differentiated good is produced in three stages.[10] The product market is characterized by monopolistic competition. Depending on parameter values, firms may have an incentive to engage in horizontal or vertical FDI. Assuming that factor costs are the same in the two countries, there is no possibility of VFDI in the usual sense. Nevertheless, VFDI *does* occur if there are technology gaps in some production stages between the two countries and/or if firms can take advantage of the superior technology by fragmenting their production process abroad. Technological differences in some production stages are considered to be the source of technology spillovers through FDI. We show that technology spillovers occur in one way or two ways if firms engage in VFDI, depending on how the three production stages are located in the two countries. Besides, we show that HFDI does not necessarily induce technology spillovers, because it is mainly motivated by saving transportation costs and hence appears even in the absence of technological differences.

The rest of this chapter is organized as follows. Section 6.2 describes the data employed in our empirical analysis. Section 6.3 introduces estimation methods. Section 6.4 provides empirical results. Section 6.5 develops a simple theoretical model of FDI and technology spillovers to explain the observed relationship in our empirical study. Section 6.6 concludes this chapter.

6.2 Data

In this section we describe the data employed in our empirical analysis.

6.2.1 Data on Patent Citations and Japanese Firms' FDI

Following Jaffe et al. (1993), Jaffe and Trajtenberg (1999), and other studies, we use patent citation data as a proxy for technology spillovers. The patent citations are collected from the dataset compiled by the National Bureau of Economic Research

[10] As the models of vertical production structure with multiple stages there are, for example, Bridgman (2012), Dixit and Grossman (1982), Kohler (2004), and Yi (2003). None of these papers, however, consider the possibility of VFDI driven by cross-country technology gaps in production stages. Baldwin and Venables (2013) consider more general structure of the GVC in production processes.

(NBER) patent database for patents at the USPTO.[11] The dataset includes information on the application date, the country name of the assignee, the main US patent class, and citations made and received for each patent. From the dataset we extract information on the patent applications and citations by Japanese MNEs and their host countries. Because of the truncated problems of citations in the NBER dataset, we concentrate our analysis on the period before 2003, though the NBER patent dataset includes data until 2006.

Our data on Japanese MNEs' activities abroad are obtained from the Basic Survey on Overseas Business Activities (BSOBA) or *Kaigai Jigyo Katsudo Kihon Chosa* conducted by the Japanese Ministry of Economic, Trade and Industry (METI). This data source provides detailed data on affiliate-level FDI activities such as the sales and purchases of affiliates of Japanese MNEs, classified by their destinations and sources, i.e., sales to (or purchases from) the local market or exports to (or imports from) the home country and a third country.

The foreign affiliates listed in the BSOBA are either foreign affiliates with at least 10% of their capital held by a Japanese parent company or those with at least 50% of their capital held by a foreign subsidiary, which in turn has at least 50% of its capital held by a Japanese parent company. These affiliates exclude those that run businesses in the financial and insurance industry or the real estate industry in host countries. According to the METI, there were approximately 15,000 foreign affiliates that responded to the survey in 2000.[12] Table 6.1 shows the top 30 host economies for Japanese MNEs in 2000, based on the number of affiliates that had completed the BSOBA.[13] As shown in the table, the United States attracts the largest number of Japanese firms' affiliates, followed by China. Asian economies as well as developed countries are popular host economies for Japanese MNEs.

Our sample covers the period between 1995 and 2003. All countries in which Japanese MNEs have at least one affiliate are included in our sample. Since the number of countries varies greatly depending on that of patent applications made, we divide our sample of the countries into two groups, Groups I and II, according to the number of USPTO patent applications made by the sample countries during the period of 1995–2003. We call Group I countries/economies "Technologically Advanced Economies," which mainly include high income countries/economies. In contrast, we call Group II countries/economies "Technologically Less Advanced Economies," which mainly include middle and low income countries. The number of patent applications in Group I is larger than 1,000, while it is less than that in Group II.[14] All countries that are categorized into each group are listed in Table 6.2.

[11] See the Bronwyn Hall's website (www.nber.org/people/bronwyn_hall?page=1&perPage=50) for the NBER patent database.

[12] See the METI website (www.meti.go.jp/english/statistics/tyo/kaigaizi/index.html) for the details of the BSOBA.

[13] About 10,100 affiliates reported full or partial information on their sales and purchases classified by the destinations and the sources in 2000.

[14] Although the number of USPTO patent applications made by China, India, Russia, and Singapore is more than 1,000 during the period, a large jump in the applications is observed after 2000,

Table 6.1 Top 30 FDI host countries/economies in the year 2000

Economy	No. of affiliates	Economy	No. of affiliates	Economy	No. of affiliates
United States	2,172	Australia	342	India	99
China	1,246	Korea	257	Vietnam	97
Thailand	692	Netherlands	248	Belgium	80
Singapore	613	France	216	New Zealand	74
Hong Kong	585	Canada	196	Chile	42
United Kingdom	509	Brazil	193		
Malaysia	477	Panama	138		
Taiwan	460	Mexico	132		
Indonesia	431	Italy	114		
Germany	363	Spain	100		

Note: The number of affiliates is those reported by respondents of the BSOBA in 2000

Table 6.2 List of countries/economies

Group I	Group II			
(Tech. Advanced Economies)	(Technologically Less Advanced Economies)			
Australia	Argentina	Ghana	Niger	Trinidad&Tobago
Austria	Bahamas	Greece	Nigeria	Tunisia
Belgium	Bahrain	Guatemala	Pakistan	Turkey
Canada	Bangladesh	Hong Kong	Panama	UAE
Denmark	Bolivia	Hungary	Papua New Guinea	Uruguay
Finland	Brazil	Iceland	Paraguay	Venezuela
France	Brunei	India	Peru	Vietnam
Germany	Cambodia	Indonesia	Poland	Zambia
Israel	Cameroon	Iran	Portugal	Zimbabwe
Italy	Chile	Ireland	Qatar	
Korea, Republic of	China	Jamaica	Romania	
Luxembourg	Colombia	Kenya	Russia	
Netherlands	Costa Rica	Kuwait	Samoa	
New Zealand	Cyprus	Laos	Saudi Arabia	
Norway	Czech	Lebanon	Senegal	
Spain	Dominican	Liberia	Singapore	
Sweden	Ecuador	Macao	Slovak	
Switzerland	Egypt	Madagascar	South Africa	
Taiwan	El Salvador	Malaysia	Sri Lanka	
United Kingdom	Ethiopia	Mexico	Tanzania	
United States	Fiji	Morocco	Thailand	

We use the Nikkei company code system to link the two data sources and collected the data on 1,445 parent companies that run at least one affiliate during the sample period. 279 parent companies out of 1,445 ones made at least one citation to USPTO patent applications from 93 countries and, on the other hand, 301 ones received at least one USPTO patent citation.

6.2.2 Types of FDI

In the literature, FDI and MNEs' activities are usually categorized into horizontal and vertical cases. In the empirical studies, there are a number of ways to measure horizontal and vertical FDI. Hummels et al. (2001) and Alfaro and Charlton (2009) use the industrial classifications to define the types of FDI. Hanson et al. (2001, 2005) utilize the firm-level database of the United States Bureau of Economic Analysis (BEA) to characterize VFDI as intra-firm flows of inputs that they observed flowing from parent companies in the United States to affiliates abroad. The method of Hanson et al. (2001, 2005) enables them to measure one-way US bilateral intra-firm trade. Using the same BSOBA dataset as in this chapter, Fukao and Wei (2008) employ the local sales ratio of the affiliates to classify vertical and horizontal FDI. In particular, if a local sales ratio of a foreign affiliate is less than the average ratio in the sample, then FDI to the affiliate is classified into VFDI. By contrast, if a local sales ratio is larger than the average ratio, FDI to the affiliate is classified into HFDI.

An advantage of the BSOBA dataset is that it allows us to measure vertical and horizontal FDI by using information on the sale of outputs and the purchase of inputs by foreign affiliates.[15] The local sales and local purchases ratios of foreign affiliates of Japanese MNEs are denoted by $ShSaHFDI$ and $ShPuHFDI$, respectively. Similarly, the sales and purchases ratios to and from Japan for foreign affiliates of Japanese MNEs are denoted by $ShSaVFDI$ and $ShPuVFDI$, respectively. Table 6.3 shows the average values of both ratios during the sample period for the subsamples of technologically advanced and less advanced economies. Looking at the ratios over the years, no evident trend is observed during the sample period. Interestingly, the table also shows that the values of $ShSaVFDI$, which indicates the vertical structure of sales from foreign affiliates, are around 10–12% in technologically advanced economies and around 20–22% in technologically less advanced economies. If we focus on $ShPuVFDI$ (i.e., the vertical structure of purchases by foreign affiliates), then the values climb up to around 40–42% in technologically advanced economies and 37–40% in technologically less advanced economies. With respect to the pur-

compared with a very limited number in the early years for these countries. We therefore categorize these four countries into the second group.

[15] One limitation of the BSOBA dataset is, however, that it does not track transactions between foreign affiliates or between foreign affiliates and the parent companies. As a result, there may exist some biases for measuring the types of FDI by using information on sale and purchase because we cannot examine flows within the boundary of a firm from our dataset.

Table 6.3 Sales and purchases ratios of affiliates abroad

	1995	1996	1997	1998	1999	2000	2001	2002	2003
	Tech. advanced economies (Group I)								
ShSaHFDI	0.761	0.747	0.735	0.757	0.761	0.759	0.751	0.752	0.745
ShSaVFDI	0.128	0.125	0.126	0.127	0.126	0.122	0.124	0.106	0.107
ShPuHFDI	0.530	0.493	0.474	0.501	0.481	0.481	0.490	0.464	0.462
ShPuVFDI	0.403	0.398	0.405	0.413	0.424	0.421	0.420	0.404	0.403
	Tech. less advanced economies (Group II)								
ShSaHFDI	0.655	0.649	0.612	0.639	0.644	0.636	0.630	0.631	0.631
ShSaVFDI	0.208	0.197	0.211	0.222	0.212	0.212	0.228	0.204	0.208
ShPuHFDI	0.524	0.482	0.464	0.512	0.494	0.493	0.509	0.530	0.536
ShPuVFDI	0.392	0.395	0.401	0.405	0.407	0.402	0.403	0.370	0.369

Source: Authors' calculation from the BSOBA data from 1995 to 2003

chase of inputs, Japanese MNEs engage in VFDI more actively in technologically advanced host countries than in technologically less advanced host countries. This evidence is consistent with Alfaro and Charlton (2009), who showed that VFDI emerges as far more prevalent between developed countries.

By exploiting information on the horizontal and vertical structures in sales and purchases of foreign affiliates, we construct new indexes of horizontal and vertical FDI, i.e., $HFDI$, $VFDI$, $PHFDI$, and $PVFDI$, in the following way:

$$
\begin{aligned}
HFDI &= ShSaHFDI \times ShPuHFDI \\
VFDI &= ShSaVFDI \times ShPuVFDI \\
PHFDI &= ShSaHFDI \times ShPuVFDI \\
PVFDI &= ShSaVFDI \times ShPuHFDI
\end{aligned}
$$

As is evident from the definition of the index, $HFDI$ measures the extent to which affiliates' purchases of intermediate inputs and sales of final goods are concentrated in the local market. Now, $HFDI$ captures the degree of "pure" HFDI. If $HFDI = 1$, a foreign affiliate makes all purchases and sales in the local market, whereas, if $HFDI = 0$, either or both of purchases and sales of the foreign affiliate become zero in the local market. Note that $HFDI = 0$ does not necessarily mean that the foreign affiliate engages in vertical activities because there is a possibility of transactions with third countries. Next $VFDI$ measures the extent to which affiliates' purchases of intermediate inputs and sales of final goods are linked to the home country (i.e., Japan), so that $VFDI$ captures the degree of "pure" VFDI. On the other hand, $PHFDI$ and $PVFDI$ capture "partially" horizontal and "partially" vertical FDI, respectively. The value of $PHFDI$ rises if an affiliate buys more intermediate goods from the home country and sells more final goods to the local market. Since the structure of sales is more important to distinguish the type of FDI than the structure of purchases, we consider that $PHFDI$ measures the degree of "partially" horizontal

FDI in terms of its horizontal sales structure. Similarly, the value of $PVFDI$ becomes large if an affiliate buys more intermediate goods from the local market and sells more final goods to the home country. Since the structure of sales is vertical in $PVFDI$, we consider that it measures the degree of "partially" vertical FDI.

We then test whether there are any differences in the effects on technology spillovers among these types of FDI.

6.3 The Empirical Model

In this section, let us explain our empirical model. Although the BSOBA is conducted every year, there are many blanks in the data on a particular firm because in some years certain respondents did not report to the METI. For this reason, we use only a pooled data in our estimation. Consequently, we run the following specification as in Branstetter (2006),

$$C_i = \beta_1 + \alpha_1 LPHost_i + \alpha_2 LPParent_i + \beta_2 FDI_i + u_i, \tag{6.1}$$

where i refers to the affiliate i, and C_i is the number of citations made (or received) by USPTO patents of the Japanese parent company that owns affiliate i. Note that $C_i = C_{i'}$ holds for affiliate i and affiliate i' if the same parent company owns affiliates i and i'. We expect that citations made by Japanese parent companies capture the technology spillovers flowing from the host countries to Japanese companies, while the citations received by them reflect the flows from Japanese companies to host countries. FDI_i in Eq. (6.1) is one of the alternative measures of the FDI types, i.e., $HFDI$, $VFDI$, $PHFDI$, and $PVFDI$ for affiliate i. In Eq. (6.1), β_1 is a constant term and u_i is an error term.

As indicated in Branstetter (2006), patent citations may rise as the "citable" host invention increases. At the same time, the higher absorptive capacity in the home country may be associated with a higher ability to understand and exploit external knowledge, and cite more external patents (Mancusi, 2008). Thus, for elucidation of the assertions we use $LPParent_i$ and $LPHost_i$, which refer to the logarithm of the count of the USPTO patent applications made by affiliate i's Japanese parent company and the host country where the affiliate i runs its business, respectively, to proxy the home absorptive capacity and "citable" host invention. Note that $LPParent_i$ is the same across affiliate i for the same parent company, and $LPHost_i$ is the same across affiliate i for the same host country.

The focus of interest in Eq. (6.1) will be the coefficient β_2. Hence, we examine if the FDI types of Japanese firms in host countries have an influence on patent citations made and received by the firm. We also investigate if there is a difference in the magnitude and sign of the coefficients between the citations made and received by the home and host countries and across the types of FDI that Japanese firms implemented.

Since the observations of a dependent variable (i.e., patent citations) are the count data, we utilize a standard estimation technique, namely, a negative binomial model discussed in Cameron and Trivedi (1998), where the data are Poisson process, but more flexible modeling of the variance to account for overdispersion than the Poisson is allowed. We use this estimation technique to acquire our basic findings and alternative estimation results.

The other challenge of estimating the effects of each of the FDI types on technology spillovers arises from the fact that patent citations may be endogenous, because unobservables in determining the types of FDI may be correlated with those in determining the citations. Besides, certain geographic factors such as distance and language may influence the citations as well as the types of FDI. Neglecting these unobserved or endogenous factors may cause biased and inconsistent estimators.[16] To address this issue, we employ an endogenous switching model.[17] In that model, the citation C_i follows a Poisson distribution, and the probability distribution for count data is given by

$$Pr(C_i, \mu_i) = \frac{\mu_i{}^{C_i} \exp(-\mu_i)}{C_i!}, \tag{6.2}$$

so that a log-linear model for the mean of C_i, μ_i, can be specified as

$$\log(\mu_i) = \beta_1 + \alpha_1 LPHost_i + \alpha_2 LPParent_i + \alpha_3 LDist_i + \alpha_4 LGDP_i \\ + \alpha_5 LCost_i + \beta_2 D_i + \epsilon_i, \tag{6.3}$$

where $LDist_i$ is the logarithm of the distance (measured as kilometers) between Japan and the host economy of affiliate i, $LGDP_i$ is the logarithm of GDP of affiliate i's host economy, $LCost_i$ is the logarithm of salary per employee of affiliate i, and ϵ_i is an unobserved heterogeneity term. $LGDP_i$ measures the market size of the host economy, and $LCost_i$ measures the labor cost of the affiliate. Instead of FDI_i in Eq. (6.1), here we use a dummy D_i (D_{HFDI_i}, D_{VFDI_i}, D_{PHFDI_i}, or D_{PVFDI_i}) for the types of FDI, which equals one for a particular type, and zero otherwise. Following Fukao and Wei (2008), we construct the dummy for a particular type of FDI such that it equals one when the value of an FDI type's index ($HFDI$, $VFDI$, $PHFDI$, or $PVFDI$) for affiliate i is greater than the average value of the particular FDI type's index in the full sample, and zero otherwise. We then use a probit model to examine how a parent firm determines its FDI type. The logic we use is that the type decision on FDI depends on factors that favor a particular type of FDI or not. The probit model can be formulated as

$$D_i^* = z_i' \gamma + \lambda \epsilon_i + u_i, \tag{6.4}$$

---

[16] See Wooldridge (2010) for dealing with endogenous problems.

[17] An estimation method of count data regression with endogenous switching is proposed by Terza (1998). Kenkel and Terza (2001) discuss an application of the method suggested by Terza (1998). See Miranda and Rabe-Hesketh (2006) for technical details of the endogenous switching model.

and

$$D_i = \begin{cases} 1, & \text{if } D_i^* > 0, \\ 0, & \text{otherwise,} \end{cases}$$

where D_i^* is an auxiliary random variable, z_i is a vector of factors which may influence the particular type of FDI. As usual, we have $u_i \sim N(0, 1)$, and u_i is independent of ϵ_i. In the so-called endogenous switching model, $Var(\epsilon_i) = \sigma^2$, and total variance is $\lambda^2\sigma^2 + 1$. If $\lambda = 0$, then D_i is considered to be exogenous. Although a Poisson distribution is used, the variance of C_i is not necessarily equal to the conditional mean, and overdispersion is allowed in this model. Using the normality assumption for ϵ_i, we have

$$Var(C_i|x_i, D_i) = E(C_i|\epsilon_i, x_i, D_i)[1 + E(C_i|\epsilon_i, x_i, D_i)(\exp(\sigma^2) - 1)],$$

where x_i is a vector of explanatory variables in Eq. (6.3) (i.e., $LPHost_i$, $LPParent_i$, $LDist_i$, $LGDP_i$, $LCost_i$, and the constant term), which implies that if $\sigma \neq 0$, then the model exhibits overdispersion, as we would expect from the negative binomial model in Eq. (6.1).[18]

In the estimation, following Fukao and Wei (2008), we include $LDist_i$ (distance), $LGDP_i$ (market size), and $LCost_i$ (labor cost) in z_i in Eq. (6.4). Among those variables, the data on salaries and the number of employees of foreign affiliates are obtained from the BSOBA. The data on distance are collected from the database of the CEPII Research Center and the data on GDP in host countries are obtained from the Penn World Table.[19]

6.4 Empirical Results

In this section, we report our estimation results. We first show the basic findings obtained by the negative binomial model. We then report the results by the endogenous switching model and discuss whether the endogeneity issue matters in our analysis. Finally, we discuss the robustness of our findings by showing the results of alternative estimations with additional explanatory variables.

6.4.1 *Basic Findings*

We first estimate Eq. (6.1) by the negative binomial model, and the results are reported in Table 6.4. The upper panel of Table 6.4 shows the estimated results for the sub-

[18] See Miranda and Rabe-Hesketh (2006) for more details.

[19] CEPII: www.cepii.fr/CEPII/en/bdd_modele/presentation.asp?id=6. Penn World table: www.rug.nl/ggdc/productivity/pwt/.

Table 6.4 Negative binomial estimates for patent citations

	Tech. advanced economies (Group I)							
	Citing				Cited			
HFDI	−0.172*** (0.029)				−0.480*** (0.047)			
VFDI		0.529*** (0.085)				1.273*** (0.15)		
PHFDI			−0.005 (0.025)				0.197*** (0.045)	
PVFDI				0.115* (0.064)				−0.120 (0.092)
LPHost	0.982*** (0.006)	0.976*** (0.005)	0.973*** (0.005)	0.973*** (0.006)	1.106*** (0.009)	1.087*** (0.009)	1.083*** (0.009)	1.081*** (0.009)
LPParent	0.963*** (0.005)	0.963*** (0.005)	0.960*** (0.005)	0.966*** (0.005)	0.502*** (0.003)	0.503*** (0.003)	0.500*** (0.003)	0.506*** (0.003)
No. of Obs	14836	14568	15441	14026	14836	14568	15441	14026
Log likelihood	−24646	−24059	−25682	−23157	−33957	−33306	−35403	−32028
Prob>chi^2	0.00	0.00	0 00	0.00	0.00	0.00	0.00	0.00
	Tech. Less Advanced Economies (Group II)							
	Citing				Cited			
HFDI	−0.573*** (0.11)				−0.684*** (0.10)			
VFDI		0.189 (0.24)				0.182 (0.20)		
PHFDI			−0.033 (0.11)				−0.338*** (0.10)	
PVFDI				1.087*** (0.21)				0.938*** (0.17)
LPHost	1.095*** (0.023)	1.085*** (0.022)	1.082*** (0.022)	1.081*** (0.023)	1.097*** (0.020)	1.112*** (0.020)	1.109*** (0.020)	1.088*** (0.020)
LPParent	1.021*** (0.023)	1.018*** (0.023)	1.022*** (0.023)	1.037*** (0.024)	0.932*** (0.019)	0.934*** (0.019)	0.934*** (0.019)	0.949*** (0.020)
No. of Obs.	18928	18870	19345	18397	18928	18870	19345	18397
Log likelihood	−3836	−3917	−3988	-3755	−5732	−5795	−5919	−5604
Prob>chi^2	0.00	0.00	0.00	0.00	0.00	0.00	0.00	0.00

Notes: (a) ***, **, and * indicate significance at the 1%, 5%, and 10% levels, respectively
(b) The values in the parentheses are standard errors
(c) A constant term is included in the estimations

sample of technologically advanced economies. We observe from the results that the estimates of $HFDI$ are significant and negative, whereas they are significantly positive for $VFDI$ both for the citing and cited. As for $PHFDI$, the estimated coefficient is insignificant for the citing, but significantly positive for the cited, whereas the coefficient of $PVFDI$ are significant and positive for the citing and insignificant for the cited.

The lower panel of Table 6.4 presents the estimated results for the subsample of technologically less advanced economies. Unlike the case of the technologically advanced economies, only the coefficients on $PVFDI$ show significantly positive, whereas the coefficients of the other types of FDI reveal negative or insignificant effects on the citing as well as the cited.

These results show that an increase in the degree of the "pure" VFDI has a significantly positive effect on technology spillovers in both directions between Japanese parent companies and their host countries if Japanese MNEs invest in high-income countries. This implies that VFDI plays a dominant role in technology spillovers with mutual effects in technologically advanced economies. When middle- and low-income countries host Japanese MNEs, an increase in the "partially" vertical FDI has a significantly positive effect on the number of patent citations in both directions between the Japanese parent companies and firms in their host countries.

6.4.2 Estimating with an Endogenous Switching Model

To deal with endogeneity issues, we simultaneously estimate both an endogenous switching model described by Eqs. (6.2) and (6.3) for technology spillovers and a probit model based on Eq. (6.4) for the decision on FDI types. We focus on the subsample of technologically advanced economies. The estimated results are summarized in Table 6.5. We first observe that the coefficient of $LCost$ is significantly positive for both "pure" VFDI (D_{VFDI}) and "partially" vertical FDI (D_{PVFDI}). This implies that VFDI to technologically advanced economies is not motivated by wage cost saving.

In terms of the endogeneity between technology spillovers and the decision on FDI types, the estimates of ρ in Table 6.5 show strong significance against the null hypothesis in two cases out of eight estimations for technologically advanced economies and in all cases for technologically less advanced economies.[20] Consequently, neglecting the endogenous issues may cause biased and inconsistent estimators (Miranda and Rabe-Hesketh, 2006). The estimations in Table 6.5 reveal that D_{VFDI} based on the endogenous switching model for both the citing and cited cases provides results similar to those based on the negative binomial model. For D_{PVFDI}, the two models also provide similar results, suggesting that more local purchases and more sales in Japan may favor Japanese parent companies with more technology spillovers from

[20] Now ρ stands for the correlation between ϵ_i and $\lambda\epsilon_i + u_i$ in Eq. (6.3), and $\rho = \lambda/\sqrt{2(\lambda^2 + 1)}$ where ρ is identified by λ.

Table 6.5 Endogenous switching estimates for technologically advanced economies

	Switching(citing)				Switching(cited)				D_{HFDI}	D_{VFDI}	D_{PHFDI}	D_{PVFDI}
D_{HFDI}	−0.084 (0.076)				−0.107 (0.082)							
D_{VFDI}		0.147*** (0.017)				0.509** (0.22)						
D_{PHFDI}			−0.099*** (0.009)				0.062 (0.048)					
D_{PVFDI}				0.151*** (0.054)				0.197 (0.13)				
$LPHost$	1.023*** (0.007)	1.020*** (0.007)	1.026*** (0.006)	1.018*** (0.006)	1.138*** (0.010)	1.134*** (0.009)	1.134*** (0.009)	1.133*** (0.009)				
$LPParent$	0.997*** (0.006)	0.999*** (0.005)	1.004*** (0.004)	0.999*** (0.006)	0.644*** (0.007)	0.647*** (0.007)	0.642*** (0.007)	0.649*** (0.007)				
$LDist$	−0.189*** (0.023)	−0.411*** (0.030)	−0.189*** (0.023)	−0.411*** (0.030)	−0.190*** (0.023)	−0.416*** (0.031)	−0.192*** (0.023)	−0.409*** (0.030)	−0.134*** (0.019)	−0.397*** (0.025)	0.006 (0.020)	−0.382*** (0.025)
$LGDP$	0.251*** (0.022)	0.047*** (0.016)	0.251*** (0.011)	0.047*** (0.016)	0.251*** (0.011)	0.047*** (0.016)	0.252*** (0.011)	0.047*** (0.016)	0.226*** (0.009)	0.061*** (0.014)	0.084*** (0.008)	0.028** (0.014)
$LCost$	−0.195*** (0.015)	0.094*** (0.022)	−0.195*** (0.015)	0.094*** (0.022)	−0.195*** (0.015)	0.094*** (0.022)	−0.194*** (0.015)	0.093*** (0.022)	−0.208*** (0.011)	0.095*** (0.018)	−0.172*** (0.011)	0.106*** (0.018)
σ	0.651*** (0.013)	0.648*** (0.012)	0.658*** (0.011)	0.646*** (0.013)	1.487*** (0.025)	1.484*** (0.025)	1.483*** (0.024)	1.487*** (0.025)				
ρ	−0.013 (0.13)	0.058 (0.058)	−0.015 (0.038)	0.078 (0.071)	−0.020 (0.025)	−0.101* (0.056)	−0.082*** (0.016)	0.018 (0.03)				
No. of Obs.	35247	35247	35247	35247	35247	35247	35247	35247	17958	17776	18803	17014
Log likelihood	−31452	−39223	−25915	−24942	−33610	−32515	−40635	−32285	−10718	−3415	−12124	−3448
Prob>chi^2	0.00	0.00	0.00	0.00	0.00	0.00	0.00	0.00	0.00	0.00	0.00	0.00

Notes: (a) ***, **, and * indicate significance at the 1%, 5%, and 10% levels, respectively
(b) The values in the parentheses are standard errors
(c) A constant term is included in the estimations
(d) D_{HFDI}, D_{VFDI}, D_{PHFDI} and D_{PVFDI} are dummy variables for the four types of FDI

the host economies. As observed for D_{HFDI} and D_{PHFDI}, the estimates become insignificant and significantly negative for citing, respectively.

Our findings imply that, for technologically advanced economies, "pure" VFDI is associated with significant technology spillovers even if we control for endogenous issues.

6.4.3 Alternative Estimations

To check the robustness of the basic findings in Sect. 6.4.1, we conduct alternative estimations for Group I countries by adding explanatory variables. We include $PROX$ (technological proximity), $CapRatio$ (capital ratio), and $Close$ (a dummy for industrial classification, which is one for the same sector and zero otherwise). We also include $LDist$ (the logarithm of the distance between Japan and host countries) and $Year$ which captures the changes in citations.

Japanese parent companies and firms in their host countries may increase their citations of each other just because Japanese parent companies and firms in their host countries change the focus of their research activities in ways that bring them "closer" to each other in the technology space (Branstetter, 2006). To control for this issue, we include a measure of technological proximity ($PROX$) in the regression. As suggested by Jaffe (1986) and Branstetter (2006), $PROX$ is constructed by

$$PROX_i = \frac{F_i F'_{host,i}}{(F_i F'_i)(F_{host,i} F'_{host,i})},$$

where $F_i = (f_{1i}, \cdots, f_{ki})$ is a vector of the cumulative count of patents obtained by affiliate i's parent firm in kth technical area[21] and $F_{host,i}$ is a vector of the aggregate count of patens obtained by all firms in the host country in which affiliate i is located.

The literature on the role of affiliate ownership in technology spillovers is limited. There are a few studies focused on the correlation between productivity and the ownership of affiliates. Javorcik (2004) and Javorcik and Spatareanu (2008) found that the correlation of productivity with FDI is stronger if the affiliate is only partially, and not fully foreign owned, because joint ownership generates more technology transfer, and wholly owned affiliates employ more sophisticated technology that is out of reach of the average domestic supplier. As indicated by Keller (2010), however, the technology gap may be a key reason for differential effects for wholly versus partially owned affiliates. $CapRatio$, which is the share of affiliate capital owned by Japanese parent companies, is included to test the effects of ownership of affiliates on technology spillovers.

As in Sect. 6.4.1, we use patent citations at the USPTO as the dependent variable and employ the negative binomial model for our estimation. The estimated results

[21] We aggregate the US patent classes into 44 fields derived by Schmoch et al.(2003).

are presented in Table 6.6.[22] The coefficients of $PROX$ are significantly positive in all cases of citing and cited. These results confirm the findings in Branstetter (2006). The coefficients of $Close$ are significantly positive in technology spillovers from host economies to Japanese MNEs, which implies that Japanese parent companies cite more patents of host economies when their affiliates run a business that is the same as or close to that of the parents. However, this is not the case for technology spillovers from Japanese MNEs to host economies, since the coefficients of $Close$ are significantly negative. The ownership variable, $CapRatio$, has positive coefficients that are mostly significant, which implies that a higher share of ownership of foreign affiliates by Japanese parent companies tends to facilitate technology spillovers in both directions between Japanese MNEs and their host economies.

The estimates of $HFDI$, $VFDI$, $PHFDI$, and $PVFDI$ for the USPTO give similar results to those we observed in Table 6.4, except for $PHFDI$ and $PVFDI$ in the cited. Specifically, the significantly positive effect of $PVFDI$ is not robust for some combinations of explanatory variables.

6.5 A Simple Model of FDI and Technology Spillovers

To explain the observed relationship between the structure of FDI and technology spillovers in the previous section, we develop a partial-equilibrium model of FDI and technology spillovers among developed economies. We consider a world of two countries, home and foreign. Foreign variables are denoted by an asterisk.

We focus on the market for a differentiated good x. Consumers in the two countries share the same preference. The preference of the representative consumer takes the standard Dixit-Stiglitz form (Dixit and Stiglitz, 1977):

$$U = \left(\sum_{j=1}^{N} x_j^{\alpha} \right)^{1/\alpha},$$

where x_j is the consumption of a variety j of good x, $\alpha = 1 - 1/\sigma$, $\sigma > 1$ is the elasticity of substitution across varieties, and N is the total number of varieties supplied in the home market. We also assume that the market size is the same in the two countries.

The demand for a variety j of good x in the home country is given by

$$x_j = (p_j^c)^{-\sigma} P^{\sigma-1} E,$$

[22] Here, we only report the estimated results with full sets of explanatory variables. The results with various combinations of the explanatory variables are available from the corresponding author upon request.

Table 6.6 Alternative estimations for technologically advanced economies

	Citing				Cited			
HFDI	−0.125*** (0.031)				−0.126** (0.053)			
VFDI		0.387*** (0.10)				0.438*** (0.17)		
PHFDI			−0.026 (0.029)				−0.228*** (0.048)	
PVFDI				0.151** (0.072)				0.298** (0.12)
LPHost	0.937*** (0.007)	0.935*** (0.006)	0.930*** (0.006)	0.933*** (0.007)	1.001*** (0.011)	0.997*** (0.010)	0.998*** (0.010)	0.996*** (0.011)
LPParent	0.944*** (0.006)	0.944*** (0.006)	0.939*** (0.006)	0.945*** (0.006)	0.362*** (0.007)	0.361*** (0.004)	0.358*** (0.004)	0.363*** (0.004)
PROX	0.904*** (0.066)	0.903*** (0.067)	0.963*** (0.065)	0.926*** (0.068)	2.962*** (0.12)	2.983*** (0.12)	3.008*** (0.12)	2.992*** (0.12)
CapRatio	0.270*** (0.061)	0.222*** (0.062)	0.295*** (0.060)	0.287*** (0.062)	0.162 (0.10)	0.150 (0.10)	0.249*** (0.10)	0.156 (0.10)
Close	0.075*** (0.023)	0.069*** (0.023)	0.070*** (0.023)	0.067*** (0.023)	−0.272*** (0.037)	−0.307*** (0.038)	−0.298*** (0.037)	−0.284*** (0.038)
LDist	0.140*** (0.026)	0.158*** (0.027)	0.142*** (0.026)	0.129*** (0.026)	0.154*** (0.039)	0.190*** (0.041)	0.148*** (0.039)	0.164*** (0.040)
Year	0.000 (0.00)	0.003 (0.005)	−0.001 (0.005)	0.001 (0.003)	0.072*** (0.007)	0.082*** (0.007)	0.076*** (0.007)	0.077*** (0.007)
No. of Obs.	6505	6330	6835	6047	6505	6330	6835	6047
Log likelihood	−20903	−20335	−21692	−19616	−27042	−26400	−28068	−25420
Prob>chi^2	0.00	0.00	0.00	0.00	0.00	0.00	0.00	0.00

Notes: (a) ***, **, and * indicate significance at the 1%, 5%, and 10% levels, respectively
(b) The values in the parentheses are standard errors
(c) A constant term is included in the estimations

where E is the total expenditure on good x in the home country (which is the same for the foreign country), p_j^c is the CIF price of variety j produced by a home firm and P is the price index for the x sector goods, which is defined as

$$P = \left[\sum_{j=1}^{n} (p_j^c)^{1-\sigma} + \sum_{k=1}^{n^*} (p_k^{*c})^{1-\sigma} \right]^{1/(1-\sigma)},$$

where n and n^* are the numbers of varieties produced by the home firms and the foreign firms, respectively, with $n + n^* = N$, and p_k^{*c} is the CIF price of variety k produced by a foreign firm.

In each country, there is one primary factor of production, labor, denoted by l. The wage rate, w, is the same in the two countries, i.e., $w = w^* \equiv \omega$. Labor is immobile across countries.

6.5.1 Production and Supply

Good x is differentiated by variety and is supplied by monopolistically competitive firms. Each firm produces one variety. The nationality of a firm is identified by the location of its headquarters.

Good x is produced in three sequential stages.[23] Intermediate inputs for good x are specific to varieties, and hence there is no market for its intermediate inputs. For simplicity we assume away the possibility of outsourcing production of intermediate inputs. All of the three production stages must be conducted in house, although firms can offshore some or all of the production stages by establishing affiliates in the other country.

The first stage of production is simply conducted by using only labor, so that one unit of an intermediate input m_1 is produced by one unit of labor: $m_1 = l_1$. The quality of the intermediate input may be differentiated. It is θ_1 if the first stage is performed in the home country and θ_1^* if it is in the foreign country, where $0 < \theta_1 \leq 1$ and $0 < \theta_1^* \leq 1$. The quality of m_1 matters when it is used in the second stage of production. The production function of an intermediate product is given by $m_2 = (\theta_1 m_1)^{\gamma} l_2^{1-\gamma}$, where m_2 stands for an intermediate product in the second stage and $\gamma \in (0, 1)$. In the production function of m_2, θ_1 is replaced by θ_1^* if m_1 produced in the foreign country is used. Moreover, in the final stage of production, m_2 and labor are used to produce a variety j of good x: $x_j = (\theta_2 m_2)^{\gamma} l_3^{1-\gamma}$, where the quality of m_2 is θ_2 (θ_2^*) if the second stage of production is performed in the home (foreign) country, where $0 < \theta_2 \leq 1$ and $0 < \theta_2^* \leq 1$. A difference in the quality of intermediate inputs m_1 and m_2 reflects the technology gap for the particular production stage between the two

[23] This means that we consider the "snake" type in the terminology of Baldwin and Venables (2013).

countries.[24] Note that the location of the production stage rather than the nationality of firms determines the quality of intermediate inputs. This may be because the information on the technology of producing intermediate inputs is locally spilled over, while it is not spilled over across countries.[25] Since the final good x is *not* differentiated in quality, the location of the final production stage does not affect characteristics of varieties.

Iceberg transportation costs apply to cross-country shipment of both intermediate inputs and final goods. For one unit of an intermediate input and a final good to arrive at a foreign destination, $\tau \geq 1$ units of an intermediate input and $t \geq 1$ units of the final good must be sent, respectively.

When a firm sets up a production stage in the country different from the country in which its headquarters is located, it engages in FDI and incurs an extra fixed cost of $\Phi/3$ units of labor per stage, where $\Phi > 0$ is exogenously given and constant.

Each monopolistically competitive firm chooses both the location of the three production stages and the price for its own variety in each market, taking the price index as given. As is well known, a monopolistically competitive firm charges a constant mark-up over the unit cost of the final good, which is given by $p_j = C_j/\alpha$, where p_j is the FOB price of variety j and C_j is the unit cost of producing variety j, which will be shown in detail below.

6.5.2 Technology Spillovers

We introduce the possibility of technology spillovers. Suppose that the quality of intermediate inputs can be upgraded by R&D. We suppose that the outcome of R&D is stochastic. Consequently, the difference in the quality of intermediate inputs arises, depending on whether R&D was successful or not.[26]

We take up the effects of spillovers from one firm's R&D outcome to other firms' product stage. As is well known, technology spillovers occur from a firm with higher technology to a firm with lower technology. We assume that when a firm uses a better quality of an ith-stage intermediate input for the production of the $(i+1)$th stage, the information on the better quality of an ith-stage intermediate input is spilled over to the $(i+1)$th stage and improves the productivity of R&D for the $(i+1)$th-stage intermediate input.

Under the above assumptions, the following lemma on spillovers holds.

---

[24] For our purpose of this chapter, we do not need to specify the cause of the technology gap between the two countries. Then, we assume that there is a technology gap between the two countries.

[25] This is different from technology spillovers that we will discuss below.

[26] The purpose of our analysis in this section is to investigate the relationship between types of FDI and technology spillovers. For this, we want to show how the technology gap between the two countries is related to FDI types and how it is also related to technology spillovers. But, we do not need to specify the details of R&D and the production in the next period after spillovers occur.

Lemma 6.1 *Technology spillovers occur only if the ith and the $(i+1)$th stages are located in different countries.*

The reason is straightforward. If the ith and the $(i+1)$th stages are located in the same country, then all firms produce the same quality of the ith-stage intermediate inputs and use them at the $(i+1)$th stage. Thus, there is no scope for technology spillovers.

One may think that technology spillovers in our model are associated with imports of intermediate inputs with better quality. However, since each intermediate input is specialized to each variety in our model, inter-firm trade of intermediate inputs does not occur. Moreover, we can argue that technology spillovers through FDI are stronger than those through imports of intermediate inputs, because FDI involves various activities more than just the transaction of intermediate inputs.

6.5.3 FDI and Technology Spillovers: HFDI

We next analyze how firms locate production stages and how international technology spillovers are associated with FDI.

We define horizontal and vertical FDI in the following way. If a firm conducts the final stage in both the home and the foreign countries, it engages in HFDI. On the other hand, if a firm conducts either or both of the first two stages in the country that is different from the country in which its headquarters is located without conducting the final stage in that country, it engages in VFDI.

We focus on the representative firm whose headquarters is located in the home country. We call it "the home firm." All firms with the same nationality behave in the same way.

We first look at HFDI. We denote the combination of locations for three production stages by three capital letters. For example, if the first stage is located in the home country, the second stage is in the foreign country, and the final stage is in the home country, then we denote this combination by HFH. Then, the possible patterns of HFDI for the home firm are $\{FFF, HFF, HHF, FHF\}$.

The unit cost function to serve the foreign market by the pattern of FFF is given by

$$C_{FFF}(\omega; \theta_1^*, \theta_2^*) = B\left((\theta_1^*)^{-\gamma}(\theta_2^*)^{-1}\right)^{\gamma} \omega, \tag{6.5}$$

where $B \equiv \{\gamma^{\gamma}(1-\gamma)^{1-\gamma}\}^{-(1+\gamma)}$ is a constant. Similarly, the unit cost functions to serve the foreign market by the patterns of HFF and HHF are given by, respectively,

$$C_{HFF}(\omega, \tau; \theta_1, \theta_2^*) = B\left(\tau^{\gamma}\theta_1^{-\gamma}(\theta_2^*)^{-1}\right)^{\gamma} \omega, \tag{6.6}$$

$$C_{HHF}(\omega, \tau; \theta_1, \theta_2) = B(\tau\theta_1^{-\gamma}\theta_2^{-1})^{\gamma}\omega. \tag{6.7}$$

Moreover, the unit cost function to serve the foreign market by exporting from the home country is

$$C_{HHH}(\omega; \theta_1, \theta_2) = B\left((\theta_1)^{-\gamma}(\theta_2)^{-1}\right)^{\gamma}\omega, \tag{6.8}$$

where the transport costs for the shipment of the final good are not included.

In the analysis of the optimal configuration of production for the foreign market, it turns out that the configuration for the home market does not matter. Thus, we just focus on the profits from supplying to the foreign market. Given the demand for a variety and pricing policy under monopolistic competition, profits of the home firm from supplying a variety to the foreign market by the patterns FFF, HFF, HHF, and HHH are given by, respectively,

$$\pi_{FFF} = \frac{\alpha^{\sigma-1}E(P^*)^{\sigma-1}}{\sigma}(C_{FFF})^{1-\sigma} - \Phi\omega, \tag{6.9}$$

$$\pi_{HFF} = \frac{\alpha^{\sigma-1}E(P^*)^{\sigma-1}}{\sigma}(C_{HFF})^{1-\sigma} - \frac{2}{3}\Phi\omega, \tag{6.10}$$

$$\pi_{HHF} = \frac{\alpha^{\sigma-1}E(P^*)^{\sigma-1}}{\sigma}(C_{HHF})^{1-\sigma} - \frac{1}{3}\Phi\omega, \tag{6.11}$$

$$\pi_{HHH} = \frac{\alpha^{\sigma-1}E(P^*)^{\sigma-1}}{\sigma}(tC_{HHH})^{1-\sigma}. \tag{6.12}$$

Note that since FHF is dominated by HHF and HFF for $\theta_i = \theta_i^* = 1$ for $i = 1, 2$, we can exclude FHF from our analysis. Then, the following lemma is obtained.

Lemma 6.2 *Suppose that $\theta_i = \theta_i^* = 1, i = 1, 2$. The home firm still has an incentive to engage in HFDI if $t > \tau^\gamma$ and Φ is sufficiently low.*

Proof It is sufficient to prove that

$$\pi_{HHH} \leq \max\left\{\pi_{FFF},\ \pi_{HFF},\ \pi_{HHF}\right\} \tag{6.13}$$

holds when $\theta_i = \theta_i^* = 1$, $i = 1, 2$. Since we focus on the incentive for one firm to choose a particular production configuration and since an individual firm takes the price index as given, we treat the price index as fixed. Then, define $A \equiv \alpha^{\sigma-1}E(P^*)^{\sigma-1}B^{1-\sigma}/\sigma$ and $\phi \equiv \Phi\omega/A$. Substitute Eqs. (6.9)–(6.12) and Eqs. (6.5)–(6.8) into Eq. (6.13) and rearrange terms to yield

$$\begin{aligned}\phi\omega^{\sigma-1} \leq \max &\left\{\left(1 - t^{1-\sigma}\right),\ \left(\tau^{\gamma^2(1-\sigma)} - t^{1-\sigma} + \frac{1}{3}\phi\omega^{\sigma-1}\right),\right.\\ &\left.\left(\tau^{\gamma(1-\sigma)} - t^{1-\sigma} + \frac{2}{3}\phi\omega^{\sigma-1}\right)\right\},\end{aligned} \tag{6.14}$$

defining the upper bound of Φ. Equation (6.14) is satisfied if

$$\phi\omega^{\sigma-1} \leq 1 - t^{1-\sigma},$$
$$\phi\omega^{\sigma-1} \leq \frac{3}{2}(\tau^{\gamma^2(1-\sigma)} - t^{1-\sigma}), \quad \text{or}$$
$$\phi\omega^{\sigma-1} \leq 3(\tau^{\gamma(1-\sigma)} - t^{1-\sigma})$$

holds, which requires that $\Phi = \phi A/\omega$ is sufficiently low for the above inequalities to hold. Since $\gamma \in (0, 1)$ and $\sigma > 1$, it holds that $\tau^{\gamma(1-\sigma)} < \tau^{\gamma^2(1-\sigma)} < 1$ for $\tau > 1$. Thus, we need $\tau^{\gamma(1-\sigma)} > t^{1-\sigma}$ or $t > \tau^{\gamma}$. *Q.E.D.*

This lemma implies that even without technology differences, firms have an incentive to engage in HFDI if transportation costs for the cross-border shipment of the final goods are sufficiently high and the additional fixed costs for FDI are sufficiently low. This is just the standard motive for the HFDI. Lemma 6.2 yields the following proposition.

Proposition 6.1 *HFDI does not necessarily induce technology spillovers.*

Proof From Lemma 6.2, HFDI occurs even in the case of no technology difference. If the technology level is the same across countries, then there is no possibility of technology spillovers. *Q.E.D.*

When the production configuration is HFF, the first and the second stages are located in different countries. Thus, Lemma 6.1 suggests that technology spillovers may occur. However, the proof of Lemma 6.2 shows that HFF can be the optimal configuration even in the absence of a technology gap. If this is the case, technology spillovers do not occur in the case of HFF.

6.5.4 FDI and Technology Spillovers: VFDI

We turn to the case of VFDI. In this case, the home firm conducts the final stage only in the home country, so that the possible patterns of VFDI are $\{FHH, FFH, HFH\}$. We obtain the following lemma.

Lemma 6.3 *Suppose that* $\theta_i = \theta_i^* = 1$ *for* $i = 1, 2$. *Then, the home firm has no incentive to engage in VFDI as long as* τ *and* Φ *are positive.*

Proof By definition, the home firm conducts the final stage in the home country for any type of VFDI. We need to examine the supply to the home market. Then, compared to the national integration (i.e., the pattern of HHH), FDI in either or both of the first two stages incurs additional transportation costs and fixed costs of FDI. Thus, in the absence of technology advantage in the foreign production, VFDI always increases production costs as long as τ and Φ are positive. *Q.E.D.*

This lemma implies that in the absence of a factor cost differential, firms have no incentive to engage in VFDI without a technology difference as long as there are positive transportation costs for intermediate inputs and FDI requires additional fixed costs.

Now, the unit cost functions for the home firm in VFDI are given by

$$C_{HFH}(\omega, \tau; \theta_1, \theta_2^*) = B\left(\tau^{1+\gamma}\theta_1^{-\gamma}(\theta_2^*)^{-1}\right)^{\gamma}\omega, \tag{6.15}$$

$$C_{FFH}(\omega, \tau; \theta_1^*, \theta_2^*) = B\left(\tau(\theta_1^*)^{-\gamma}(\theta_2^*)^{-1}\right)^{\gamma}\omega, \tag{6.16}$$

$$C_{FHH}(\omega, \tau; \theta_1^*, \theta_2) = B(\tau^{\gamma}(\theta_1^*)^{-\gamma}\theta_2^{-1})^{\gamma}\omega. \tag{6.17}$$

In order to simplify the analysis, we assume that $t = 1$, so that firms have no incentive to locate the final stage of production for the foreign market separately from that for the home market. It is then shown that as long as the final stage is performed in a single location, firms have no incentive to conduct either or both of the first two stages at more than one location. Given this, profits of the home firm in production configurations $k = HFH$, FFH, FHH, and HHH are given by, respectively.

$$\Pi_{HFH} = \frac{\alpha^{\sigma-1}E\{(P)^{\sigma-1} + (P^*)^{\sigma-1}\}}{\sigma}(C_{HFH})^{1-\sigma} - \frac{1}{3}\Phi\omega, \tag{6.18}$$

$$\Pi_{FFH} = \frac{\alpha^{\sigma-1}E\{(P)^{\sigma-1} + (P^*)^{\sigma-1}\}}{\sigma}(C_{FFH})^{1-\sigma} - \frac{2}{3}\Phi\omega, \tag{6.19}$$

$$\Pi_{FHH} = \frac{\alpha^{\sigma-1}E\{(P)^{\sigma-1} + (P^*)^{\sigma-1}\}}{\sigma}(C_{FHH})^{1-\sigma} - \frac{1}{3}\Phi\omega, \tag{6.20}$$

$$\Pi_{HHH} = \frac{\alpha^{\sigma-1}E\{(P)^{\sigma-1} + (P^*)^{\sigma-1}\}}{\sigma}(C_{HHH})^{1-\sigma}, \tag{6.21}$$

where Π_k denotes the home firm's total profits when it engages in VFDI with configuration k. Then, we can prove the following proposition on the relationship between VFDI and technology spillovers.[27]

Proposition 6.2 *VFDI of the configuration HFH by the home firm may induce technology spillovers in both directions. Other types of VFDI can induce technology spillovers in one direction.*

Proof First, we derive the conditions for HFH to be chosen. Define $G \equiv \alpha^{\sigma-1}E\{(P)^{\sigma-1} + (P^*)^{\sigma-1}\}B^{1-\sigma}/\sigma$ and $\psi \equiv \Phi\omega/G$. It is shown from Eqs. (6.8), (6.15), (6.18), and (6.21) that $\Pi_{HFH} \geq \Pi_{HHH}$ holds if and only if

$$(\theta_2^*/\tau^{1+\gamma})^{\gamma(\sigma-1)} - (\theta_2)^{\gamma(\sigma-1)} \geq \frac{\omega^{\sigma-1}\psi}{3(\theta_1)^{\gamma^2(\sigma-1)}}. \tag{6.22}$$

It is also shown from Eqs. (6.15), (6.16), (6.18), and (6.19) that $\Pi_{HFH} \geq \Pi_{FFH}$ holds if and only if

[27] To simplify the analysis, we assume that firms treat technology spillovers as pure externality and do not take the effects of technology spillovers into account in their decision on production locations. Including technology spillovers in firms' profits will not alter the qualitative results.

$$(\theta_1^*)^{\gamma^2(\sigma-1)} - (\theta_1/\tau)^{\gamma^2(\sigma-1)} \leq \frac{\omega^{\sigma-1}\psi}{3(\theta_2^*/\tau)^{\gamma(\sigma-1)}} \tag{6.23}$$

and from Eqs. (6.15), (6.17), (6.18), and (6.20) that $\Pi_{HFH} \geq \Pi_{FHH}$ holds if and only if

$$(\theta_1)^\gamma (\theta_2^*/\tau) \geq (\theta_1^*)^\gamma \theta_2. \tag{6.24}$$

Since $\theta_2 < \theta_2^*$ is necessary for Eq. (6.22) to hold, Lemma 6.1 implies that technology spillovers in R&D occur for m_2 from the foreign country to the home country. On the other hand, $\theta_1 < \theta_1^*$ can be consistent with the inequality Eq. (6.23) if the gap between θ_1 and θ_1^* is sufficiently small, τ is sufficiently low, and ψ is sufficiently high. Thus, the technology spillovers in R&D for m_1 from the home country to the foreign country may not occur. On the other hand, if $\theta_1 > \theta_1^*$ holds, however, they do occur. It is easy to prove that $\theta_1 > \theta_1^*$ and $\theta_2 < \theta_2^*$ satisfy Eq. (6.24) and that $\theta_1 < \theta_1^*$ and $\theta_2 < \theta_2^*$ can satisfy Eq. (6.24) if $\theta_1^* \leq (\theta_2^*/\tau\theta_2)^{1/\gamma}\theta_1$ holds. Moreover, in order for Eqs. (6.22) and (6.23) to hold simultaneously, we need

$$\left((\theta_1^*)^\gamma (\theta_2^*/\tau)\right)^{\gamma(\sigma-1)} - ((\theta_1)^\gamma \theta_2)^{\gamma(\sigma-1)} \leq 2\left((\theta_1/\tau)^\gamma (\theta_2^*/\tau)\right)^{\gamma(\sigma-1)},$$

which can be consistent with Eq. (6.24).

We next derive the conditions for FHH to be chosen. It is shown from Eqs. (6.8), (6.17), (6.20), and (6.21) that $\Pi_{FHH} \geq \Pi_{HHH}$ holds if and only if

$$(\theta_1^*/\tau)^{\gamma^2(\sigma-1)} - (\theta_1)^{\gamma^2(\sigma-1)} \geq \frac{\omega^{\sigma-1}\psi}{3(\theta_2)^{\gamma(\sigma-1)}}. \tag{6.25}$$

It is also shown from Eqs. (6.16), (6.17), (6.19), and (6.20) that $\Pi_{FHH} \geq \Pi_{FFH}$ holds if and only if

$$(\theta_2^*/\tau)^{\gamma(\sigma-1)} - (\theta_2/\tau^\gamma)^{\gamma(\sigma-1)} \leq \frac{\omega^{\sigma-1}\psi}{3(\theta_1^*)^{\gamma^2(\sigma-1)}} \tag{6.26}$$

and from Eqs. (6.15), (6.17), (6.18), and (6.20) that $\Pi_{FHH} \geq \Pi_{HFH}$ holds if and only if

$$(\theta_1)^\gamma (\theta_2^*/\tau) \leq (\theta_1^*)^\gamma \theta_2. \tag{6.27}$$

In order for Eqs. (6.25) and (6.26) to hold simultaneously, we need

$$\left((\theta_1^*)^\gamma (\theta_2^*/\tau)\right)^{\gamma(\sigma-1)} + ((\theta_1)^\gamma \theta_2)^{\gamma(\sigma-1)} \leq 2\left((\theta_1^*/\tau)^\gamma \theta_2\right)^{\gamma(\sigma-1)},$$

which can be consistent with Eq. (6.27). Since $\theta_1 < \theta_1^*$ is necessary for Eq. (6.25) to hold and satisfies Eq. (6.27), this implies from Lemma 6.1 that technology spillovers in R&D occur for m_1 from the foreign country to the home country.

We finally derive the conditions for FFH to be chosen. It yields from Eqs. (6.8), (6.16), (6.19), and (6.21) that $\Pi_{FFH} \geq \Pi_{HHH}$ holds if and only if

$$\left((\theta_1^*)^\gamma (\theta_2^*/\tau)\right)^{\gamma(\sigma-1)} - (\theta_1^\gamma \theta_2)^{\gamma(\sigma-1)} \geq \frac{2\omega^{\sigma-1}\psi}{3}. \tag{6.28}$$

Also, from Eqs. (6.16), (6.17), (6.19), and (6.20) it holds that $\Pi_{FFH} \geq \Pi_{FHH}$ if and only if

$$(\theta_2^*/\tau)^{\gamma(\sigma-1)} - (\theta_2/\tau^\gamma)^{\gamma(\sigma-1)} \geq \frac{\omega^{\sigma-1}\psi}{3(\theta_1^*)^{\gamma^2(\sigma-1)}} \tag{6.29}$$

and from Eqs. (6.15), (6.16), (6.18), and (6.19) it holds that $\Pi_{FFH} \geq \Pi_{HFH}$ if and only if

$$(\theta_1^*)^{\gamma^2(\sigma-1)} - (\theta_1/\tau)^{\gamma^2(\sigma-1)} \geq \frac{\omega^{\sigma-1}\psi}{3(\theta_2^*/\tau)^{\gamma(\sigma-1)}}. \tag{6.30}$$

Since $\theta_2 < \theta_2^*$ is necessary for Eq. (6.29) to hold and satisfies Eq. (6.28), this implies from Lemma 6.1 that technology spillovers occur in R&D for m_2 from the foreign country to the home country. *Q.E.D.*

This proposition shows that if home firms engage in VFDI in the configuration of HFH, technology spillovers occur from the foreign country to the home country. Technology spillovers in the opposite direction may also occur but do not necessarily. For other types of VFDI, we expect that technology spillovers occur only in one direction from the foreign country to the home country.

Note that if the wage rates between the two countries are sufficiently different, then firms may have an incentive to engage in VFDI even in the absence of a technology difference, but VFDI does not induce international technology spillovers. This situation corresponds to the typical North-South VFDI rather than the North-North VFDI. Then, this never undermines our argument on the relationship between VFDI and technology spillovers. That is, North-South VFDI does not necessarily involve international technology spillovers.

6.6 Conclusion

In this chapter, we have investigated how the structure of MNEs' activities affects technology spillovers between MNEs and their host countries by using detailed firm-level data on Japanese MNEs and patent citation data. We propose new specifications of FDI by information on sales and purchases of foreign affiliates of MNEs. We define pure HFDI as FDI with a high share of both purchases of intermediate inputs and sales of outputs in the local market and pure VFDI as FDI with a high share of transactions (i.e., both purchases of intermediate inputs and sales of outputs) with the home country. In addition, partially horizontal and partially vertical FDI are defined.

Our estimation results reveal that when a technologically advanced country hosts Japanese MNEs, an increase in the degree of pure VFDI has a significantly positive effect on technology spillovers as measured by patent citations in both directions between the host country and Japanese MNEs. In contrast, pure HFDI has no significant effect or significantly negative effects on technology spillovers in either direction. We also find that VFDI by Japanese firms to technologically advanced countries is not based on factor price differentials.

To explain the mechanism for the observed relationship between the structure of FDI and technology spillovers, we have developed a simple model of FDI and technology spillovers, in which a good is produced in multiple stages. Our model reveals that VFDI among technologically advanced economies would be associated with international technology spillovers, while HFDI does not necessarily induce technology spillovers.

The results indicate that technology spillovers from FDI occur among technologically advanced economies. In particular, VFDI plays an important role in technology spillovers. We come to the conclusion that technologically advanced countries can gain knowledge flow from MNEs' activities both as the home country and as the host country when FDI involves the geographical fragmentation of the production process.

Another finding of this chapter is that when the host country is a technologically less advanced country, any types of FDI do not have positive effects on technology spillovers. One possible explanation for this finding is that we have focused on technology spillovers measured by patent citations. Since patent applications are made to be counted as "spillovers," indigenous firms in technologically less advanced countries do not largely benefit from technology spillovers in our definition. Another possible explanation for the finding is that it reflects the stringency of intellectual property right (IPR) protection in host countries. Branstetter et al. (2006) and Wakasugi and Ito (2009) find that the stronger protection of IPR in host countries has a positive effect on technology transfer from parent firms to their foreign affiliates. Nagaoka (2009) also finds a positive effect of stronger patent protection on expanding the scope of the recipients of technology transfer. Taking these empirical findings into account, we notice that the weaker protection of IPR in developing countries generally hinders technology spillovers from FDI in our measurement.

Since our findings are based on Japanese MNEs' data, we suggest testing whether our findings could be applicable to other countries' MNEs through examining detailed data on MNEs in other countries.

Chapter 7
Do Deep Regional Trade Agreements Enhance International Technology Spillovers? Depth, Breadth, and Heterogeneity

7.1 Introduction

In Chap. 5, we examine the relationship between bilateral trade patterns and international technology spillovers. In Chap. 6, we analyze how horizontal and vertical foreign direct investment (FDI) of multinational enterprises (MNEs) affects technology spillovers between themselves and firms in host countries. Both chapters analyze the issues from theoretical and empirical points of view. Each chapter shows that international trade or FDI is an important channel of international technology spillovers, but the effect on them is heterogeneous, depending on the type of trade patterns or the structure of FDI. In both chapters we measure technology spillovers using patent citation data.

In this chapter, we shed light on the role of deep regional trade agreements (RTAs) in international technology spillovers. As is well known in the field of international economics, trade creation and trade diversion are the most popular effects of signing an RTA (Viner 1950). The dynamic effects of RTAs such as the effects on technology adoption and technology diffusion have been examined by relatively recent studies (e.g., Bustos 2011; Das and Andriamananjara 2006; Ederington and McCalman 2008; Schiff and Wang 2003).

As Jinji et al. (2019a) argue, RTAs may facilitate cross-border technology spillovers both directly and indirectly. The indirect effects of RTAs on cross-border technology spillovers are through international trade in goods and FDI. Since RTAs, particularly deep RTAs with investment provisions, stimulate international trade and FDI, they can facilitate cross-border technology spillovers through an increase in bilateral trade and FDI. A more direct link between RTAs and cross-border technology spillovers may arise from the deep nature of recent RTAs. As examined in Chap. 2, recent RTAs tend to be deeper than old ones. Many RTAs include provisions related to technology, such as trade-related aspects of intellectual property rights (TRIPS), intellectual property right (IPR), innovation policy, and research and development (R&D). Moreover, some RTAs explicitly include provisions that stimulate

N. Jinji et al., *Deep Integration, Global Firms, and Technology Spillovers*,
Advances in Japanese Business and Economics 26,
https://doi.org/10.1007/978-981-16-5210-3_7

technology spillovers. For example, the United States-Peru Free Trade Agreement includes a provision on the promotion of innovation and technological development (Article 16.12), which encourages the engagement in collaborative scientific research projects and transfer of technology.

Using patent citations as a proxy for technology spillovers, Jinji et al. (2019a) empirically examine whether RTAs actually enhance international technology spillovers. They use panel data on patent citations at the USPTO for 114 countries/economies for the period 1991–2007. The focus of their study is on whether the depth of RTAs that is measured by the legal enforceability information on the policy areas in the WTO-X group matters for technology spillovers among member countries/economies of RTAs.[1] They show that the depth of integration actually influences technology spillovers. Interestingly, they find that deeper integration in a broad sense has a greater impact on technology spillovers than do technology-related policy areas. They classify 26 out of 38 policy areas in the WTO-X group into three subsets by utilizing the technique of the factor analysis. Then, they construct a new measure of the nature of deep RTAs by calculating the ratio of the sum of the points of legally enforceable WTO-X policy areas included in each subset that are covered by RTAs to the total points of all legally enforceable WTO-X policy areas covered by the same RTAs. They interpret the first subset as the set of policy areas representing a healthy economic environment in a general sense and the second subset as the set of policy areas representing basic social and economic conditions. The WTO-X policy areas included in these two subsets are not directly related to technology spillovers. On the other hand, the third subset is interpreted as the set of policy areas directly related to competition and technology. Their finding is that the estimated coefficients of the indexes for the first two subsets tend to be larger than those for the third subset.

The analysis in this chapter extends and enriches the study by Jinji et al. (2019a) in several ways. First, as in Jinji et al. (2019a) and Chaps. 5 and 6 of this book, we use patent citations as a proxy of technology spillovers.[2] We extend the observation period until 2015. Thus, our observation period is 25 years from 1991 to 2015. The eight-year extension of the observation period from Jinji et al. (2019a) is important because more recent RTAs tend to be much deeper. Second, when we estimate the model, we include directional country-pair fixed effects, which are not included in the analysis in Jinji et al. (2019a), as well as time-varying citing and cited countries fixed effects. As we discuss below, the inclusion of country-pair fixed effects is particularly important to address the endogeneity issue (Baier and Bergstrand 2007). Third, we include intra-national citation data in the analysis, which are not included in the estimations of Jinji et al. (2019a). This is essential to measure the effect of RTAs, as argued by Dai et al. (2014). Finally, although Jinji et al. (2019a) restrict the measurement of deep RTAs to the WTO-X policy areas, we include policy areas in

[1] See Chap. 2 for the details of the policy areas in WTO-extra (WTO-X) and WTO-plus (WTO+) groups.

[2] This approach was pioneered by Jaffe et al. (1993) and has been employed by a number of studies (e.g., Branstetter 2006; Cappelli and Montobbio 2020; Hall et al. 2001; Haruna et al. 2010; Jaffe and Trajtenberg 1999; Jinji et al. 2013, 2015; Li 2014; MacGarvie 2006; Maurseth and Verspagen 2002; Murata et al. 2014; Peri 2005).

both WTO+ and WTO-X groups and employ the classification of the policy areas in terms of the depth and breadth of RTAs proposed by Limão (2016).[3]

In this chapter, we first estimate the effects of the depth and breadth indexes of RTAs on bilateral patent citations. With regard to the depth of RTAs, we use the indexes in the fields of tariffs, non-tariff barriers (NTBs), the behind-the-border policies (BBPs), and other policies (OPs). On the other hand, as for the breadth of RTAs, we construct indexes for services, technology, investment/capital, labor, and non-economic policies (NEPs) fields. Throughout this chapter, we employ the Poisson pseudo-maximum likelihood (PPML) estimator with time-varying citing country fixed effects, time-varying cited country fixed effects, and citing-cited-pair fixed effects, which is recommended in the gravity literature (Anderson and van Wincoop 2003; Head and Mayer 2014; Santos Silva and Tenreyro 2006, 2011; Yotov et al. 2016).

We next analyze the heterogeneous effects of individual RTAs. In the trade literature, a number of previous studies find the heterogeneous effects of RTAs on trade in goods by the type of agreements (Roy 2010; Vicard 2009) and by the characteristics of country-pairs and particular countries (Baier et al. 2019; Behar and Cirera-i Crivillé 2013; Cheong et al. 2015; Vicard 2011). Although Jinji et al. (2019a) investigate the heterogeneous effects of RTAs on technology spillovers by the type of agreements (i.e., customs union versus free trade agreement) and by the characteristics of country-pairs (i.e., North and South combinations), the heterogeneous effects of individual RTAs on technology spillovers have not been investigated. As major sources of international technology spillovers, we focus on RTAs signed by the United States and European countries, such as the North American Free Trade Agreement (NAFTA), the European Community (EC)/European Union (EU), RTAs with the United States, and FTAs with the EC/EU.

The main findings of this chapter are as follows. First, we find that the estimated coefficient on the RTA dummy is positive and highly significant, which confirms the finding by Jinji et al. (2019a) and even strengthens their finding by showing that the significantly positive effect of the RTA dummy is kept even if directional country-pair fixed effects are included. Second, we find that the coefficients on the depth indexes other than the OP index are positive and highly significant, suggesting that technology spillovers among signatories of RTAs are stronger as RTAs are deeper. However, when each of the depth indexes is estimated together with the RTA dummy, the coefficient on the depth index becomes insignificant, which suggests that the additional effect of including the depth policy areas may be small or even negligible. A possible reason for the insignificant additional effect of the depth policy areas is that since most of the recent RTAs tend to become deeper and deeper, the estimated average effect of the RTA dummy partly captures the impact of the depth policy areas on technology spillovers. The problem of multicollinearity may affect the result.

Third, the estimated coefficients on the breadth indexes are all positive and statistically significant, suggesting that technology spillovers among members of RTAs become stronger as RTAs cover more policy areas with legal enforceability in each of

[3] See Chap. 2 for the details of the depth and breadth of RTAs by Limão (2016).

the breadth fields. However, similar to the depth indexes, when the breadth indexes are estimated with the RTA dummy, all of them lose their significance. Therefore, the additional effects of including legally enforceable provisions in services, technology, investment/capital, labor, or NEP fields on cross-border technology spillovers may be small or insignificant. Since some of the specific provisions in these fields actually strengthen regulations, this result implies that the same level of the index in each breadth field may include both the positive and negative effects on technology spillovers.

Finally, with regard to the heterogeneous effects of the RTAs signed by the United States and the EU, we find that the impact of NAFTA on bilateral technology spillovers is particularly strong. By contrast, the impacts of the EU and EU enlargement on technology spillovers are weak or not positive. On the other hand, both the RTAs with the United States and the FTAs with the EU enhance technology spillovers. Thus, the results suggest that signing RTAs with technologically advanced countries, such as the United States and major European countries, is effective in stimulating cross-border technology spillovers.

The remainder of the chapter is organized as follows. In Sect. 7.2, we explain the empirical framework. In Sect. 7.3, we describe the data employed in our empirical analysis. In Sect. 7.4, we present our empirical results. Section 7.5 concludes the chapter.

7.2 Empirical Framework

In this section, we explain our empirical framework to examine the effects of deep RTAs on international technology spillovers.

7.2.1 The Depth and Breadth Indexes

We first explain how we measure the contents of deep RTAs. As explained in Chap. 2, Horn et al. (2010) identify 52 policy areas covered by RTAs and classify them into two groups: WTO-plus (WTO+) and WTO-extra (WTO-X) (See Table 2.1 in Chap. 2 for the details of the WTO+ and WTO-X policy areas). Then, Limão (2016) proposes recategorizing the WTO+ and WTO-X policy areas from the viewpoints of the depth and breadth of RTAs. The depth of RTAs is measured by four fields: (a) import tariffs, (b) NTBs, (c) BBPs, and (d) OPs. On the other hand, the breadth of RTAs is measured by five fields: (a) services, (b) technology, (c) investment/capital, (d) labor, and (e) NEPs. Which policy areas are classified into each field of the depth and breadth measures is shown in Table 2.2 in Chap. 2.

For each field of the depth measure, we construct the following index:

$$RTA\_Depth\_d\_index_{ijt} = \frac{\sum_{p \in \Theta^d} Max\_LE^p_{ijt}}{2K^d}, \tag{7.1}$$

where $Depth\_d \in \{Tariff, NTB, BBP, OP\}$ indicates the fields of the depth measure, Θ^d is the set of policy areas that consist of the field $d \in \{Tariff, NTB, BBP, OP\}$, $Max\_LE^p_{ijt} \in \{0, 1, 2\}$ is the maximum point of the LE index of policy area p in all RTAs of which countries i and j are members in year t if they sign any common RTAs, and K^d is the number of policy areas in field d. Note that $2K^d$ in the denominator of Eq. (7.1) is the total points of the LE index of policy areas in field d if all LE indexes are equal to two in field d. Thus, $RTA\_Depth\_d\_index_{ijt}$ takes the value between zero and one.

Similar to the depth measure, we construct the following index for each field of the breadth measure:

$$RTA\_Breadth\_c\_index_{ijt} = \frac{\sum_{p \in \Theta^c} Max\_LE^p_{ijt}}{2K^c}, \tag{7.2}$$

where $Breadth\_c \in \{GATS, Tech, Cap, Lab, non-EP\}$ indicates the fields of the breadth measure, Θ^c is the set of policy areas that consist of the field $c \in \{GATS, Tech, Cap, Lab, non-EP\}$, $Max\_LE^p_{ijt} \in \{0, 1, 2\}$ is the maximum point of the LE index of policy area p in all RTAs of which countries i and j are members in year t if they sign any common RTAs, and K^c is the number of policy areas in field c.

7.2.2 RTA Dummies

Let us next explain our RTA dummies. In addition to the usual RTA dummy, we use various dummies to capture the heterogeneous effects of individual RTAs by decomposing the RTA dummy.

First of all, $RTA\ dummy_{ijt}$ is a dummy variable that takes the value of unity if countries i and j both belong to the same RTA in t and zero otherwise. Next, we decompose the $RTA\ dummy_{ijt}$ in two ways. The first decomposition is to take into account the NAFTA and the EC/EU. That is, we set $NAFTA_{ijt}$, which is a dummy variable that takes the value of unity if countries i and j both belong to the NAFTA in t and zero otherwise. Similarly, EU_{ijt} is a dummy variable that takes the value of unity if they both belong to the EC/EU in t and zero otherwise. Furthermore, we set $Other\_RTA_{ijt}$, which is a dummy variable that takes the value of unity if they both belong to the same RTA other than the NAFTA and the EC/EU in t and zero otherwise.

Next, our second decomposition of the RTA dummy is to take into account RTAs signed by the United States other than the NAFTA and EU enlargement from 1995. We construct $RTA\_with\_US_{ijt}$, which is a dummy variable that takes the value of unity if either of countries i and j is the United States and the two countries belong to the same RTA other than the NAFTA in t and zero otherwise. $EU\_Enlarge_{ijt}$ is a dummy variable that takes the value of unity if at least one of the two countries (i and j) becomes a member of the EU in or after 1995 and both they are the members of the EU in year t and zero otherwise. Moreover, $FTA\_with\_EU_{ijt}$ is a dummy variable that takes the value of unity if either of countries i and j is a member of the EC/EU in t and the other country is not a member of the EC/EU in t but countries i and j belong to the same FTA in t and zero otherwise. Finally, $non\_US\_EU\_RTA_{ijt}$ is a dummy variable that takes the value of unity if they belong to the same RTA in t and $NAFTA_{ijt} = EU_{ijt} = RTA\_with\_US_{ijt} = EU\_Enlarge_{ijt} = FTA\_with\_EU_{ijt} = 0$ holds for them in t and zero otherwise.[4]

In addition, we use the GATT/WTO dummy. That is, $WTO\ dummy_{ijt}$ is a dummy variable that takes the value of unity if both of countries i and j are GATT/WTO members in t and zero otherwise.

7.2.3 Empirical Model and Strategy

We next specify a model of knowledge flows between countries and discuss our empirical strategy to estimate the model.

We first measure technology spillovers from country j to country i at time t by extending the framework proposed by Jaffe et al. (1993), Jaffe and Trajtenberg (1999), and Peri (2005). Let Φ_{ijt} be the actual flow of knowledge from country j to country i at time t in terms of the actual effects on the research output in country i. Then, we assume that Φ_{ijt} depends on both the knowledge stock in country j at t, K_{jt}, and the research ability of firms in country i at t, Q_{it}, as follows:

$$\Phi_{ijt} = (Q_{it})^{\alpha_1}(\tilde{\phi}_{ijt}K_{jt})^{\alpha_2}, \tag{7.3}$$

where $\tilde{\phi}_{ijt} \in [0, 1]$ is the degree of accessibility for firms in country i to the knowledge stock in country j at t. Thus, $(\tilde{\phi}_{ijt}K_{jt})$ is the effective unit of country j's knowledge stock from the perspective of firms in country i. Parameters α_1 and α_2 are both positive. For notational simplicity, we relabel $\tilde{\phi}_{ijt}$ as $\phi_{ijt} \equiv (\tilde{\phi}_{ijt})^{\alpha_2}$.

The degree of accessibility for firms in country i to the knowledge stock in country j at t, ϕ_{ijt}, depends on the *economic distance* between countries i and j, which is affected by not only bilateral geographical distance but also other potential *resistance factors* (Peri 2005, p. 310). The resistance factors include both time-invariant and time-varying country-pair specific characteristics. The time-invariant country-pair specific characteristics include bilateral geographical distance, the use of a common

[4] Note that in the second decomposition we do not set a dummy variable for the country-pairs of which both countries were the members of the EC/EU before 1995. However, with the use of country-pair fixed effects in our estimations, this omission of the dummy variable for the old members of the EC/EU does not affect the estimations, because this dummy always takes the value of unity during our observation period.

language, and so on. On the other hand, the time-varying country-pair specific characteristics, which affect the economic distance between two countries, are typically represented by the membership of the same RTA and that of GATT/WTO.

Let $\boldsymbol{x}_{ijt}$ be a set of bilateral country characteristics. Then, we have

$$\begin{aligned}\phi_{ijt} &= \phi(\boldsymbol{x}_{ijt}) \\ &= e^{\xi_{ij}} e^{\gamma_1(RTA\ dummies_{ijt})} e^{\gamma_2(DRTA\_index_{ijt})} \\ &\quad \times e^{\gamma_3(WTO\ dummy_{ijt})},\end{aligned} \tag{7.4}$$

where ξ_{ij} denotes the time-invariant country-pair specific characteristics and $DRTA\_index_{ijt}$ denotes various indexes of the depth and breadth of RTAs.

Since Φ_{ijt}, Q_{it}, and K_{jt} in Eq. (7.3) are not directly observable, we need to use some proxies for those variables in our analysis. We use C_{ijt}, the number of patent citations made by the patents of country i to those of country j at time t, as a proxy for Φ_{ijt}. Moreover, following the gravity literature (Head and Mayer 2014; Yotov et al. 2016), we capture Q_{it} by the time-varying citing country fixed effects, $\tilde{\mu}_{it}$, and K_{jt} by the time-varying cited country fixed effects, $\tilde{\nu}_{jt}$. According to Peri (2005), we assume the following relationship between C_{ijt} and Φ_{ijt}:

$$C_{ijt} = \tilde{\lambda}_{ij} \Phi_{ijt} e^{\epsilon_{ijt}}, \tag{7.5}$$

where $\tilde{\lambda}_{ij}$ denotes the time-invariant individual effect associated with patent citations between the two countries and $e^{\epsilon_{ijt}}$ is an error term with zero-mean distribution.

Substitute Eqs. (7.3) and (7.4), $\tilde{\mu}_{it}$ and $\tilde{\nu}_{jt}$ into Eq. (7.5) to obtain

$$\begin{aligned}C_{ijt} &= \tilde{\lambda}_{ij} (\tilde{\mu}_{it})^{\alpha_1} (\tilde{\nu}_{it})^{\alpha_2} e^{\xi_{ij}} e^{\gamma_1(RTA\ dummies_{ijt})} e^{\gamma_2(DRTA\_index_{ijt})} \\ &\quad \times e^{\gamma_3(WTO\ dummy_{ijt})} e^{\epsilon_{ijt}}.\end{aligned} \tag{7.6}$$

This equation is quite similar to the standard gravity equation that specifies the relationship between the volume of bilateral trade and the market sizes of the two countries with bilateral geographical distance (Anderson and van Wincoop 2003; Head and Mayer 2014; Yotov et al. 2016). By redefining the fixed effects variables, Eq. (7.6) can be rewritten as

$$\begin{aligned}C_{ijt} = \exp\Big(&\gamma_1 RTA\ dummies_{ijt} + \gamma_2 DRTA\_index_{ijt} + \gamma_3 WTO\ dummy_{ijt} \\ &+ \zeta_{ij} + \mu_{it} + \nu_{jt} + \epsilon_{ijt}\Big).\end{aligned} \tag{7.7}$$

Equation (7.7) is our estimation equation for the analysis in Sect. 7.4. In this equation, we use the RTA dummy and the decomposed RTA dummies that we construct in Sect. 7.2.2. We also use the depth and breadth indexes that we construct in Sect. 7.2.1 for $DRTA\_index_{ijt}$. In the estimations, we make use of one-year lagged variables for $RTA\ dummies_{ijt}$, $DRTA\_index_{ijt}$, and $WTO\ dummy_{ijt}$.

In the estimations, we employ the PPML estimator with time-varying citing country fixed effects, time-varying cited country fixed effects, and directional country-pair fixed effects, recommended in the gravity literature (Anderson and van Wincoop 2003; Head and Mayer 2014; Santos Silva and Tenreyro 2006, 2011; Yotov et al. 2016). As is popularly argued in the gravity literature, the use of PPML estimator with time-varying country fixed effects can address the issues of many observations with zero value for the dependent variable and unobservable multilateral resistance terms. Now there is one important issue that we should address the potential endogeneity of RTAs. Possible sources of such endogeneity are the existence of an omitted variable bias and reverse causality (Baier and Bergstrand 2007). Baier and Bergstrand (2007) and Yotov et al. (2016) recommend the use of country-pair fixed effects to take "the unobservable linkages between the endogenous trade policy covariate and the error term in gravity regressions" (Yotov et al. 2016, p.21) into account. We follow their recommendation and include citing-cited-country-pair fixed effects in our estimations to address the endogeneity issue.

7.3 Description of the Data

The data on patent citations are taken from the Global 2019 edition of the EPO Worldwide Patent Statistical Database (PATSTAT). We extract the patent statistics of the USPTO from the PATSTAT.[5] This dataset includes information on the application date, the country name of the assignee, the main US patent class, and citations made and received for each patent. We use patent citation data from 1991 to 2015 for our analysis.

The sample includes all countries and economies that are included in the USPTO data during the observation period. Our sample covers 243 countries and economies, which are listed in Table 7.1. We then construct a panel of 11,667 pairs of the citing and cited countries/economies for 25 years from 1991 to 2015.

Data on RTAs are taken from the database provided by Mario Larch (Egger and Larch 2008),[6] and data on the content of RTAs are taken from the World Bank's website.[7]

Table 7.2 shows the descriptive statistics of the variables.

7.4 Empirical Results

In this section, we report our estimation results.

---

[5] We also extract the patent statistics of the EPO and use them for a robustness check.

[6] www.ewf.uni-bayreuth.de/en/research/RTA-data/index.html.

[7] This dataset was originally provided by Horn et al. (2010) and extended by Hofmann et al. (2019) (datacatalog.worldbank.org/dataset/content-deep-trade-agreements).

Table 7.1 Sampled countries/economies

No.	Country/Economy	No.	Country/Economy	No.	Country/Economy	No.	Country/Economy
1	Afghanistan	64	Dominican Rep.	126	Liberia	187	Saint Kitts & Nevis
2	Aland Islands	65	Ecuador	127	Libya	188	Saint Lucia
3	Albania	66	Egypt	128	Liechtenstein	189	Saint Pierre and Miquelon
4	Algeria	67	El Salvador	129	Lithuania		
5	American Samoa	68	Equatorial Guinea	130	Luxembourg	190	Saint Vincent & the Grenadines
6	Andorra	69	Eritrea	131	Macao		
7	Angola	70	Estonia	132	Madagascar	191	Samoa
8	Anguilla	71	Eswatini	133	Malawi	192	San Marino
9	Antarctica	72	Ethiopia	134	Malaysia	193	Sao Tome & Principe
10	Antigua and Barbuda	73	Falkland Islands	135	Maldives	194	Saudi Arabia
11	Argentina	74	Faroe Islands	136	Mali	195	Senegal
12	Armenia	75	Fiji	137	Malta	196	Serbia & Montenegro
13	Aruba	76	Finland	138	Marshall Islands	197	Seychelles
14	Australia	77	France	139	Martinique	198	Sierra Leone
15	Austria	78	French Guiana	140	Mauritania	199	Singapore
16	Azerbaijan	79	French Polynesia	141	Mauritius	200	Sint Maarten
17	Bahamas	80	French Southern Territories	142	Mexico	201	Slovakia
18	Bahrain			143	Micronesia	202	Slovenia
19	Bangladesh	81	Gabon	144	Moldova	203	Solomon Islands
20	Barbados	82	Gambia	145	Monaco	204	Somalia
21	Belarus	83	Georgia	146	Mongolia	205	South Africa
22	Belgium	84	Germany	147	Montenegro	206	Spain
23	Belize	85	Ghana	148	Montserrat	207	Sri Lanka
24	Benin	86	Gibraltar	149	Morocco	208	Sudan (the)
25	Bermuda	87	Greece	150	Mozambique	209	Suriname
26	Bhutan	88	Greenland	151	Myanmar	210	Svalbard & Jan Mayen
27	Bolivia	89	Grenada	152	Namibia		
28	Bonaire, Sint Eustatius & Saba	90	Guadeloupe	153	Nauru	211	Sweden
		91	Guam	154	Nepal	212	Switzerland
29	Bosnia and Herzegovina	92	Guatemala	155	Netherlands	213	Syrian Arab Rep.
30	Botswana	93	Guernsey	156	Netherlands antilles	214	Taiwan
31	Bouvet Island	94	Guinea	157	New Caledonia	215	Tajikistan
32	Brazil	95	Guyana	158	New Zealand	216	Tanzania
33	British Indian Ocean Territory	96	Haiti	159	Nicaragua	217	Thailand
		97	Heard Islands & McDonald Islands	160	Niger (the)	218	Togo
34	Brunei Darussalam			161	Nigeria	219	Tokelau
35	Bulgaria	98	Holy See	162	Niue	220	Tonga
36	Burkina Faso	99	Honduras	163	Norfolk Island	221	Trinidad & Tobago
37	Burundi	100	Hong Kong	164	Northern Mariana Islands	222	Tunisia
38	Cabo Verde	101	Hungary			223	Turkey
39	Cambodia	102	Iceland	165	Norway	224	Turkmenistan
40	Cameroon	103	India	166	Oman	225	Turks & Caicos

(continued)

Table 7.1 (continued)

No.	Country/Economy	No.	Country/Economy	No.	Country/Economy	No.	Country/Economy
41	Canada	104	Indonesia	167	Pakistan		Islands
42	Cayman Islands	105	Iran	168	Palau	226	Tuvalu
43	Central African Republic	106	Iraq	169	Palestine, State of	227	Uganda
		107	Ireland	170	Panama	228	Ukraine
44	Chad	108	Isle of Man	171	Papua New Guinea	229	UAE
45	Chile	109	Israel	172	Paraguay	230	United Kingdom
46	China	110	Italy	173	Peru	231	US Minor Outlying Islands
47	Christmas Island	111	Jamaica	174	Philippines		
48	Cocos Islands	112	Japan	175	Pitcairn	232	United States
49	Colombia	113	Jersey	176	Poland	233	Uruguay
51	Congo	114	Jordan	177	Portugal	234	Uzbekistan
52	Congo, Dem. Rep.	115	Kazakhstan	178	Puerto Rico	235	Vanuatu
53	Cook Islands	116	Kenya	179	Qatar	236	Venezuela
54	Costa Rica	117	Kiribati	180	Rep. of North Macedonia	237	Viet Nam
55	Cote d'Ivoire	118	Korea, Dem. People's Rep.			238	Virgin Islands, British
56	Croatia			181	Reunion	239	Virgin Islands, US
57	Cuba	119	Korea, Rep. of	182	Romania	240	Wallis and Futuna
58	Curacao	120	Kuwait	183	Russian Federation	241	Yemen
59	Cyprus	121	Kyrgyzstan	184	Rwanda	242	Zambia
60	Czechia	122	Laos	185	Saint Barthelemy	243	Zimbabwe
61	Denmark	123	Latvia	186	Saint Helena, Ascension & Tristan da Cunha		
62	Djibouti	124	Lebanon				
63	Dominica	125	Lesotho				

7.4.1 The Depth of RTAs

First, we estimate the impact of the depth of RTAs on bilateral technology spillovers. The results obtained are reported in Table 7.3. Column (1) shows that the estimated coefficient on the RTA dummy is positive and highly significant. This result confirms the finding by Jinji et al. (2019a) and strengthens their finding by showing that the significantly positive effect of the RTA dummy remains even when directional country-pair fixed effects are included. Signing an RTA increases bilateral citation of patents by 4.8% on average.[8]

The effects of the four depth indexes are shown in columns (2)–(5). The coefficients on the first three depth indexes are positive and highly significant. The estimated coefficient on RTA_Tariff_index is 0.042. Since this index consists of two policy areas with four points in total, an increase in one policy area from zero points to two points (i.e., a change from no legal enforceability to legally enforceable

[8] $(e^{0.047} - 1) \times 100 \approx 4.8$.

Table 7.2 Descriptive statistics

Variable	No. of Obs	Mean	Std. Dev.	Min	Max
C_{ijt}	291,675	527.023	28134.360	0	4,677,583
$RTA\ dummy_{ij,t-1}$	291,675	0.206	0.405	0	1
$RTA\_Tariff\_index_{ij,t-1}$	291,675	0.121	0.325	0	1
$RTA\_NTB\_index_{ij,t-1}$	291,675	0.095	0.272	0	1
$RTA\_BBP\_index_{ij,t-1}$	291,675	0.073	0.220	0	1
$RTA\_OP\_index_{ij,t-1}$	291,675	0.035	0.150	0	1
$RTA\_GATS\_index_{ij,t-1}$	291,675	0.073	0.261	0	1
$RTA\_Tech\_index_{ij,t-1}$	291,675	0.045	0.147	0	0.667
$RTA\_Cap\_index_{ij,t-1}$	291,675	0.068	0.225	0	1
$RTA\_Lab\_index_{ij,t-1}$	291,675	0.049	0.194	0	1
$RTA\_nonEP\_index_{ij,t-1}$	291,675	0.022	0.095	0	0.556
$WTO\ dummy_{ij,t-1}$	291,675	0.567	0.500	0	1
$NAFTA_{ij,t-1}$	291,675	0.0004	0.021	0	1
$EU_{ij,t-1}$	291,675	0.035	0.185	0	1
$RTA\_with\_US_{ij,t-1}$	291,675	0.001	0.032	0	1
$EU\_Enlarge_{ij,t-1}$	291,675	0.005	0.070	0	1
$FTA\_with\_EU_{ij,t-1}$	291,675	0.051	0.220	0	1
$Other\_RTA_{ij,t-1}$	291,675	0.172	0.378	0	1
$non\_US\_EU\_RTA_{ij,t-1}$	291,675	0.151	0.358	0	1

policy area) raises bilateral citation of patents by 2.1% on average.[9] Similarly, the estimated coefficients of the RTA_NTB_index and the RTA_BBP_index are 0.059 and 0.066, where RTA_NTB_index and RTA_BBP_index consist of five policy areas and six policy areas, respectively. Thus, an increase in one policy area from zero points to two points raises bilateral citation of patents by 1.0% for the NTB index and 1.4% for the BBP index, respectively.[10] Only the estimated coefficient on the RTA_OP_index is insignificant.

Columns (6) and (8) show the results on estimations when the RTA dummy and each of RTA_NTB_index, RTA_BBP_index, or RTA_OP_index are jointly used as explanatory variables. The results may suffer from the problem of multicollinearity as the correlations among the RTA dummy and the depth indexes are high. In column (6), both the RTA dummy and the RTA_NTB_index become insignificant, whereas in columns (7) and (8) the coefficient on the RTA dummy is positive and significant but that on the RTA_BBP_index or the RTA_OP_index is insignificant. These results imply that the additional effect of including the depth policy areas in the fields of NTB, BBP, and OP may be small or even insignificant. A possible reason for the insignificant additional effect of the depth policy areas is

9 $(e^{0.042} - 1) \times (1/4) \times 2 \times 100 \approx 2.1$.

10 $(e^{0.059} - 1) \times (1/10) \times 2 \times 100 \approx 1.0$ and $(e^{0.066} - 1) \times (1/12) \times 2 \times 100 \approx 1.4$.

Table 7.3 The impact of the depth indexes on technology spillovers

	(1)	(2)	(3)	(4)	(5)	(6)	(7)	(8)
$RTA\ dummy_{ij,t-1}$	0.047***					0.021	0.044**	0.049***
	(0.011)					(0.029)	(0.022)	(0.012)
$RTA\_Tariff\_index_{ij,t-1}$		0.042***						
		(0.011)						
$RTA\_NTB\_index_{ij,t-1}$			0.059***			0.036		
			(0.013)			(0.037)		
$RTA\_BBP\_index_{ij,t-1}$				0.066***			0.006	
				(0.020)			(0.039)	
$RTA\_OP\_index_{ij,t-1}$					0.043			−0.029
					(0.072)			(0.065)
$WTO\ dummy_{ij,t-1}$	0.263**	0.264**	0.264**	0.264**	0.263**	0.264**	0.263**	0.263**
	(0.108)	(0.108)	(0.108)	(0.108)	(0.108)	(0.108)	(0.108)	(0.108)
Citing country-year FE	Yes	Yes	Yes	Yes	Yes	Yes	Yes	Yes
Cited country-year FE	Yes	Yes	Yes	Yes	Yes	Yes	Yes	Yes
Directional country-pair FE	Yes	Yes	Yes	Yes	Yes	Yes	Yes	Yes
No. of observations	236,953	236,953	236,953	236,953	236,953	236,953	236,953	236,953

Notes: (a) Estimations were implemented using Stata command `ppmlhdfe`
(b) ***, **, and * indicate statistical significance at the 1%, 5%, and 10% levels, respectively
(c) Standard errors clustered by country-pair are in parentheses
(d) The regressions include a constant term

that most of the RTAs that have recently been signed tend to be increasingly deeper. Thus, we can conclude that the estimated average effect of the RTA dummy partly captures the impact of the depth policy areas on technology spillovers.

By contrast, the estimated coefficient on the WTO dummy is positive and highly significant in all columns, and its magnitude is large. If both countries are members of GATT/WTO, then bilateral citations of patents are on average 30.2% higher than those in other types of country-pairs.[11]

7.4.2 The Breadth of RTAs

We next estimate the impact of the breadth of RTAs on bilateral technology spillovers. Estimated results are shown in Table 7.4. Columns (1)–(5) indicate the individual effect of the five breadth indexes: RTA_GATS_index, RTA_Tech_index, RTA_Cap_index, RTA_Lab_index, and RTA_nonEP_index. The estimated coefficients are positive and statistically significant for all of them. For example, the estimated coefficient on the RTA_GATS_index is 0.045 and the GATS field consists of just one policy area, so that an increase in this index from zero points to two points raises cross-border citations of patents by 4.6%.[12] Since the coefficient on the RTA_Tech_index is 0.084 and the technology field consists of six policy areas, an increase in one technology-related policy area from zero points to two points raises bilateral citations of patents by 1.5%.[13] Similarly, since the coefficient on the RTA_Cap_index is 0.045 and the investment/capital field is comprised of three policy areas, an increase in one investment/capital policy area from zero points to two points raises bilateral citations of patents by 1.5%.[14] On the other hand, the impact of the labor-related policy fields becomes much larger. The estimated coefficient on the RTA_Lab_index is 0.133. The labor field consists of four policy areas, so that a rise in one labor-related policy area from zero point to two points causes bilateral citations of patents by 3.6% to increase.[15] The larger impact of the RTAs with legally enforceable labor-related policy areas than those with technology and investment/capital policy areas implies that the movement of workers across countries stimulated by signing RTAs is an important channel of technology spillovers. In column (5), the coefficient on the RTA_nonEP_index is 0.189, where the NEP field consists of nine policy areas, so an increase in one NEP policy area from zero point to two points raises bilateral citations of patents by 2.3%.[16]

Compared with the results above, the results presented in columns (6)–(10) indicate that all of them lose their statistical significance when the breadth indexes are

---

11 $(e^{0.264} - 1) \times 100 \approx 30.2$.

12 $(e^{0.045} - 1) \times (1/2) \times 2 \times 100 \approx 4.6$.

13 $(e^{0.084} - 1) \times (1/12) \times 2 \times 100 \approx 1.5$.

14 $(e^{0.045} - 1) \times (1/6) \times 2 \times 100 \approx 1.5$.

15 $(e^{0.133} - 1) \times (1/8) \times 2 \times 100 \approx 3.6$.

16 $(e^{0.189} - 1) \times (1/18) \times 2 \times 100 \approx 2.3$.

Table 7.4 The impact of the breadth indexes on technology spillovers

	(1)	(2)	(3)	(4)	(5)	(6)	(7)	(8)	(9)	(10)
$RTA\ dummy_{ij,t-1}$						0.032 (0.025)	0.060*** (0.022)	0.051* (0.028)	0.041*** (0.011)	0.042*** (0.016)
$RTA\_GATS\_index_{ij,t-1}$	0.045*** (0.011)					0.016 (0.027)				
$RTA\_Tech\_index_{ij,t-1}$		0.084** (0.036)					−0.039 (0.062)			
$RTA\_Cap\_index_{ij,t-1}$			0.045*** (0.012)					−0.004 (0.029)		
$RTA\_Lab\_index_{ij,t-1}$				0.133*** (0.047)					0.044 (0.046)	
$RTA\_nonEP\_index_{ij,t-1}$					0.189*** (0.064)					0.039 (0.085)
$WTO\ dummy_{ij,t-1}$	0.264** (0.108)	0.264** (0.108)	0.264** (0.108)	0.263** (0.108)	0.263** (0.108)	0.264** (0.108)	0.263** (0.108)	0.263** (0.108)	0.263** (0.108)	0.263** (0.108)
Citing country-year FE	Yes	Yes	Yes	Yes	Yes	Yes	Yes	Yes	Yes	Yes
Cited country-year FE	Yes	Yes	Yes	Yes	Yes	Yes	Yes	Yes	Yes	Yes
Directional country-pair FE	Yes	Yes	Yes	Yes	Yes	Yes	Yes	Yes	Yes	Yes
No. of observations	236,953	236,953	236,953	236,953	236,953	236,953	236,953	236,953	236,953	236,953

Notes: (a) Estimations were implemented using Stata command `ppmlhdfe`
(b) ***, **, and * indicate statistical significance at the 1%, 5%, and 10% levels, respectively
(c) Standard errors clustered by country-pair are in parentheses
(d) The regressions include a constant term

estimated with the RTA dummy. This means that the additional effect of including legally enforceable policy areas in services, technology, investment/capital, labor, or NEP field on bilateral technology spillovers may be negligible. However, it should be noted that the problem of multicollinearity may distort the estimated coefficients of the breadth indexes. Moreover, the inclusion of legally enforceable policy areas in services, technology, investment/capital, labor, or NEP field does not necessarily increase bilateral citations of patents because some of the policy areas in these fields actually strengthen regulations. The same level of the index in each breadth field may include not only the positive effect but also the negative effect on technology spillovers. Consequently, the positive impact of the breadth index may be weakened.

Note that the estimated coefficient on the WTO dummy in Table 7.4 is almost the same as that in Table 7.3.

7.4.3 Heterogeneous Effects of RTAs by the United States and the EU

Our next focus is on the heterogeneous effects of the RTAs signed by the United States and the EU. Table 7.5 shows the estimated results. Column (1) shows the effects of the NAFTA and the EU. Interestingly, while the estimated coefficient on the $NAFTA$ dummy is positive and highly significant, that of the EU dummy is negative and significant. NAFTA increases bilateral citations of patents among Canada, Mexico, and the United States by 28.5% on average.[17] The NAFTA membership is fairly comparable in magnitude to the GATT/WTO membership.

Column (2) reports the effects of RTAs with the United States, EU enlargement, and FTAs with the EU. RTAs with the United States, other than NAFTA, have on average a positive and significant effect on bilateral patent citations. Moreover, although the impact of EU enlargement is insignificant, FTAs with the EU affect positively bilateral patent citations on average. These results suggest that the impact of NAFTA is much larger than that of other RTAs.

7.4.4 Robustness Check

The large impact of NAFTA and the small one of the EU on bilateral citations of patents shown in the previous subsection may be due to the use of the USPTO data. In other words, one may suspect that the home bias may cause the heterogeneous effects between NAFTA and the EU.

To check the robustness of the finding in the previous subsection, we employ the EPO data and construct the dataset, so that the same country-pairs are included in both the USPTO and the EPO citations. Then, we estimate the same specifications

[17] $(e^{0.251} - 1) \times 100 \approx 28.5$.

Table 7.5 Heterogeneous effects of RTAs by the United States and the EU

	(1)	(2)
$NAFTA_{ij,t-1}$	0.251***	0.259***
	(0.090)	(0.092)
$EU_{ij,t-1}$	−0.089*	
	(0.046)	
$Other\_RTA_{ij,t-1}$	0.040***	
	(0.011)	
$RTA\_with\_US_{ij,t-1}$		0.054***
		(0.011)
$EU\_Enlarge_{ij,t-1}$		0.078
		(0.075)
$FTA\_with\_EU_{ij,t-1}$		0.093***
		(0.023)
$non\_US\_EU\_RTA_{ij,t-1}$		−0.009
		(0.025)
$WTO\ dummy_{ij,t-1}$	0.263**	0.264**
	(0.108)	(0.108)
Citing country-year FE	Yes	Yes
Cited country-year FE	Yes	Yes
Directional country-pair FE	Yes	Yes
No. of observations	236,953	236,953

Notes: (a) Estimations were implemented using Stata command `ppmlhdfe`
(b) ***, **, and * indicate statistical significance at the 1%, 5%, and 10% levels respectively
(c) Standard errors clustered by country-pair are in parentheses
(d) The regressions include a constant term

with those in Table 7.5 for both the USPTO and the EPO citations. The results are reported in Table 7.6. Columns (1) and (2) show the results of the USPTO citations, and columns (3) and (4) show those of the EPO citations.

Comparing the estimated coefficients on the $NAFTA$ dummy in columns (1)–(2) and columns (3)–(4), the coefficient is positive in both columns (3)–(4) and significant in column (4), although the magnitude becomes smaller in columns (3)–(4). By contrast, the coefficient on the EU dummy is negative and significant in both columns (1) and (3). The estimated coefficient on the EU enlargement dummy is insignificant in both columns (2) and (4). Moreover, whereas the coefficient on the FTA_with_EU dummy is positive and significant in column (2), it is negative and insignificant in column (4).

We conclude that the findings in Table 7.5 are not due to the home bias and that these findings are robust.

Table 7.6 Robustness check: USPTO citations versus EPO citations

	(1)	(2)	(3)	(4)
	USPTO	USPTO	EPO	EPO
$NAFTA_{ij,t-1}$	0.251***	0.259***	0.128	0.196*
	(0.090)	(0.092)	(0.114)	(0.115)
$EU_{ij,t-1}$	−0.094*		−0.149***	
	(0.046)		(0.043)	
$Other\_RTA_{ij,t-1}$	0.040***		−0.081***	
	(0.011)		(0.026)	
$RTA\_with\_US_{ij,t-1}$		0.054***		−0.010
		(0.011)		(0.034)
$EU\_Enlarge_{ij,t-1}$		0.078		−0.053
		(0.075)		(0.061)
$FTA\_with\_EU_{ij,t-1}$		0.093***		−0.039
		(0.024)		(0.032)
$non\_US\_EU\_RTA_{ij,t-1}$		−0.010		−0.070*
		(0.026)		(0.036)
$WTO\ dummy_{ij,t-1}$	0.269**	0.270**	0.664***	0.665***
	(0.110)	(0.110)	(0.207)	(0.207)
Citing country-year FE	Yes	Yes	Yes	Yes
Cited country-year FE	Yes	Yes	Yes	Yes
Directional country-pair FE	Yes	Yes	Yes	Yes
No. of observations	98,546	98,546	84,578	84,578

Notes: (1) Estimations were implemented using Stata command `ppmlhdfe`
(2) ***, **, and * indicate statistical significance at the 1%, 5%, and 10% levels, respectively
(3) Standard errors clustered by country-pair are in parentheses
(4) The regressions include a constant term

7.5 Conclusion

In this chapter, we investigated the impact of deep RTAs on international technology spillovers, employing patent citations as a proxy of technology spillovers. We extended and enriched the research by Jinji et al. (2019a) in several ways. The focus of our research is on the impacts of the depth and breadth of RTAs and the heterogeneous effects of individual RTAs on international technology spillovers.

Our main findings are as follows. First, we confirmed the finding by Jinji et al. (2019a) that RTAs significantly enhance international technology spillovers measured by bilateral patent citations. We actually strengthened their finding by deriving the one that the significantly positive coefficient on the RTA dummy is kept even when the model is estimated with directional country-pair fixed effects.

Second, we found that deep RTAs with higher coverage of policy areas in the depth fields such as tariffs, NTBs, and BBPs, and those with higher coverage of policy areas in the breadth fields such as services, technology, investment/capital, labor, and NEPs at the legally enforceable level have positive effects on international technology spillovers. The additional effects of including the depth or breadth policy areas may be small or even negligible. This may be because the estimated average effect of the RTA dummy partly captures the impact of the depth policy areas on technology spillovers as recent RTAs tend to be increasingly deeper. Moreover, with regard to the breadth fields, the same level of the breadth index may include both the positive and negative effects on technology spillovers, as some policy areas actually strengthen rather than relax regulations. Finally, we found that the NAFTA has a strongly positive impact on international spillovers, whereas the impacts of the EU and EU enlargement on technology spillovers are weak or not positive. However, the RTAs with the United States and the FTAs with the EU both positively affect technology spillovers.

Our empirical results imply that signing deep RTAs with higher coverage of the depth or breadth policy areas is quite effective to enhance bilateral technology spillovers. In addition, signing RTAs with technologically advanced countries, such as the United States and major European countries, is also effective in stimulating cross-border technology spillovers.

Chapter 8
Conclusion and Policy Implications

After about a quarter century of countries having pursued deep regional integration through negotiating on deep regional trade agreements (RTAs), we observed a number of historical events that symbolize the curbing of the trend of globalization in 2016. On June 24, 2016, the people of the United Kingdom voted to leave the European Union (EU) in a referendum. On November 8, 2016, Mr. Donald Trump, who proposed the "America First" policy and a number of protectionist policies, such as the withdrawal from the Trans-Pacific Partnership Agreement and the construction of a substantial wall on the United States–Mexico border, during his presidential campaign, won the US presidential election.

Since then, it seems that the world has been taking "a momentary pause" (Baier et al. 2019), at least until 2020, in the trend toward deep integration. For example, after the Brexit referendum in 2016, the United Kingdom struggled for more than three years to decide whether and when it would actually leave the EU. Finally, it withdrew from the EU on January 31, 2020. On the other hand, the Trump administration of the United States implemented various unprecedented protectionist policies. It increased tariffs on imports from China, which was retaliated by China and resulted in a trade war. As pledged in Mr. Trump's election campaign, the United States withdrew from the Trans-Pacific Partnership Agreement on January 23, 2017, and suspended negotiations with the EU for the Transatlantic Trade and Investment Partnership Agreement. Moreover, the Trump administration re-negotiated over the NAFTA with Canada and Mexico and signed a new agreement called the United States–Mexico–Canada Agreement, which entered into force on July 1, 2020. With regard to trade negotiations, the Trump administration emphasized bilateralism rather than multilateralism or pluralism.

In 2020, due to the spread of COVID-19, major countries closed national borders and implemented lockdown policies to limit the movement of people both across and within countries. Shortages of masks and other medical materials made it difficult to

N. Jinji et al., *Deep Integration, Global Firms, and Technology Spillovers*,
Advances in Japanese Business and Economics 26,
https://doi.org/10.1007/978-981-16-5210-3_8

maintain free trade in those goods. Moreover, there has been a surge in protectionism for trade in COVID-19 vaccines. Like all other countries, the countries producing the vaccines want to vaccinate their people against COVID-19 as quickly as possible. For example, then US President Donald Trump signed an executive order to use US-made vaccines to meet their domestic demand first in December 2020. The European Commission announced in January 2021 that the EU was to introduce tighter rules over the exports of COVID-19 vaccines to non-EU countries. In March 2021, those tighter export measures were extended to June 2021.

In contrast to the waves of protectionism due to COVID-19, moves toward deep integration were partially regained in 2020. For example, the Regional Comprehensive Economic Partnership (RCEP), which has been negotiated by 10 Association of South-East Asian Nations (ASEAN) countries and six Asia-Pacific countries (Australia, China, India, Japan, New Zealand, and South Korea) since 2012, was signed by 15 countries excluding India on November 15, 2020. It is expected that RCEP will enter into force by the end of 2021. Moreover, in a foreign policy speech in February 2021, US President Joe Biden stated that the United States would work with the international community to tackle global challenges, such as the COVID-19 pandemic and climate change, and to advance freedom and dignity for people in the world. In spite of this US departure from unilateralism, the so-called "economic decoupling" between the United States and China may be accelerated.

So, the world economy seems to be currently in the mixed situation of slowly regaining the momentum of globalization and protectionism/nationalism. The main topics in this book, namely, deep integration, global firms, and technology spillovers, will continue to be important issues in economic research. In this chapter, we summarize the findings from the analyses in the book and discuss the issues for future research.

This final chapter of the book is organized as follows. In Sect. 8.1, we summarize the main findings in this book. In Sect. 8.2, we discuss policy implications that are obtained from our findings. Finally, the issues for future research are discussed in Sect. 8.3.

8.1 Summary of the Main Findings

In this section, we summarize the main findings of the research outlined in Chaps. 2–7.

8.1.1 The Trend of Deep Regional Integration in the Asia-Pacific Region

In Chap. 2, we investigated the trend of deep regional integration in the Asia-Pacific region from the perspective of the depth and breadth of regional integration. The depth measure consists of four fields: import tariffs; non-tariff barriers (NTBs); behind the border policies (BBPs); and other policies (OPs). Each of those fields includes a number of policy areas. For example, the BBPs field includes five policy areas: state trading enterprises; state aid; public procurement; anti-corruption; and competition policy. On the other hand, the breadth measure consists of five fields: services; technology; investment/capital; labor; and non-economic policies (NEPs), each of which includes a number of policy areas. For example, the field of technology includes six policy areas: trade-related aspects of intellectual property rights (TRIPS); intellectual property right (IPR); innovation policies; economic policy dialogue; information society; and research and technology.

We found that the depth and breadth of RTAs signed by ASEAN countries, China, and Japan are quite heterogeneous. Specifically, the heterogeneity is significant in the fields of the NTBs and the BBPs in the depth measure and in the fields of investment/capital and labor in the breadth measure. Although RTAs signed by ASEAN countries include more NTB policy areas in the 2000s, an improvement in the inclusion of the BBP policy areas is small. Moreover, RTAs signed by China indicate a large improvement in the inclusion of both NTBs and BBPs in the 2000s, but the coverage of the legally enforceable BBP index is still low even in 2010–2015, compared with RTAs signed by Japan, the United States, and European countries. By contrast, RTAs signed by Japan in 2010–2015 show almost the same level of the coverage of the NTB and BBP policy areas as those by the United States and European countries. As for the breadth measure, on the other hand, the coverage of the investment/capital policy areas is much narrower for RTAs signed by China than those signed by ASEAN countries and Japan even in 2010–2015. Moreover, the coverage of the labor policy areas is almost the same among ASEAN countries, China, and Japan in 2000–2009, whereas the coverage becomes much wider for RTAs signed by Japan than those signed by ASEAN countries and China in 2010–2015.

8.1.2 Firm Performance and the Choice of Globalization Mode

In Chaps. 3 and 4, we examined how a firm's choice of globalization mode, such as export, foreign outsourcing (FO), and foreign direct investment (FDI), is associated with firm performance. We use various measures of firm performance, which include labor productivity (LP), total factor productivity (TFP), Tobin's q, and the ratio of patent stock to tangible fixed capital. The last measure is a proxy of the ratio of intangible to tangible assets. With regard to the measure of globalization activities, we employ the ratio of the size of a firm's globalization activity to the size of its domestic sales. The size of its activity is measured by the value of exports, sales of foreign affiliates, and costs of FO. This measure can capture the relative importance of a particular type of globalization activity (i.e., export, FDI, or FO) for a firm in relation to the size of its domestic activity. In addition, we construct indexes to measure the relative choice of globalization modes, such as the ratio of export sales to foreign affiliate sales and the ratio of outsourcing costs to foreign affiliate sales.

Our main findings in Chap. 3 are as follows. First, we found that an increase in LP or Tobin's q enhances the size of export or FDI relative to its domestic sales, whereas it does not necessarily induce a firm to expand its FO relative to its domestic sales. These results imply that exporters and multinational enterprises (MNEs) are likely to be more productive and have higher Tobin's q than non-globalized firms, but firms that engage in FO are not necessarily superior in LP or Tobin's q to non-globalized firms. It seemed that our result does not clearly indicate a difference between LP and Tobin's q in terms of the effects on firms' globalization. Second, we found important differences between LP and Tobin's q on a firm's relative choice among modes of globalization. Specifically, an increase in LP tends to motivate a firm to choose more FDI and less exporting, but does not affect the choice between FDI and FO. By contrast, an increase in Tobin's q tends to motivate a firm to choose more FDI and less FO, but does not affect the choice between exporting and FDI. Third, we also found that Tobin's q and intangible asset intensity work in a different way when one tries to capture the importance of the knowledge capital in the choice of globalization mode. Headquarters companies with relatively higher intangible assets tend to favor FDI over exporting and outsourcing. In other words, a difference in the intangible asset intensity is important to the choice between exporting and FDI as well as to the choice between FDI and FO. In this way, we revealed the differences among various measures of firm performance in the effects of globalization activity.

In Chap. 4, we further investigated the effects of Tobin's q on a firm's choice of globalization mode. We distinguished between total FDI and horizontal FDI (HFDI) through taking advantage of the feature of our dataset that allows us to observe detailed information on sales of foreign affiliates of Japanese MNEs. We measure total FDI by total sales of foreign affiliates and HFDI by sales of foreign affiliates excluding exports to Japan. Then, employing a number of different estimation techniques, we confirmed that Tobin's q is negatively and significantly correlated with the ratio of FO to the total FDI. This strongly supports the prediction by Chen et al. (2012) that a higher Tobin's q is associated with a higher FDI engagement relative to FO by MNEs. In contrast, little evidence was found on a definite relationship between Tobin's q and the ratio of exports to HFDI. It implies that the imperfect contractibility of knowledge capital and a higher technology transfer cost actually matter for knowledge-capital intensive firms to choose between exports and FDI, because these factors weaken the positive relationship between Tobin's q and the ratio of FDI to exports.

We also confirmed that the relationship between Tobin's q and the firm's choice of globalization mode fairly differs from that of TFP. We found that TFP is negatively and significantly correlated with the ratio of exports to HFDI, whereas no significant relationship existed between TFP and the ratio of FO to the total FDI. The former result is consistent with the theoretical prediction of Helpman et al. (2004), but the latter result differs from the prediction of Antràs and Helpman (2004).

8.1.3 The Impact of Trade/FDI on Technology Spillovers

We explored the impact of international trade and FDI on international technology spillovers in Chaps. 5 and 6. To measure international technology spillovers we used patent citation data throughout this book. Patent citations are references to existing patents included in patent documents. The advantage of using patent citations as a proxy of technology spillovers is that it is a direct measure of knowledge flows (Hall et al. 2001).

In Chap. 5, we focused on the relationship between the bilateral trade structure and technology spillovers. We first conducted a theoretical analysis using a two-country model of monopolistic competition with quality differentiation, in which inter- and intra-industry trade patterns endogenously arise. Our model predicted that the bilateral trade pattern is horizontal intra-industry trade (HIIT) when the two countries have access to a similar level of technology, while it is vertical intra-industry trade (VIIT) when there is a technological difference between them. If the technological difference is sufficiently large, then the bilateral trade pattern becomes one-way (or inter-industry) trade. As for the relationship between trade patterns and international technology spillovers, our model predicted that technology spillovers are highest when the bilateral trade pattern is HIIT, followed by VIIT and one-way trade. We tested these theoretical predictions using European and Japanese patent data and found that the predictions are supported by empirical results. Specifically, an increase in the share of intra-industry trade in the bilateral trade has a positive effect on the number of patent citations between the two countries. HIIT has a larger effect on spillovers than VIIT. On the other hand, the effects of one-way trade on the number of citations are much weaker than those of IIT.

In Chap. 6, we examined how the structure of MNEs' activity in terms of horizontal and vertical FDI affects technology spillovers between MNEs and firms in their host economies using firm-level data on Japanese MNEs and patent citation data. We constructed new measures of FDI by exploiting information on sales and purchases of foreign affiliates of MNEs. Pure vertical (horizontal) FDI was defined as FDI with a high share of transactions (i.e., both purchases of inputs and sales of outputs) with the source country (in the local market). Partially vertical and horizontal FDI was also defined. We then estimated the effects of these types of FDI on technology spillovers captured by patent citations and found that pure vertical FDI plays a dominant role in technology spillovers in both directions between Japanese MNEs and their high-income host countries. More specifically, when technologically advanced economies host Japanese MNEs, an increase in the degree of pure vertical FDI has significantly positive effects on technology spillovers in both directions between the MNEs and their host countries. Moreover, partially vertical FDI (i.e., FDI with a higher share of purchase of intermediate inputs in the local market and a higher share of sales of outputs to the home country) also has positive and significant effects on technology spillovers from the high-income host countries to the MNEs. By contrast, we found no evidence of a positive impact of pure horizontal FDI on technology spillovers between the MNEs and their host countries.

Although a number of previous studies have identified international trade and FDI as important channels of international technology spillovers, the analyses in Chaps. 5 and 6 suggest that the degree of technology spillovers depends substantially on the subdivided patterns or structure of bilateral trade or FDI.

8.1.4 Deep Regional Integration and Technology Spillovers

Finally, we analyzed the impact of regional integrations on international technology spillovers in Chap. 7. The focus of our analysis was on the impacts of the depth and breadth of RTAs and the heterogeneous effects of individual RTAs on international technology spillovers measured by cross-country patent citations. With regard to the depth of RTAs, we used the indexes in the areas of tariffs, NTBs, BBPs, and OPs. On the other hand, as for the breadth of RTAs, we constructed indexes for services, technology, investment/capital, labor, and NEPs areas. Moreover. we analyzed the heterogeneous effects of individual RTAs. As major sources of international technology spillovers, we focused on RTAs signed by the United States and European countries, such as the North American Free Trade Agreement (NAFTA), the European Community (EC)/European Union (EU), RTAs with the United States, and FTAs with the EC/EU.

Then, in addition to the positive effect of the RTA dummy, we found that deep RTAs with a higher coverage ratio of policy areas in the depth fields such as tariffs, NTBs, and BBPs, and those with a higher coverage ratio of policy areas in the breadth fields such as services, technology, investment/capital, labor, and NEPs, at the legally enforceable level have positive effects on international technology spillovers. The additional effects of including the depth or breadth policy areas may be small or even negligible. This may be because the estimated average effect of the RTA dummy partly captures the impact of the depth policy areas on technology spillovers as recent RTAs become deep. Moreover, with regard to the breadth fields, the same level of the breadth index may have both positive and negative effects on technology spillovers, as some specific policy areas in the breadth fields strengthen rather than relax regulations. Finally, we found that the impact of NAFTA on bilateral technology spillovers is particularly strong, whereas the impacts of the EU and the EU enlargement on technology spillovers are weak or not positive. However, the RTAs with the United States and the FTAs with the EU both positively affect technology spillovers.

8.2 Policy Implications

We can obtain a number of important policy implications from our findings in Chaps. 2–7. In this section, we discuss two areas of policy implications: policies to support the globalization activities of firms; and policies to facilitate international technology spillovers.

8.2.1 Policies to Support the Globalization Activities of Firms

First important policy implications are obtained from the analysis of the effects of firm performance on the choice of a firm's globalization mode. Although existing empirical studies have primarily focused on the relationship between a firm's productivity and its choice of globalization mode, our findings illuminate the potential importance of Tobin's q on firms' globalization activities. In particular, we found that a difference in Tobin's q affects the choice of a firm between FDI and FO, whereas that a difference in productivity is relatively less important to the firm's choice between those two activities.

Firms with lower Tobin's q are relatively more active in FO than in FDI. Generally, policies to facilitate FO will benefit the domestic economy, because FO contributes to improving the competitiveness of outsourcers through reducing their production costs. Since relatively lower values of Tobin's q imply that the firms do not efficiently utilize their capital, deregulation and expansion of supportive services to small and medium enterprises may be helpful. For example, providing information on regulations, business customs, and the law in foreign countries and helping to find a potential outsourcing partner may also enhance gains from FO through reducing the fixed costs of outsourcing.

On the other hand, firms with lower Tobin's q may be reluctant to enhance FDI because they have difficulties in financing costs of investment, as indicated by the low value of Tobin's q. Thus, policies to create a financing mechanism for FDI will help those firms facilitate outward FDI.

In both cases, Tobin's q of individual firms provides useful information for policy makers of the firms' home country about what kind of policy is required to support their globalization activities. Since the ratio of intangible to tangible assets gives similar information, it can be used as an alternative indicator of Tobin's q. Therefore, in addition to the indexes of productivities, such as LP and TFP, policy makers should pay much attention to data on Tobin's q and the ratio of intangible to tangible assets when they consider policies to support the globalization activities of firms.

8.2.2 Policies to Facilitate International Technology Spillovers

We next discuss policy implications for facilitating international technology spillovers. As previous studies have shown, international trade and FDI are both important channels of international technology spillovers (Keller, 2004). However, our empirical findings suggest that the patterns of trade and the structure of FDI matter for the flows of knowledge across countries. Therefore, to facilitate international technology spillovers, it is not enough to merely increase the volume of bilateral trade or the level of inward or outward FDI relative to GDP. Policy makers should also pay much attention to the patterns of bilateral trade and the structure of MNEs' activities.

More specifically, our findings indicate that IIT or VFDI is primarily associated with international technology spillovers. With regard to international trade, HIIT with technologically advanced countries may be effective in enhancing spillovers of technological knowledge. On the other hand, as for FDI, both pure VFDI and partially vertical FDI are positively associated with international technology spillovers. This is true for not only the host economies of FDI but also the source economies of FDI. Thus, information on the structure of outward FDI as well as that of inward FDI will provide useful information on what extent of technology spillovers can be expected.

Furthermore, our research suggests that there is a more active role for governments in facilitating international technology spillovers. That is, our empirical results imply that signing deep RTAs with higher coverage of the depth or breadth policy areas is quite effective in enhancing bilateral technology spillovers. A number of previous studies have suggested that the stringency of the IPR protection in host countries is important to technology spillovers. For example, Branstetter et al. (2006) and Wakasugi and Ito (2009) find that stronger protection of IPR in host countries has a positive effect on technology transfer from parent firms to their foreign affiliates. Nagaoka (2009) also finds a positive effect of stronger patent protection on expanding the scope of the recipients of technology transfer. In addition to the importance of IPR protection, our research suggests that including other policy areas of the depth and breadth fields in RTAs may play an important role in facilitating flows of technological knowledge among members of the RTAs.

In addition, we found that the impact of RTAs on bilateral technology spillovers is quite heterogeneous across RTAs. This finding is in line with previous studies on the heterogeneous effects of RTAs on trade in goods (see, e.g., Baier et al. 2019; Behar and Cirera-i Crivillé 2013; Cheong et al. 2015; Vicard 2011). In the case of technology spillovers, our analysis indicates that signing RTAs with technologically advanced countries, such as the United States, is effective in stimulating cross-border technology spillovers. RTAs with EU countries may also facilitate technology spillovers, but it may be true only for RTAs between EU and non-EU countries. More analyses will be required to identify the causes of the heterogeneous effects of RTAs on technology spillovers.

8.3 Direction for Future Research

In this final section, we discuss the issues for future research.

8.3.1 *Political Trilemma of the World Economy*

The first issue for future research is the potential incompatibility of deep integration with the sovereignty of nation states and democracy. This issue was originally raised by Rodrik (2000) as the "political trilemma of the world economy" as an analogy of the trilemma of international finance. As is well known, the trilemma of international finance tells us that countries cannot simultaneously maintain the following three policy goals: independent monetary policies; fixed exchange rates; and an open account to international flows of capital. Countries can pick at most any two of the three policy goals.

Rodrik (2011) slightly revises his argument in Rodrik (2000) and states that sovereign nation states, democratic politics, and deep international economic integration (or hyper-globalization) are mutually incompatible. Countries can choose at most two of these three options. This is the "political trilemma of the world economy." This argument implies that deep RTAs may possibly be incompatible with national democracy. Only shallow RTAs can be compatible with the sovereignty of nations and democracy.

Rodrik's (2011) argument on the political trilemma of the world economy may explain why many British people voted "Leave" at the Brexit referendum in 2016. According to Sampson (2017), the "Leave" vote was an assertion of national identity. He argues that Brexit is "a democratic response to the erosion of British sovereignty caused by EU membership" (Sampson 2017, p. 180).

Thus, it is a significant issue for deep regional integration whether the hypothesis of the political trilemma of the world economy proposed by Rodrik (2000, 2011) holds both theoretically and empirically. Aizenman and Ito (2020) empirically address this issue. They construct a set of indexes that measure the levels of globalization, national sovereignty, and democracy for 139 countries in the period 1975–2016. Using these indexes, they empirically test the hypothesis of the political trilemma of the world economy by examining whether the trilemma variables are linearly related. The indexes indicate that developed and developing countries have gone through different paths of development in pursuing these three policy goals. Specifically, they find that there is a linear negative relationship between globalization and national sovereignty for developed countries, while the democratization index stays constant during the sample period, suggesting that those countries have faced a dilemma rather than a trilemma. By contrast, all three variables are linearly correlated for developing countries, indicating that they are indeed in a trilemma relationship.

The study by Aizenman and Ito (2020) is the first important attempt in this field. More analyses on this topic by various approaches can be conducted. In particular, studies focused on the post-2016 period will be important because of the possible regime changes. Moreover, interdisciplinary research from both theoretical and empirical analyses will be required to uncover economic and non-economic impacts of deep regional integration and people's responses to deep regional integration.

8.3.2 National Security and Non-trade Issues

The next issue for future research is national security and non-trade issues in relation to international trade.

The relationship between national security and trade policy became a controversial issue when the Trump Administration imposed tariffs on imports of steel and aluminum in 2018. On March 8, 2018, then-President Donald Trump issued two proclamations, imposing 25% ad valorem tariffs on steel products and 10% ad valorem tariffs on aluminum products, which took effect on March 23, 2018.[1] The imposition of these tariffs was based on the Section 232 investigation report by the U.S. Department of Commerce released on January 11, 2018 (U.S. Department of Commerce 2018). The report concluded that certain types of steel and aluminum products imported into the United States threaten to impair the national security of the country, as defined in Section 232 of the Trade Expansion Act of 1962 as amended, and recommended that the President take immediate action to adjust the level of these imports through quotas or tariffs.

Against the restrictions on steel and aluminum imports by the United States, disputes at the World Trade Organization (WTO) were initiated by a number of countries including China, India, the European Union, Norway, Russia, Switzerland, and Turkey. National security is a major issue in other recent WTO disputes as well, such as disputes between Russia and Ukraine, between Saudi Arabia and Qatar, and between Japan and Korea.[2]

In the legal text of the WTO Agreements, the General Agreement on Tariffs and Trade (GATT 1947) includes a provision on security exceptions (Article XXI). Besides, the General Agreement on Trade in Services (GATS) and the Agreement on Trade-Related Aspects of Intellectual Property Rights (TRIPS Agreement) include a similar security exception.[3] However, no panel report in the GATT/WTO dispute settlement procedure invoking Article XXI has been adopted until 2019. In April 2019, the panel report on the case between Russia and Ukraine was adopted as the first panel report involving Article XXI.[4] In this dispute, Ukraine argued that Russia's restrictions on the transit of Ukrainian goods through Russian territory violated various provisions of the GATT/WTO rules and Russia's Accession Protocol to the WTO. However, the panel decided that Article XXI justified the Russian measures (Prazeres 2020).

Although the issue of trade restrictions for national security reasons has been much debated in international economic law literature (e.g., Lester and Zhu 2019;

---

[1] See the web site of the U.S. Department of Commerce (www.commerce.gov/section-232-investigation-effect-imports-steel-us-national-security) for the details of the Section 232 report.

[2] *Russia – Measures Concerning Traffic in Transit* (WT/DS512), *Saudi Arabia – Measures concerning the Protection of Intellectual Property Rights* (WT/DS567), *Japan – Measures related to the Exportation of Products and Technology to Korea* (WT/DS590).

[3] See Article XIV bis in GATS and Article 73 in TRIPS Agreement. With regard to the history of the security exception in the GATT/WTO, see Lester and Zhu (2019) and Pinchis-Paulsen (2020).

[4] Panel Report, *Russia – Measures Concerning Traffic in Transit*, WT/DS512/R.

Pinchis-Paulsen 2020; Prazeres 2020), there are few economic studies on this issue. Taking into account the importance of this issue from the economic point of view, such economic research is worth conducting.

In addition to the issue of trade and national security, human rights and other non-trade issues have also been discussed in relation to international trade. In particular, as seen in Chap. 2, RTAs tend to include ever more provisions on non-trade issues, as RTAs get deeper. Whereas the coverage of such provisions (e.g., provisions on environmental law, health, and human rights) is still very low, it is argued that the role of RTAs in governing countries' compliance with those non-trade issues is important. For example, Spilker and Böhmelt (2013) show that RTAs including "hard" human rights standards have a potential to reduce human rights violations substantially, while most human rights treaties are ineffective in ensuring countries' compliance with human rights standards. Hafner-Burton (2005) shows a similar role of RTAs in countries' compliance with human rights standards. Although a number of studies on the impact of RTAs on non-trade issues have been conducted in the fields of political science and international relations (e.g., Hafner-Burton 2005; Milewicz et al. 2018; Spilker and Böhmelt 2013), economic research on related issues will contribute to understanding the role of RTAs in addressing those issues.

8.3.3 *Network Dynamics of Deep RTAs from the Perspective of Depth and Breadth in Relation to Technology Spillovers*

The final issue for future research is network dynamics of deep RTAs and their implication for technology spillovers.

In Chaps. 2 and 7, we discussed the trend of RTAs and the effects of deep RTAs on the technology spillovers. With respect to the trend of RTAs or the surge of deep RTAs, a number of existing studies have focused more on the process of forming RTAs, because this process has been becoming increasingly dynamic and complicated (Bartesaghi et al. 2020; Sopranzetti 2018; Wonnacott 1996; Zhu et al. 2014).

In the hub-and-spoke system developed by Wonnacott (1975), a hub country (e.g., the United States) has two overlapping bilateral agreements with two spoke countries (e.g., Canada and Mexico), each of which has a bilateral relationship with the hub country. In such a system, the hub country may hold its dominant position by benefiting at the expense of its relatively poor neighbors (Wonnacott 1996). However, this definition of the "hub" has changed, because we observe some cases in which a group of countries (e.g., members of the EU) rather than a single hub country jointly negotiates an RTA with a third country in looking for a better hub position. As a result, the hub-and-spoke effects become multilayered, and the interaction becomes even more complicated (Sopranzetti 2018). On the other hand, a number of studies make challenges in detecting "communities" and "community cores" in international trade networks. The main purpose of these challenges is to understand the evolution of the network and to find rich dynamics over time both inter- and intra-communities (Bartesaghi et al. 2020; Zhu et al. 2014). Following these lines of the network analysis, we provide a description of the evolution of the network to show the global dynamics of RTA network and to reveal how communities appear, disappear, reemerge, and converge.

Figures 8.1 and 8.2 present dynamic changes of the communities of network for the depth and breadth indexes as to RTAs for the period 1990–2015, respectively. In order to analyze the characteristics of RTAs' global dynamics, we use the definition of the depth and breadth of RTAs by Limão (2016) and just focus on WTO-extra (WTO–X) policy areas.[5] We obtain 158 nodes and 5,102 edges for the undirected network of the depth (Fig. 8.1) and 158 nodes and 4,974 edges for the undirected network of the breadth (Fig. 8.2). In order to detect the communities we employ Gephi, network analysis software, where the Louvain community detection algorithm is used to detect communities with the modularity optimization method.[6]

As shown in Fig. 8.1a, only several limited communities are observed in 1990. Those limited communities are related to Caribbean Community and Common Market (CARICOM), EU enlargement, the Central American Common Market (CACM), and the Agreement on Trade and Commercial Relations between the governments of Australia and Papua New Guinea (PATCRA). In 1990, most countries, including the United States, were scattered individually in the network of the depth of RTAs. The number of communities increases and the network system of those communities becomes more complex through the 1990s and 2000s. In 2015 (Fig. 8.1d), by contrast, many countries get involved in one or more RTAs. The network density increased from 0.029 in 1990 to 0.398 in 2015. The Asia-Oceania community and the community of the Gulf countries are also observed in 2015. Furthermore, EU countries are still dominant and held the core position of the communities.

Figure 8.2 shows similar patterns in the network of the breadth. There are only several limited communities in 1990, and the network system evolves in the 1990s and 2000s. In 2015, the position of the communities for EU countries seems to be strengthened more in the network of the breadth index (Fig. 8.2d) than in the network of the depth index (Fig. 8.1d).

The network analysis approach is useful not only for illustrating the process of network dynamics of RTAs but also for examining the effects of the evolution of the RTA networks. For example, Sopranzetti (2018) analyzes the effect of the hub-and-spoke nature of RTAs on bilateral trade. She considers the effects of the country's position in the RTA networks on the bilateral trade of the hub country. Interestingly, she finds that an increase in the number of spoke countries has a negative effect on the trade of the hub country. On the other hand, if signing new RTAs makes a country more central or less constrained in the network, then these new agreements have a strongly positive impact on the country's bilateral trade. Then, we may be able to gain some new insights from applying the network analysis approach to the analysis of the relationship between the evolution of the RTA networks and technology spillovers.

---

[5] See Table 2.1 in Chap. 2 for the details of the WTO–X policy areas.

[6] See https://gephi.org/tutorials/gephi-tutorial-quick_start.pdf.

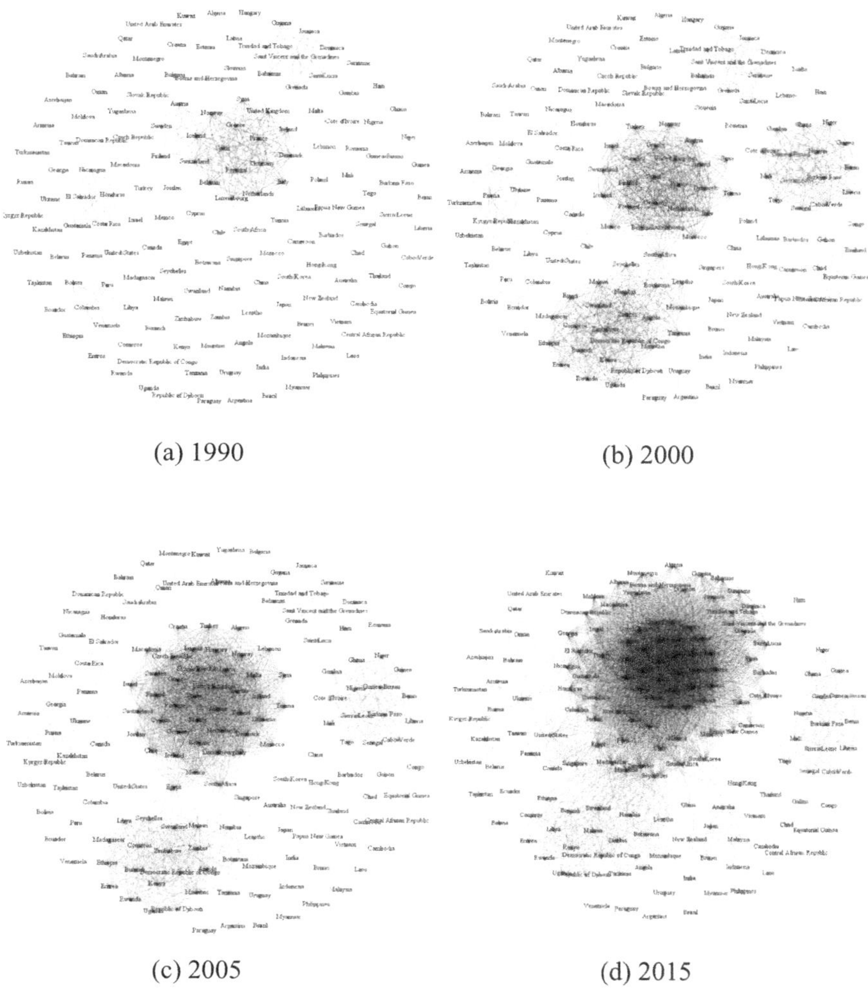

Fig. 8.1 Dynamic changes of the communities of network for the depth indexes, 1990–2015. *Note* Figures are depicted using the WTO–X policy areas in the depth indexes. We detect communities in the network using the Louvain community detection algorithm by Gephi. *Source* Authors' creation from the Content of Deep Trade Agreement database

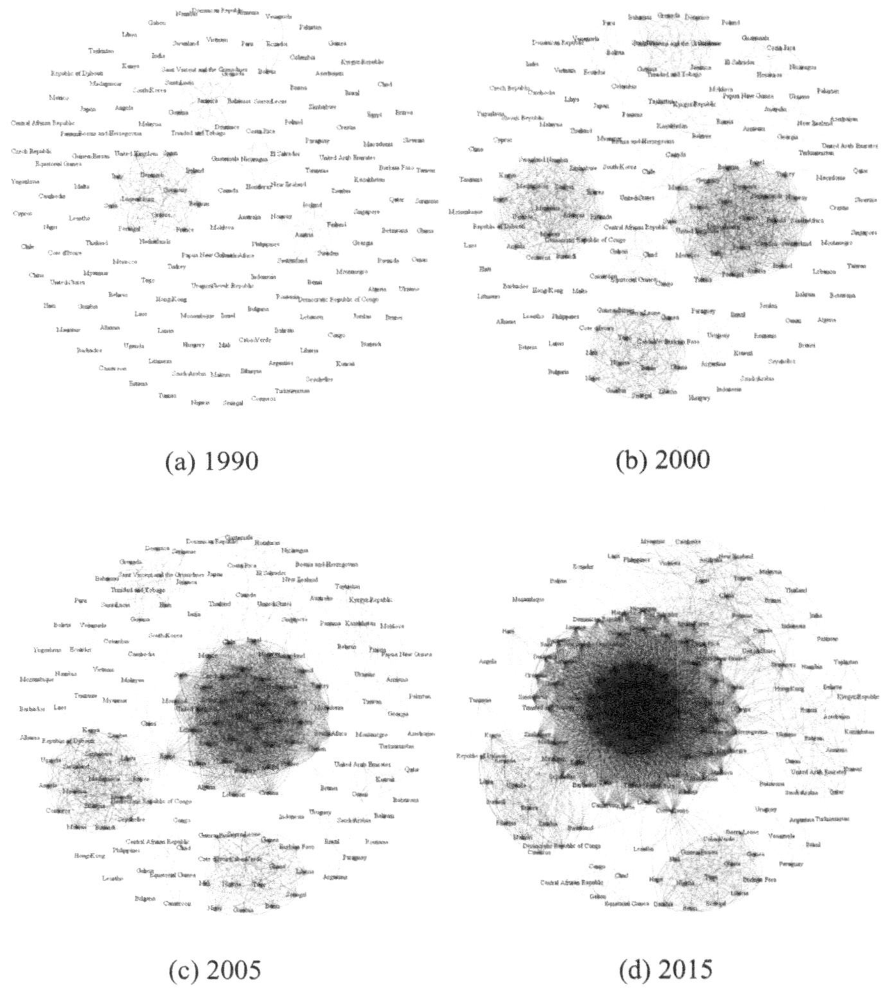

Fig. 8.2 Dynamic changes of the communities of network for the breadth indexes, 1990–2015. *Note* Figures are depicted using the WTO–X policy areas in the breadth indexes. We detect communities in the network using the Louvain community detection algorithm by Gephi. *Source* Authors' creation from the Content of Deep Trade Agreement database

References

Abel AB, Blanchard OJ (1986) The present value of profits and cyclical movements in investment. Econometrica 54(2):249–273
Abel AB, Eberly JC (1994) A unified model of investment under uncertainty. Am Econ Rev 84(5):1369–1384
Abel AB, Eberly JC (2011) How q and cash flow affect investment without frictions: An analytic explanation. Rev Econ Stud 78(4):1179–1200
Acharya RC, Keller W (2009) Technology transfer through imports. Can J Econ 42(4):1411–1448
Aghion P, Howitt P (1992) A model of growth through creative destruction. Econometrica 60(2):323–351
Aghion P, Bloom N, Blundell R, Griffith R, Howitt P (2005) Competition and innovation: An inverted-U relationship. Quart J Econ 120(2):701–728
Aghion P, Antràs P, Helpman E (2007) Negotiating free trade. J Int Econ 73(1):1–30
Aitken BJ, Harrison AE (1999) Do domestic firms benefit from direct foreign investment? Evidence from Venezuela. Amer Econ Rev 89(3):605–618
Aizenman J, Ito H (2020) The political-economy trilemma. Open Econ Rev 31(5):945–975
Alfaro L, Charlton A (2009) Intra-industry foreign direct investment. Am Econ Rev 99(5):2096–2119
Alfaro L, Chor D, Antras P, Conconi P (2019) Internalizing global value chains: A firm-level analysis. J Polit Econ 127(2):508–559
Amador J, Cabral S (2016) Global value chains: A survey of drivers and measures. J Econ Surv 30(2):278–301
Anderson JE, van Wincoop E (2003) Gravity with gravitas: A solution to the border puzzle. Am Econ Rev 93(1):170–192
Ando M (2021) Demand and supply shocks of COVID-19 and international production networks: Evidence from Japan's machinery trade, ERIA Discussion Paper Series No. 366
Ando M, Kimura F (2012) How did the Japanese exports respond to two crises in the international production networks? The global financial crisis and the great East Japan earthquake. Asian Econ J 26(3):261–287
Ando M, Kimura F (2013) Production linkage of Asia and Europe via Central and Eastern Europe. J Econ Integr 28(2):204–240
Ando M, Kimura F (2014) Evolution of machinery production networks: Linkage of North America with East Asia. Asian Econ Papers 13(3):121–160

N. Jinji et al., *Deep Integration, Global Firms, and Technology Spillovers*,
Advances in Japanese Business and Economics 26,
https://doi.org/10.1007/978-981-16-5210-3

Antoniades A (2015) Heterogeneous firms, quality, and trade. J Int Econ 95(2):263–273
Antràs P (2003) Firms, contracts, and trade structure. Quart J Econ 118(4):1375–1418
Antràs P, Chor D (2013) Organizing the global value chain. Econometrica 81(6):2127–2204
Antràs P, Helpman E (2004) Global sourcing. J Polit Econ 112(3):552–580
Antràs P, Helpman E (2008) Contractual frictions and global sourcing. In: Marin D, Verdier T, Helpman E (eds) The Organization of Firms in a Global Economy. Harvard University Press, Cambridge, MA, pp 9–54
Arrow KJ (1962) Economic welfare and the allocation of resources for invention. In: Nelson R (ed) The Rate and Direction of Inventive Activity. Princeton University Press, Princeton, NJ, pp 609–625
Atalay E, Hortaçsu A, Syverson C (2014) Vertical integration and input flows. Am Econ Rev 104(4):1120–1148
Atkeson A, Burstein AT (2010) Innovation, firm dynamics, and international trade. J Polit Econ 118(3):433–484
Aw BY, Roberts MJ, Xu DY (2011) R&D investment, exporting, and productivity dynamics. Am Econ Rev 101(4):1312–1344
Bagwell K, Staiger RW (1999) An economic theory of GATT. Am Econ Rev 89(1):215–248
Bagwell K, Staiger RW (2002) The Economics of the World Trading System. The MIT Press, Cambridge, MA
Bagwell K, Staiger RW (2005) Multilateral trade negotiations, bilateral opportunism and the rules of GATT/WTO. J Int Econ 67(2):268–294
Bagwell K, Staiger RW (2010) The world trade organization: Theory and practice. Ann Rev Econ 2(1):223–256
Baier SL, Bergstrand JH (2007) Do free trade agreements actually increase members' international trade? J Int Econ 71(1):72–95
Baier SL, Yotov YV, Zylkin T (2019) On the widely differing effects of free trade agreements: Lessons from twenty years of trade integration. J Int Econ 116:206–226
Baldwin R (1995) A domino theory of regionalism. In: Baldwin R, Haapara有anta P, Kiander J (eds) Expanding Membership of the European Union. Cambridge University Press, Cambridge, UK, pp 25–47
Baldwin R (2006) Globalisation: The great unbundling(s). In: Globalisation Challenges for Europe: Report by the Secretariat of the Economic Council – Part I. Finnish Prime Minister's Office Publications, Helsinki, pp 11–54
Baldwin R (2011) 21st century regionalism: Filling the gap between 21st century trade and 20th century trade rules, World Trade Organization Staff Working Paper ERSD–2011–08
Baldwin R (2016) The Great Convergence: Information Technology and the New Globalization. Harvard University Press, Cambridge, MA
Baldwin R (2016) The world trade organization and the future of multilateralism. J Econ Perspect 30(1):95–116
Baldwin R (2019) The Globotics Upheaval: Globalization, Robotics, and the Future of Work. Weidenfeld & Nicolson, London, UK
Baldwin R, Harrigan J (2011) Zeros, quality, and space: Trade theory and trade evidence. Am Econ J: Microecon 3(2):60–88
Baldwin R, Okubo T (2014) Networked FDI: Sales and sourcing patterns of Japanese foreign affiliates. World Econ 37(8):1051–1080
Baldwin R, Venables AJ (2013) Spiders and snakes: Offshoring and agglomeration in the global economy. J Int Econ 90(2):245–254
Barrios S, Görg H, Strobl E (2011) Spillovers through backward linkages from multinationals: Measurement matters! Eur Econ Rev 55(6):862–875
Bartesaghi P, Clemente GP, Grassi R (2020) Community structure in the world trade network based on communicability distances. J Econ Inter Coord
Behar A, Cirera-i Crivillé L (2013) Does it matter who you sign with? Comparing the impacts of North-South and South-South trade agreements on bilateral trade. Rev Int Econ 21(4):765–782

Bernard AB, Jensen JB (1995) Exporters, jobs, and wages in U.S. manufacturing: 1976–1987. Brookings Papers on Economic Activity. Microeconomics 1995:67–112

Bernard AB, Jensen JB (1999) Exceptional exporter performance: Cause, effect, or both? J Int Econ 47(1):1–25

Bernard AB, Jensen JB, Redding SJ, Schott PK (2007) Firms in international trade. J Econ Perspect 21(3):105–130

Bernard AB, Jensen JB, Schott PK (2009) Importers, exporters, and multinationals: A portrait of firms in the U.S. that trade goods. In: Dunne T, Jensen JB, Roberts MJ (eds) Producer Dynamics: New Evidence from Micro Data, University of Chicago Press, Chicago, IL

Bernard AB, Jensen JB, Redding SJ, Schott PK (2012) The empirics of firm heterogeneity and international trade. Ann Rev Econ 4(1):283–313

Bernard AB, Jensen JB, Redding SJ, Schott PK (2018) Global firms. J Econ Lit 56(2):565–619

Bhagwati J (1991) The World Trading System at Risk. Princeton University Press, Princeton, NJ

Bhagwati J (1992) Regionalism versus multilateralism. World Econ 15(5):535–556

Bhagwati J (2004) In Defense of Globalization. Oxford University Press, Oxford, UK

Blalock G, Gertler PJ (2008) Welfare gains from foreign direct investment through technology transfer to local suppliers. J Int Econ 74(2):402–421

Blundell R, Griffith R, Van Reenen J (1999) Market share, market value and innovation in a panel of British manufacturing firms. Rev Econ Stud 66(3):529–554

Boffa M, Jansen M, Solleder O (2019) Do we need deeper trade agreements for GVCs or just a BIT? World Econ 42(6):1713–1739

Brainard SL (1993) A simple theory of multinational corporations and trade with a trade-off between proximity and concentration, NBER Working Paper No. 4269

Brainard SL (1997) An empirical assessment of the proximity-concentration trade-off between multinational sales and trade. Am Econ Rev 87(4):520–544

Branstetter L (2006) Is foreign direct investment a channel of knowledge spillovers? Evidence from Japan's FDI in the United States. J Int Econ 68(2):325–344

Branstetter LG, Fisman R, Foley CF (2006) Do stronger intellectual property rights increase international technology transfer? Empirical evidence from U.S. firm-level panel data. Quart J Econ 121(1):321–349

Bridgman B (2012) The rise of vertical specialization trade. J Int Econ 86(1):133–140

Bustos P (2011) Trade liberalization, exports, and technology upgrading: Evidence on the impact of MERCOSUR on Argentinian firms. Am Econ Rev 101(1):304–340

Cameron AC, Trivedi PK (1998) Regression Analysis of Count Data. Cambridge University Press, New York, NY

Cameron AC, Trivedi PK (2009) Microeconometrics: Using Stata, 2nd Edn STATA Press, College Station

Cappelli R, Montobbio F (2020) Geographical distance puzzle in patent citations: Intensive versus extensive margins. Appl Econ Lett 27(10):771–777

Carvalho VM, Nirei M, Saito YU, Tahbaz-Salehi A (2021) Supply chain disruptions: Evidence from the Great East Japan earthquake. Quart J Econ 136(2):1255–1321

Chen Y, Horstmann IJ, Markusen JR (2012) Physical capital, knowledge capital, and the choice between FDI and outsourcing. Can J Econ 45(1):1–15

Cheong J, Kwak DW, Tang KK (2015) Heterogeneous effects of preferential trade agreements: How does partner similarity matter? World Dev 66:222–236

Cherniwchan J, Copeland BR, Taylor MS (2017) Trade and the environment: New methods, measurements, and results. Ann Rev Econ 9:59–85

Chernozhukov V, Hansen C (2008) Instrumental variable quantile regression: A robust inference approach. J Econom 142(1):379–398

Chernozhukov V, Hong H (2002) Three-step censored quantile regression and extramarital affairs. J Am Stat Assoc 97(459):872–882

Chernozhukov V, Fernández-Val I, Kowalski AE (2015) Quantile regression with censoring and endogeneity. J Econom 186(1):201–221

Cipollina M, Salvatici L (2010) Reciprocal trade agreements in gravity models: A meta-analysis. Rev Int Econ 18(1):63–80
Clerides SK, Lach S, Tybout JR (1998) Is learning by exporting important? Micro-dynamic evidence from Colombia, Mexico, and Morocco. Quart J Econ 113(3):903–947
Coe DT, Helpman E (1995) International R&D spillovers. Eur Econ Rev 39(5):859–887
Cohen WM (2010) Fifty years of empirical studies of innovative activity and performance. In: Hall BH, Rosenberg N (eds) Handbook of the Economics of Innovation, vol 1. Elsevier, Amsterdam, The Netherlands, pp 129–213
Cooley TF, Greenwood J, Yorukoglu M (1997) The replacement problem. J Monet Econ 40(3):457–499
Copeland BR, Taylor MS (2003) Trade and the Environment: Theory and Evidence. Princeton University Press, Princeton, NJ
Copeland BR, Taylor MS (2004) Trade, growth, and the environment. J Econ Lit 42(1):7–71
Costantini J, Melitz M (2008) The dynamics of firm-level adjustment to trade liberalization. In: Marin D, Verdier T, Helpman E (eds) The Organization of Firms in a Global Economy. Harvard University Press, Cambridge, MA, pp 107–141
Costinot A, Vogel J, Wang S (2013) An elementary theory of global supply chains. Rev Econ Stud 80(1):109–144
DaDalt PJ, Donaldson JR, Garner JL (2003) Will any q do? J Finan Res 26(4):535–551
Dai M, Yotov YV, Zylkin T (2014) On the trade-diversion effects of free trade agreements. Econ Lett 122(2):321–325
Das GG, Andriamananjara S (2006) Hub-and-spokes free trade agreements in the presence of technology spillovers: An application to the western hemisphere. Rev World Econ 142(1):33–66
d'Aspremont C, Jacquemin A (1988) Cooperative and noncooperative R & D in duopoly with spillovers. Am Econ Rev 78(5):1133–1137
Deardorff AV (2001) Fragmentation in simple trade models. N Am J Econ Finance 12(2):121–137
Deardorff AV, Stern RM (2002) What you should know about globalization and the world trade organization. Rev Int Econ 10(3):404–423
Defever F, Toubal F (2013) Productivity, relationship-specific inputs and the sourcing modes of multinationals. J Econ Behav Organ 94:345–357
Diamond J (1997) Guns, Germs and Steel: The Fates of Human Societies. W.W. Norton & Company Inc, New York, NY
Dixit A, Norman V (1980) Theory of International Trade. Cambridge University Press, Cambridge, UK
Dixit AK, Grossman GM (1982) Trade and protection with multistage production. Rev Econ Stud 49(4):583–594
Dixit AK, Stiglitz JE (1977) Monopolistic competition and optimum product diversity. Am Econ Rev 67(3):297–308
Dufrenot G, Mignon V, Tsangarides C (2010) The trade-growth nexus in the developing countries: A quantile regression approach. Rev World Econ 146(4):731–761
Dür A, Baccini L, Elsig M (2014) The design of international trade agreements: Introducing a new dataset. Rev Int Org 9(3):353–375
Dwyer DW (2001) Plant-level productivity and the market value of a firm, Center for Economic Research, U.S. Census Bureau. Working Paper 01–03
Eaton J, Kierzkowski H (1984) Oligopolistic competition, product variety and international trade. In: Kierzkowski H (ed) Monopolistic Competition and International Trade. Oxford University Press, Oxford, pp 69–83
Eaton J, Kortum S (1996) Trade in ideas: Patenting and productivity in the OECD. J Int Econ 40(3–4):251–278
Eaton J, Kortum S (1999) International technology diffusion: Theory and measurement. Int Econ Rev 40(3):537–570
Eckel C, Neary JP (2010) Multi-product firms and flexible manufacturing in the global economy. Rev Econ Stud 77(1):188–217

Ederington J, McCalman P (2008) Endogenous firm heterogeneity and the dynamics of trade liberalization. J Int Econ 74(2):422–440
Egger P, Larch M (2008) Interdependent preferential trade agreement memberships: An empirical analysis. J Int Econ 76(2):384–399
Ekholm K, Forslid R, Markusen JR (2007) Export-platform foreign direct investment. J Eur Econ Assoc 5(4):776–795
Espitia A, Mattoo A, Rocha N, Ruta M, Winkler D (2021) Pandemic trade: COVID-19, remote work and global value chains. World Econ Early View Article
Falvey RE (1981) Commercial policy and intra-industry trade. J Int Econ 11(4):495–511
Falvey RE, Kierzkowski H (1987) Product quality, intra-industry trade and (im)perfect competition. In: Kierzkowski H (ed) Protection and Competition in International Trade. Basil Blackwell, Oxford, pp 143–161
Farzanegan MR, Feizi M, Gholipour HF (2021) Globalization and the outbreak of COVID-19: An empirical analysis. J Risk Finan Manag 14(3):105
Federico S (2010) Outsourcing versus integration at home or abroad and firm heterogeneity. Empirica 37(1):47–63
Feenstra RC (2016) Advanced International Trade: Theory and Evidence, 2nd Edn Princeton University Press, Princeton, NJ
Figueiredo E, Lima LR, Schaur G (2016) The effect of the Euro on the bilateral trade distribution. Emp Econ 50(1):17–29
Flam H, Helpman E (1987) Vertical product differentiation and North-South trade. Am Econ Rev 77(5):810–822
Fontagné L, Freudenberg M (1997) Intra-industry trade: Methodological issues reconsidered, CEPII Working papers, No. 1997-01
Fontagné L, Mayer T, Zignago S (2005) Trade in the triad: How easy is the access to large markets? Can J Econ 38(4):1401–1430
Fontagné L, Freudenberg M, Gaulier G (2006) A systematic decomposition of world trade into horizontal and vertical IIT. Rev World Econ 142(3):459–475
Fosfuri A, Motta M, Rønde T (2001) Foreign direct investment and spillovers through workers' mobility. J Int Econ 53(1):205–222
Freund C (2000) Multilateralism and the endogenous formation of preferential trade agreements. J Int Econ 52(2):359–376
Freund C, Ornelas E (2010) Regional trade agreements. Ann Rev Econ 2(1):139–166
Fukao K, Wei Y (2008) How do the location determinants of vertical FDI and horizontal FDI differ? Hi-Stat Discussion Paper Series No. 233. Institute of Economic Research, Hitotsubashi University
Fukao K, Ishido H, Ito K (2003) Vertical intra-industry trade and foreign direct investment in East Asia. J Jpn Int Econ 17(4):468–506
Fukuda S, Cong J, Okui M, Okuda K (1999) Long term loans and investment in Japan: An empirical analysis based on the panel data of Japanese firms, Discussion Paper No. 1999–08. Japanese Institute for Posts and Telecommunications Policy (in Japanese)
Furusawa T, Konishi H (2007) Free trade networks. J Int Econ 72(2):310–335
Gala VD, Julio B (2012) Convergence in corporate investments, Unpublished manuscript, London Business School
Gaulier G, Zignago S (2008) BACI: a world database of international trade at the product-level: the 1995–2004 Version, CEPII Working Paper
Gervais A (2015) Product quality and firm heterogeneity in international trade. Can J Econ 48(3):1152–1174
Gilbert R (2006) Looking for Mr. Schumpeter: Where are we in the competition-innovation debate? In: Jaffe AB, Lerner J, Stern S (eds) Innovation Policy and the Economy, vol 6. MIT Press, Cambridge, MA, pp 159–215
Goel RK, Haruna S (2011) Cost-reducing R&D with spillovers and trade. J Inst Theor Econ 167(2):314–326

Görg H, Strobl E (2001) Multinational companies and productivity spillovers: A meta-analysis. Econ J 111(475):F723–F739

Goto A, Motohashi K (2007) Construction of a Japanese patent database and a first look at Japanese patenting activities. Res Policy 36(9):1431–1442

Greenaway D, Kneller R (2007) Firm heterogeneity, exporting and foreign direct investment. Econ J 117(517):F134–F161

Greenaway D, Hine R, Milner C (1994) Country-specific factors and the pattern of horizontal and vertical intra-industry trade in the UK. Weltwirtschaftliches Archiv/Rev World Econ 130(1):77–100

Greenaway D, Hine R, Milner C (1995) Vertical and horizontal intra-industry trade: A cross industry analysis for the United Kingdom. Econ J 105(433):1505–1518

Grossman GM, Helpman E (1990) Comparative advantage and long-run growth. Am Econ Rev 80(4):796–815

Grossman GM, Helpman E (1991) Innovation and Growth in the Global Economy. The MIT Press, Cambridge, MA

Grossman GM, Helpman E, Szeidl A (2005) Complementarities between outsourcing and foreign sourcing. Am Econ Rev 95(2):19–24

Grossman GM, Helpman E, Szeidl A (2006) Optimal integration strategies for the multinational firm. J Int Econ 70(1):216–238

Grossman SJ, Hart OD (1986) The costs and benefits of ownership: A theory of vertical and lateral integration. J Polit Econ 94(4):691–719

Häckner J (2000) A note on price and quantity competition in differentiated oligopolies. J Econ Theory 93(2):233–239

Haddad M, Harrison A (1993) Are there positive spillovers from direct foreign investment?: Evidence from panel data for Morocco. J Dev Econ 42(1):51–74

Hafner-Burton EM (2005) Trading human rights: How preferential trade agreements influence government repression. Int Organ 59(3):593–629

Hall BH, Jaffe AB, Trajtenberg M (2001) The NBER patent citation data file: Lessons, insights and methodological tools. In: Jaffe AB, Trajtenberg M (eds) Patents, Citations, and Innovations. The MIT Press, Cambridge, MA, pp 403–460

Hall BH, Jaffe A, Trajtenberg M (2005) Market value and patent citations. Rand J Econ 36(1):16–38

Hall BH, Thoma G, Torrisi S (2007) The market value of patents and R&D: Evidence from European firms, NBER Working Paper No. 13426

Hanson GH, Mataloni RJ, Slaughter MJ (2001) Expansion strategies of U.S. multinational firms. In: Collins S, Rodrik D (eds) Brookings trade forum 2001. Brookings Institution Press, Washington, DC, pp 245–282

Hanson GH, Mataloni RJ Jr, Slaughter MJ (2005) Vertical production networks in multinational firms. Rev Econ Stat 87(4):664–678

Hao L, Naiman DQ (2007) Quantile Regression. SAGE Publications, Thousand Island

Hart O, Moore J (1990) Property rights and the nature of the firm. J Polit Econ 98(6):1119–1158

Haruna S, Goel RK (2015) R&D strategy in international mixed duopoly with research spillovers. Aust Econ Pap 54(2):88–103

Haruna S, Goel RK (2017) Output subsidies in mixed oligopoly with research spillovers. J Econ Finance 41(2):235–256

Haruna S, Jinji N, Zhang X (2010) Patent citations, technology diffusion, and international trade: Evidence from Asian countries. J Econ Finance 34(4):365–390

Hashmi AR (2013) Competition and innovation: The inverted-U relationship revisited. Rev Econ Stat 95(5):1653–1668

Haskel JE, Pereira SC, Slaughter MJ (2007) Does inward foreign direct investment boost the productivity of domestic firms? Rev Econ Stat 89(3):482–496

Hausman JA, Hall BH, Griliches Z (1984) Econometric models for count data with an application to the patents-R&D relationship. Econometrica 52(4):909–938

Havránek T, Iršová Z (2011) Estimating vertical spillovers from FDI: Why results vary and what the true effect is. J Int Econ 85(2):234–244
Hayakawa K, Mukunoki H (2021) Impacts of COVID-19 on global value chains. Dev Econ 59(2):154–177
Hayakawa K, Machikita T, Kimura F (2012) Globalization and productivity: A survey of firm-level analysis. J Econ Surv 26(2):332–350
Hayashi F, Inoue T (1991) The relation between firm growth and q with multiple capital goods: Theory and evidence from panel data on Japanese firms. Econometrica 59(3):731–753
Head K, Mayer T (2014) Gravity equations: Workhorse, toolkit, and cookbook. In: Gopinath G, Helpman E, Rogoff K (eds) Handbook of International Economics, vol 4. Elsevier, Amsterdam, The Netherlands, pp 131–195
Head K, Ries J (2003) Heterogeneity and the FDI versus export decision of Japanese manufacturers. J Jpn Int Econ 17(4):448–467
Helble M, Okubo T (2008) Heterogeneous quality firms and trade costs, World Bank Policy Research Working Paper No. 4550
Helpman E (1981) International trade in the presence of product differentiation, economies of scale and monopolistic competition. J Int Econ 11(3):305–340
Helpman E (1984) A simple theory of international trade with multinational corporations. J Polit Econ 92(3):451–471
Helpman E (1985) Multinational corporations and trade structure. Rev Econ Stud 52(3):443–457
Helpman E (2006) Trade, FDI, and the organization of firms. J Econ Lit 44(3):589–630
Helpman E, Krugman PR (1985) Market structure and foreign trade: Increasing returns, imperfect competition, and the international economy. The MIT Press, Cambridge, MA
Helpman E, Melitz MJ, Yeaple SR (2004) Export versus FDI with heterogeneous firms. Am Econ Rev 94(1):300–316
Hennessy CA (2004) Tobin's q, debt overhang, and investment. J Finance 59(4):1717–1742
Herguera I, Lutz S (1998) Oligopoly and quality leapfrogging. World Econ 21(1):75–94
Hofmann C, Osnago A, Ruta M (2019) The content of preferential trade agreements. World Trade Rev 18(3):365–398
Honoré BE (1992) Trimmed LAD and least squares estimation of truncated and censored regression models with fixed effects. Econometrica 60(3):533–565
Hopenhayn HA (1992) Entry, exit, and firm dynamics in long run equilibrium. Econometrica 60(5):1127–1150
Horn H, Mavroidis PC, Sapir A (2010) Beyond the WTO? An anatomy of EU and US preferential trade agreements. World Econ 33(11):1565–1588
Horstmann I, Markusen JR (1987) Licensing versus direct investment: A model of internalization by the multinational enterprise. Can J Econ 20(3):464–481
Horstmann IJ, Markusen JR (1992) Endogenous market structures in international trade (natura facit saltum). J Int Econ 32(1–2):109–129
Hu AG, Jaffe AB (2003) Patent citations and international knowledge flow: The cases of Korea and Taiwan. Int J Ind Organ 21(6):849–880
Huber PJ (1981) Robust Statistics. Wiley, New York, NY
Hummels D, Ishii J, Yi KM (2001) The nature and growth of vertical specialization in world trade. J Int Econ 54(1):75–96
International Monetary Fund (IMF) (2021) World Economic Outlook: Managing Divergent Recoveries, April 2021. International Monetary Fund, Washington, DC. www.imf.org/en/Publications
Iršová Z, Havránek T (2013) Determinants of horizontal spillovers from FDI: Evidence from a large meta-analysis. World Dev 42:1–15
Jaffe AB (1986) Technological opportunity and spillovers of R&D: Evidence from firms' patents, profits and market value. Am Econ Rev 76(5):984–1001
Jaffe AB, Trajtenberg M (1996) Flows of knowledge from universities and federal laboratories: Modeling the flow of patent citations over time and across institutional and geographic boundaries. Proc Natl Acad Sci 93(23):12671–12677

Jaffe AB, Trajtenberg M (1999) International knowledge flows: Evidence from patent citations. Econ Innov New Technol 8(1–2):105–136
Jaffe AB, Trajtenberg M, Henderson R (1993) Geographic localization of knowledge spillovers as evidenced by patent citations. Quart J Econ 108(3):577–598
Jaffe AB, Trajtenberg M, Fogarty MS (2000) Knowledge spillovers and patent citations: Evidence from a survey of inventors. Am Econ Rev Pap Proc 90(2):215–218
Javorcik BS (2004) Does foreign direct investment increase the productivity of domestic firms? In search of spillovers through backward linkages. Am Econ Rev 94(3):605–627
Javorcik BS, Spatareanu M (2008) To share or not to share: Does local participation matter for spillovers from foreign direct investment? J Dev Econ 85(1–2):194–217
Jinji N (2021) What does regional economic integration deliver? Int Econ Adv Artic
Jinji N, Zhang X, Haruna S (2013) The effect of regional trade agreements on technology spillovers through international trade. In: Egashira S (ed) Globalism and Regional Economy. Routledge, Abingdon, UK, pp 83–100
Jinji N, Zhang X, Haruna S (2015) Trade patterns and international technology spillovers: Evidence from patent citations. Rev World Econ 151(4):635–658
Jinji N, Zhang X, Haruna S (2019) Do deeper regional trade agreements enhance international technology spillovers? World Econ 42(8):2326–2363
Jinji N, Zhang X, Haruna S (2019) Does a firm with higher Tobin's q prefer foreign direct investment to foreign outsourcing? N Am J Econ Finance 50:101044
Jinji N, Sawada Y, Zhang X, Haruna S (2021) Deep regional trade agreements and cross-border technology transfer: Theory and evidence, Kyoto University, Graduate School of Economics Discussion Paper Series No. E–20–008
Johnson RC (2012) Trade and prices with heterogeneous firms. J Int Econ 86(1):43–56
Jones RW, Kierzkowski H (1990) The role of services in production and international trade: A theoretical framework. In: Jones RW, Krueger AO (eds) The Political Economy of International Trade: Essays in Honor of Robert E. Baldwin. Basil Blackwell, Oxford, UK, pp 31–48
Jovanovic B (1982) Selection and the evolution of industry. Econometrica 50(3):649–670
Kamien MI, Muller E, Zang I (1992) Research joint ventures and R&D cartels. Am Econ Rev 82(5):1293–1306
Keller W (1998) Are international R&D spillovers trade-related?: Analyzing spillovers among randomly matched trade partners. Eur Econ Rev 42(8):1469–1481
Keller W (2004) International technology diffusion. J Econ Lit 42(3):752–782
Keller W (2010) International trade, foreign direct investment, and technology spillovers. In: Hall BH, Rosenberg N (eds) Handbook of the Economics of Innovation, vol 2. Elsevier, Amsterdam, The Netherlands, pp 793–829
Keller W, Yeaple SR (2009) Multinational enterprises, international trade, and productivity growth: Firm-level evidence from the United States. Rev Econ Stat 91(4):821–831
Keller W, Yeaple SR (2013) The gravity of knowledge. Am Econ Rev 103(4):1414–1444
Kemp MC, Wan HYJ (1976) An elementary proposition concerning the formation of customs unions. J Int Econ 6(1):95–97
Kenkel DS, Terza JV (2001) The effect of physician advice on alcohol consumption: Count regression with an endogenous treatment effect. J Appl Economet 16(2):165–184
Kimura F, Ando M (2003) Fragmentation and agglomeration matter: Japanese multinationals in Latin America and East Asia. N Am J Econ Finance 14(3):287–317
Kimura F, Ando M (2005) Two-dimensional fragmentation in East Asia: Conceptual framework and empirics. Int Rev Econ & Finance 14(3):317–348
Kimura F, Kiyota K (2006) Exports, FDI, and productivity: Dynamic evidence from Japanese firms. Rev World Econ 142(4):695–719
Koenker R (2005) Quantile Regression. Cambridge University Press, Cambridge, UK
Koenker R, Bassett GJ (1978) Regression quantiles. Econometrica 46(1):33–50
Kohler WK (2004) International outsourcing and factor prices with multistage production. Econ J 114(494):C166–C185

Kohler WK, Smolka M (2012) Global sourcing: Evidence from Spanish firm-level data. In: Stern RM (ed) Quantitative Analysis of Newly Evolving Patterns of International Trade: Fragmentation, Offshoring of Activities, and Vertical Intra-industry Trade. World Scientific, Hackensack, pp 139–193

Krishna P (1998) Regionalism and multilateralism: A political economy approach. Quart J Econ 113(1):227–251

Krugman PR (1979) Increasing returns, monopolistic competition, and international trade. J Int Econ 9(4):469–479

Krugman PR (1980) Scale economies, product differentiation, and the pattern of trade. Am Econ Rev 70(5):950–959

Kugler M, Verhoogen E (2012) Prices, plant size, and product quality. Rev Econ Stud 79(1):307–339

Kwak DW (2010) Instrumental variable quantile regression method for endogenous treatment effect, Unpublished manuscript

Laget E, Osnago A, Rocha N, Ruta M (2020) Deep trade agreements and global value chains. Rev Ind Org 57:379–410

Lambertini L (1997) Intraindustry trade under vertical product differentiation. Keio Econ Stud 34(2):51–69

Lawrence RZ (1996) Regionalism, Multilateralism, and Deeper Integration. Brookings Institution, Washington, DC

Leahy D, Neary JP (1997) Public policy towards R&D in oligopolistic industries. Am Econ Rev 87(4):642–662

Leahy D, Neary JP (1999) R&D spillovers and the case for industrial policy in an open economy. Oxf Econ Pap 51(1):40–59

Lee S (2007) Endogeneity in quantile regression models: A control function approach. J Econ 141(2):1131–1158

Lester S, Zhu H (2019) A proposal for 'rebalancing' to deal with 'national security' trade restrictions. Fordham Int Law J 42:1451–1474

Li YA (2014) Borders and distance in knowledge spillovers: Dying over time or dying with age? – Evidence from patent citations. Eur Econ Rev 71:152–172

Limão N (2016) Preferential trade agreements. In: Bagwell K, Staiger RW (eds) Handbook of Commercial Policy, vol 1B. Elsevier, Amsterdam, The Netherlands, pp 279–367

Liu Z, Ma H (2021) Input trade liberalization and markup distribution: Evidence from China. Econ Inq 59(1):344–360

Lu Y, Tao Z, Zhu L (2017) Identifying FDI spillovers. J Int Econ 107(1):75–90

MacGarvie M (2006) Do firms learn from international trade? Rev Econ Stat 88(1):46–60

Maggi G (2014) International trade agreements. In: Gopinath G, Helpman E, Rogoff K (eds) Handbook of International Economics, vol 4. Elsevier, Amsterdam, The Netherlands, pp 317–390

Mancusi ML (2008) International spillovers and absorptive capacity: A cross-country cross-sector analysis based on patents and citations. J Int Econ 76(2):155–165

Mandel BR (2010) Heterogeneous firms and import quality: Evidence from transaction-level prices, International Finance Discussion Papers No. 991, Board of Governors of the Federal Reserve System

Markusen JR (1984) Multinationals, multi-plant economies, and the gains from trade. J Int Econ 16(3–4):205–226

Markusen JR (1995) The boundaries of multinational enterprises and the theory of international trade. J Econ Perspect 9(2):169–189

Markusen JR (2002) Multinational Firms and the Theory of International Trade. The MIT Press, Cambridge, MA

Markusen JR, Maskus KE (2002) Discriminating among alternative theories of the multinational enterprise. Rev Int Econ 10(4):694–707

Markusen JR, Maskus KE (2003) General-equilibrium approaches to the multinational enterprise: A review of theory and evidence. In: Choi EK, Hartigan JC (eds) Handbook of International Trade. Blackwell Publishing, Oxford, UK, pp 320–349

Markusen JR, Venables AJ (1998) Multinational firms and the new trade theory. J Int Econ 46(2):183–203
Markusen JR, Venables AJ (2000) The theory of endowment, intra-industry and multi-national trade. J Int Econ 52(2):209–234
Mattoo A, Rocha N, Ruta M (eds) (2020) Handbook of Deep Trade Agreements. World Bank, Washington, DC
Maurseth PB, Verspagen B (2002) Knowledge spillovers in Europe: A patent citations analysis. Scand J Econ 104(4):531–545
Mayer T, Ottaviano GI (2007) The Happy Few: The Internationalisation of European Firms. New facts based on firm-level evidence, Bruegel Blueprint Series
Melitz MJ (2003) The impact of trade on intra-industry reallocations and aggregate industry productivity. Econometrica 71(6):1695–1725
Melitz MJ, Ottaviano GI (2008) Market size, trade, and productivity. Rev Econ Stud 75(1):295–316
Meyer KE, Sinani E (2009) When and where does foreign direct investment generate positive spillovers? A meta-analysis. J Int Bus Stud 40(7):1075–1094
Milewicz K, Hollway J, Peacock C, Snidal D (2018) Beyond trade: The expanding scope of the nontrade agenda in trade agreements. J Conflict Resolut 62(4):743–773
Ministry of Economy, Trade, and Industry (METI) (2019) White Paper on International Economy and Trade 2019. www.meti.go.jp/english/report/data/wp2019/wp2019.html
Miranda A, Rabe-Hesketh S (2006) Maximum likelihood estimation of endogenous switching and sample selection models for binary, ordinal, and count variables. Stand Genomic Sci 6(3):285–308
Morck R, Yeung B (1991) Why investors value multinationality. J Bus 64(2):165–187
Motta M, Thisse JF, Cabrales A (1997) On the persistence of leadership or leapfrogging in international trade. Int Econ Rev 38(4):809–824
Mukunoki H, Tachi K (2006) Multilateralism and hub-and-spoke bilateralism. Rev Int Econ 14(4):658–674
Murakami Y, Otsuka K (2020) Governance, information spillovers, and productivity of local firms: Toward an integrated approach to foreign direct investment and global value chains. Dev Econ 58(2):134–174
Murata Y, Nakajima R, Okamoto R, Tamura R (2014) Localized knowledge spillovers and patent citations: A distance-based approach. Rev Econ Stat 96(5):967–985
Nagaoka S (2009) Does strong patent protection facilitate international technology transfer? Some evidence from licensing contracts of Japanese firms. J Technol Transf 34(2):128–144
Neary JP (2003) Globalization and market structure. J Eur Econ Assoc 1(2–3):245–271
Neary JP, Leahy D (2000) Strategic trade and industrial policy towards dynamic oligopolies. Econ J 110(463):484–508
Neary JP, O'Sullivan P (1999) Beat 'em or join 'em? export subsidies versus international research joint ventures in oligopolistic markets. Scandinavian J Econ 101(4):577–596
Neves PC, Sequeira TN (2018) Spillovers in the production of knowledge: A meta-regression analysis. Res Policy 47(4):750–767
Newman C, Rand J, Talbot T, Tarp F (2015) Technology transfers, foreign investment and productivity spillovers. Eur Econ Rev 76:168–187
Nicholas T (2003) Why Schumpeter was right: Innovation, market power, and creative destruction in 1920s America. J Econ Hist 63(4):1023–1058
Norbäck PJ (2001) Multinational firms, technology and location. J Int Econ 54(2):449–469
Obashi A (2011) Resiliency of production networks in Asia: Evidence from the Asian Crisis. In: Evenett SJ, Mikic M, Ratnyake R (eds) Trade-led Growth: A Sound Strategy for Asia. United Nations Publication, New York, NY, pp 29–52
Ohyama M (1972) Trade and welfare in general equilibrium. Keio Econ Stud 9(2):37–73
Olley GS, Pakes A (1996) The dynamics of productivity in the telecommunications equipment industry. Econometrica 64(6):1263–1297
Olper A, Raimondi V (2009) Patterns and determinants of international trade costs in the food industry. J Agric Econ 60(2):273–297

Orefice G, Rocha N (2014) Deep integration and production networks: An empirical analysis. World Econ 37(1):106–136
Ornelas E (2005) Endogenous free trade agreements and the multilateral trading system. J Int Econ 67(2):471–497
Osnago A, Rocha N, Ruta M (2017) Do deep trade agreements boost vertical FDI? World Bank Econ Rev 30(Supplement_1):S119–S125
Osnago A, Rocha N, Ruta M (2019) Deep trade agreements and vertical FDI: The devil is in the details. Can J Econ 52(4):1558–1599
Ottaviano G, Tabuchi T, Thisse JF (2002) Agglomeration and trade revisited. Int Econ Rev 43(2):409–435
Palia D, Lichtenberg F (1999) Managerial ownership and firm performance: A re-examination using productivity measurement. J Corp Finan 5(4):323–339
Panagariya A (1999) The regionalism debate: An overview. World Econ 22(4):455–476
Panagariya A (2000) Preferential trade liberalization: The traditional theory and new developments. J Econ Lit 38(2):287–331
Perfect SB, Wiles KW (1994) Alternative constructions of Tobin's q: An empirical comparison. J Empir Financ 1(3–4):313–341
Peri G (2005) Determinants of knowledge flows and their effect on innovation. Rev Econ Stat 87(2):308–322
Pinchis-Paulsen M (2020) Trade multilateralism and U.S. national security: The making of the GATT security exceptions. Michigan J Int Law 41(1):109–193
Prazeres TL (2020) Trade and national security: Rising risks for the WTO. World Trade Rev 19(1):137–148
Qiu LD, Tao Z (1998) Policy on international R&D cooperation: Subsidy or tax? Eur Econ Rev 42(9):1727–1750
Ramondo N, Rappoport V, Ruhl KJ (2016) Intrafirm trade and vertical fragmentation in US multinational corporations. J Int Econ 98(1):51–59
Rodrik D (1997) Has Globalization Gone Too Far? Institute for International Economics, Washington, DC
Rodrik D (2000) How far will international economic integration go? J Econ Perspect 14(1):177–186
Rodrik D (2011) The Globalization Paradox: Democracy and the Future of the World Economy. W.W. Norton & Company, New York, NY
Rodrik D (2018) What do trade agreements really do? J Econ Perspect 32(2):73–90
Romer PM (1990) Endogenous technological change. J Polit Econ 98(5, pt. 2):S71–S102
Rousseeuw P, Yohai V (1984) Robust regression by means of S-estimators. In: Franke J, Härdle W, Martin RD (eds) Robust and Nonlinear Time Series Analysis. Springer, New York, NY, pp 256–272
Rousseeuw PJ, Leroy AM (1987) Robust Regression and Outlier Detection. Wiley, New York, NY
Roy J (2010) Do customs union members engage in more bilateral trade than free-trade agreement members? Rev Int Econ 18(4):663–681
Saggi K, Yildiz HM (2010) Bilateralism, multilateralism, and the quest for global free trade. J Int Econ 81(1):26–37
Sampson T (2016) Dynamic selection: An idea flows theory of entry, trade, and growth. Quart J Econ 131(1):315–380
Sampson T (2017) Brexit: The economics of international disintegration. J Econ Perspect 31(4):163–184
Samuelson PA (2004) Where Ricardo and Mill rebut and confirm arguments of mainstream economists supporting globalization. J Econ Perspect 18(3):135–146
Santos Silva J, Tenreyro S (2006) The log of gravity. Rev Econ Stat 88(4):641–658
Santos Silva J, Tenreyro S (2011) Further simulation evidence on the performance of the Poisson pseudo-maximum likelihood estimator. Econ Lett 112(2):220–222
Saunders-Hastings PR, Krewski D (2016) Reviewing the history of pandemic influenza: Understanding patterns of emergence and transmission. Pathogens 5(4):66

Schiff M, Wang Y (2003) NAFTA, technology diffusion and productivity in Mexico. Cuadernos de Economía 40(121):469–476

Schmoch U, Laville F, Patel P, Frietsch R (2003) Linking technology areas to industrial sectors. DG Research, Final Report to the European Commission

Schumpeter JA (1942) Capitalism, Socialism and Democracy. Harper & Brothers Publishers, New York, NY

Shaked A, Sutton J (1984) Natural oligopolies and international trade. In: Kierzkowski H (ed) Monopolistic Competition and International Trade. Oxford University Press, Oxford, pp 34–50

Shrestha N, Shad MY, Ulvi O, Khan MH, Karamehic-Muratovic A, Nguyen USD, Baghbanzadeh M, Wardrup R, Aghamohammadi N, Cervantes D, Nahiduzzaman KM, Zaki RA, Haque U (2020) The impact of COVID-19 on globalization. One Health 11:100180

Singh J (2007) Asymmetry of knowledge spillovers between MNCs and host country firms. J Int Bus Stud 38(5):764–786

Sopranzetti S (2018) Overlapping free trade agreements and international trade: A network approach. World Econ 41(6):1549–1566

Spilker G, Böhmelt T (2013) The impact of preferential trade agreements on governmental repression revisited. Rev Int Org 8(3):343–361

Stiglitz JE (2002) Globalization and Its Discontents. W.W. Norton & Company, New York, NY

Stiglitz JE (2006) Making Globalization Work. W.W. Norton & Company, New York, NY

Stiglitz JE (2018) Globalization and Its Discontents Revisited: Anti Globalization in the Era of Trump. W.W. Norton & Company, New York, NY

Suzumura K (1992) Cooperative and noncooperative R&D in an oligopoly with spillovers. Am Econ Rev 82(5):1307–1320

Sveikauskas L (2007) R&D and productivity growth: A review of the literature, U.S. Bureau of Labor Statistics Working Papers 408

Terza JV (1998) Estimating count data models with endogenous switching: Sample selection and endogenous treatment effects. J Economet 84(1):129–154

Timmer MP, Erumban AA, Los B, Stehrer R, De Vries GJ (2014) Slicing up global value chains. J Econ Perspect 28(2):99–118

Tobin J (1969) A general equilibrium approach to monetary theory. J Money Credit Bank 1(1):15–29

Todo Y (2006) Knowledge spillovers from foreign direct investment in R&D: Evidence from Japanese firm-level data. J Asian Econ 17(6):996–1013

Todo Y (2011) Quantitative evaluation of the determinants of export and FDI: Firm-level evidence from Japan. World Econ 34(3):355–381

Todo Y, Miyamoto K (2006) Knowledge spillovers from foreign direct investment and the role of local R&D activities: Evidence from Indonesia. Econ Dev Cult Change 55(1):173–200

Todo Y, Nakajima K, Matous P (2015) How do supply chain networks affect the resilience of firms to natural disasters? Evidence from the Great East Japan Earthquake. J Reg Sci 55(2):209–229

Tomiura E (2007) Foreign outsourcing, exporting, and FDI: A productivity comparison at the firm level. J Int Econ 72(1):113–127

Ugur M, Churchill SA, Luong HM (2020) What do we know about R&D spillovers and productivity? Meta-analysis evidence on heterogeneity and statistical power. Res Policy 49(1):103866

US Department of Commerce (2018) The Effect of Imports of Steel on the National Security: An Investigation Conducted under Section 232 of the Trade Expansion Act of 1962, As Amended. www.commerce.gov/section-232-investigation-effect-imports-steel-us-national-security

Venables AJ (1999) Fragmentation and multinational production. Eur Econ Rev 43(4–6):935–945

Verardi V, Croux C (2009) Robust regression in Stata. Stand Genomic Sci 9(3):439–453

Vicard V (2009) On trade creation and regional trade agreements: Does depth matter? Rev World Econ 145(2):167–187

Vicard V (2011) Determinants of successful regional trade agreements. Econ Lett 111(3):188–190

Viner J (1950) The Customs Union Issue. Carnegie Endowment for International Peace, New York, NY

Wagner J (2006) Export intensity and plant characteristics: What can we learn from quantile regression? Rev World Econ 142(1):195–203
Wagner J (2007) Exports and productivity: A survey of the evidence from firm-level data. World Econ 30(1):60–82
Wagner J (2012) International trade and firm performance: A survey of empirical studies since 2006. Rev World Econ 148(2):235–267
Wakasugi R (ed) (2014) Internationalization of Japanese Firms: Evidence from Firm-level Data. Springer, New York, NY
Wakasugi R, Ito B (2009) The effects of stronger intellectual property rights on technology transfer: Evidence from Japanese firm-level data. J Technol Transf 34(2):145–158
Wakasugi R (2010) Tanaka A (2010) Activities of Japanese multinationals with productivity heterogeneity. Int Econ 14:128–142
Wakasugi R, Tanaka A (2012) Productivity heterogeneity and internationalization: Evidence from Japanese firms. Millennial Asia 3(1):45–70
Wonnacott RJ (1975) Canada's future in a world of trade blocs: A proposal. Can Public Policy 1(1):118–130
Wonnacott RJ (1996) Trade and investment in a hub-and-spoke system versus a free trade area. World Econ 19(3):237–252
Wooldridge JM (2010) Econometric Analysis of Cross Section and Panel Data, 2nd Edn The MIT Press, Cambridge, MA
World Intellectual Property Organization (WIPO) (2020) World Intellectual Property Indicators 2020. World Intellectual Property Organization, Geneva
World Trade Organization (WTO) (2011) World Trade Report 2011: The WTO and Preferential Trade Agreements: From Co-existence to Coherence. World Trade Organization, Geneva, Switzerland
Xu B, Wang J (1999) Capital goods trade and R&D spillovers in the OECD. Can J Econ 32(5):1258–1274
Yeaple SR (2003) The complex integration strategies of multinationals and cross country dependencies in the structure of foreign direct investment. J Int Econ 60(2):293–314
Yeaple SR (2003b) The role of skill endowments in the structure of U.S. outward foreign direct investment. Rev Econ Stat 85(3):726–734
Yeaple SR (2009) Firm heterogeneity and the structure of U.S. multinational activity. J Int Econ 78(2):206–215
Yi KM (2003) Can vertical specialization explain the growth of world trade? J Polit Econ 111(1):52–102
Yohai VJ (1987) High breakdown-point and high efficiency robust estimates for regression. Ann Stat 15(2):642–656
Yomogida M (2004) Vertical intra-industry trade and factor proportions. Hitotsubashi J Econ 45(1):67–79
Yotov YV, Piermartini R, Monteiro JA, Larch M (2016) An Advanced Guide to Trade Policy Analysis: The Structural Gravity Model, Online Revised Version. World Trade Organization, Geneva, Switzerland
Zhu Z, Cerina F, Chessa A, Caldarelli G, Riccaboni M (2014) The rise of China in the international trade network: A community core detection approach. PLoS ONE 9(8):e105496

Index

N. Jinji et al., *Deep Integration, Global Firms, and Technology Spillovers*,
Advances in Japanese Business and Economics 26,
https://doi.org/10.1007/978-981-16-5210-3

The manufacturer's authorised representative in the EU is Springer Nature Customer Service Centre GmbH, Europaplatz 3, 69115 Heidelberg, Germany. If you have any concerns regarding our products, please contact ProductSafety@springernature.com

Printed and bound by CPI Group (UK) Ltd, Croydon, CR0 4YY
30/09/2026
02225287-0002